KCC LEARNING CENTER

D0476759

Disability Politics and Community Care

of related interest

Housing Options for Disabled People
Edited by Ruth Bull
Preface by Baroness Masham
ISBN 1 85302 454 6

Community Care Practice and the Law, Third Edition
Michael Mandelstam
ISBN 1 84310 233 1

Growing Up with Disability
Edited by Carol Robinson and Kirsten Stalker
ISBN 1 85302 568 2
Research Highlights in Social Work 34

Advocacy and Learning Disability
Edited by Barry Gray and Robin Jackson
ISBN 1 85302 942 4

A Supported Employment Workbook
Using Individual Profiling and Job Matching
Steve Leach
ISBN 1 84310 052 5

Inclusive Research with People with Learning Disabilities
Past, Present and Futures
Jan Walmsley and Kelley Johnson
ISBN 1 84310 061 4

Disability Politics and Community Care

Mark Priestley

Jessica Kingsley Publishers
London and Philadelphia

00047905
JD050133
£15.35
382.4941 PRI
ROBY
REF

All rights reserved. No part of this publication may be reproduced in any material
form (including photocopying or storing it in any medium by electronic means and
whether or not transiently or incidentally to some other use of this publication)
without the written permission of the copyright owner except in accordance with the
provisions of the Copyright, Designs and Patents Act 1988 or under the terms of a
licence issued by the Copyright Licensing Agency Ltd, 90 Tottenham Court Road,
London, England W1T 4LP. Applications for the copyright owner's written permission
to reproduce any part of this publication should be addressed to the publisher.
Warning: The doing of an unauthorised act in relation to a copyright work may result
in both a civil claim for damages and criminal prosecution.

The right of Mark Priestley to be identified as author of this work has been asserted
by him in accordance with the Copyright, Designs and Patents Act 1988.

First published in the United Kingdom in 1999 by
Jessica Kingsley Publishers
116 Pentonville Road
London N1 9JB, UK
and
400 Market Street, Suite 400
Philadelphia, PA 19106, USA

www.jkp.com

Second impression 1999
Printed digitally since 2005

Copyright © 1999 Mark Priestley

Library of Congress Cataloging in Publication Data
A CIP catalogue record for this book is available from the Library of Congress

British Library Cataloguing in Publication Data
Priestley, Mark
Disability politics and community care
1.Handicapped – Care 2.Handicapped – Government policy
I.Title
362.4

ISBN-13: 978 1 85302 652 2
ISBN-10: 1 85302 652 2

Contents

List of Tables

List of Figures

Acknowledgements

This book would not have been possible without the assistance of a great many people. Thanks are due to Martin Milligan, Swapna McNeill and the 'Association of Blind Asians' for inspiration by example; to Ken Davis, Maggie Davis, Dave Gibbs, Rob Jackson and Ken Smith for trust and cooperation; to Colin Barnes, Geof Mercer, Vic Finkelstein, Fiona Williams and Mike Oliver for thoughtful comments; to Jan and the boys for their patience and, above all, to those disabled men and women in Derbyshire who shared with me their experiences of community care and integrated living.

A Note on Terminology

The choice of appropriate terminology is not just a semantic decision. It is also a political one. Disabled people within the movement have frequently criticised the choices made by writers in the past. They have also promoted alternative definitions. In Britain, the most influential and widely quoted is that produced by the Union of the Physically Impaired Against Segregation (UPIAS/Disability Alliance 1976) who argued, after Paul Hunt (1966) and Vic Finkelstein (1975), that it is necessary to distinguish between impairment and 'the social situation called disability'. Thus:

> In our view, it is society which disables physically impaired people. Disability is something imposed on top of our impairments, by the way we are unnecessarily isolated and excluded from full participation in society. Disabled people are therefore an oppressed group in society. (UPIAS/Disability Alliance 1976, p.3)

The definitions which they proposed read as follows:

> IMPAIRMENT: is defined as lacking part or all of a limb, or having a defective limb, organ or mechanism of the body.

> DISABILITY: is the disadvantage or restriction of activity caused by a contemporary social organisation which takes little or no account of people who have physical impairments and thus excludes them from participation in the mainstream of social activities.

In 1981 these definitions were adopted, in a slightly modified form, by the newly formed British Council of Organisations of Disabled People (now the British Council Of Disabled People, BCODP). They were also proposed for adoption at the first World Congress of the Disabled Peoples' International (DPI). After lengthy discussions amongst delegates from various countries about the language to be used the following definitions were agreed:

> DISABILITY: is the functional limitation within the individual caused by physical, mental or sensory impairment.

> HANDICAP: is the loss or limitation of opportunities to take part in the normal life of the community on an equal level with others due to physical and social barriers.

For linguistic reasons, the British delegation opted to replace the terms 'disability' and 'handicap' with 'impairment' and 'disability' respectively.

In 1993, the United Nations General Assembly drew directly on the representations of disabled peoples' organisations in drawing up its new *Standard Rules on the Equalization of Opportunities for Persons with Disabilities* (Resolution 48/96, 20 December 1993). Paragraph 18 develops the DPI definitions and the original UPIAS wording by stating that:

> The term 'handicap' means the loss or limitation of opportunities to take part in the life of the community on an equal level with others. It describes the encounter between the person with a disability and the environment. The purpose of this term is to emphasize the focus on the shortcomings in the environment and in many organized activities in society, for example, information, communication and education, which prevent persons with disabilities from participating on equal terms.

There has been a great deal of cross-cultural debate about the use of terminology, much of it very heated. Writers within the American speaking world have tended to favour terms like 'persons with disabilities' (see for example Albrecht 1992). However, social model writers in Britain have rejected this construction in order to emphasise that 'disability' is not 'with' the individual but with the social and physical environment in which that person operates (e.g. Barnes 1991). To add further confusion, disabled Americans have increasingly joined in rejecting the term 'handicap'. Consequently, in much contemporary writing the word 'disability' is used interchangeably to denote *both* an individual impairment *and* a form of institutional oppression.

For the purpose of clarity, and taking into account the context of the study, I have chosen to adopt the definitions of the British disabled peoples' movement (specifically, the BCODP definitions). Thus, the terms 'impairment' and 'disability' are used where the UN Rules employ 'disability' and 'handicap' respectively. Inevitably this gives rise to occasional confusions of terminology in the use of quotations from other writers (particularly those from other countries). However, this use of language best describes my own view of disability and is entirely consistent with the definitions employed by the disabled people's organisations who contributed to this study.

CHAPTER I

Introduction

The disabled peoples' movement has struggled hard to gain acceptance for the idea that disability can be considered as a form of institutional discrimination or collective social oppression. As these 'social model' ideas have gained political currency so they have engendered a profound reexamination of British social policy. Although disabled people in Britain have won some recent concessions towards anti-discriminatory legislation, the bulk of disability policy making continues to reproduce disabling discourses of dependency, individualism and otherness. It is not surprising then, that the enabling values of the disabled people's movement have frequently come into conflict with traditional ways of thinking about disability policy. Indeed, there is much evidence to suggest that the implementation of 'community care' reforms during the 1990s has served to heighten, rather than reduce, these conflicts. As Morris (1993a, p.ix) concludes: 'A political and ideological battle is being waged...between government and national disability organisations, between social service authorities and local disability organisations, and, most importantly, within the daily lives of disabled individuals... The terrain of this battle is...named "community care".'

The analysis presented in this book arose directly from the concerns of disabled people within this battleground. Specifically, it was prompted by the experiences of disabled people involved with the Derbyshire Coalition of Disabled People (DCDP) and the Derbyshire Centre for Integrated Living (DCIL). Their perception was that a significant conflict of values had arisen between themselves and the local commissioning authorities over the provision of support services to disabled people in the locality. This difference of values, it was suggested, had been exacerbated by recent community care reforms and by the imposition of service contracting. This study examines how such conflicts arise and what they might teach us about disability policy making.

DCDP was Britain's first coalition of disabled people and the Derbyshire Centre for Integrated Living, Britain's first CIL. Since the mid 1980s DCIL has sought to design and deliver services to disabled people based on the principles of participation, integration and true equality. Their commitment to integrated living represents a radical departure from traditional modes of welfare production. They have attempted to develop support services that respond to the social causes of disability and they have sought to involve disabled people themselves as key participants in the production of their own welfare. In this way, integrated living blurs the administratively constructed boundaries between 'providers' and 'users' and brings into question the whole concept of 'services'.

In many ways, the growth of organisations like DCIL, within the movement for independent/integrated living, has been a remarkable success story. Many hundreds of disabled people have been able to extricate themselves from the disabling social relations of institutionalised service provision and to exercise greater choice and control over the production of their own welfare. In theory, the implementation of community care legislation, the growing assertiveness of the disabled people's movement and the move from state provision to consumerist marketisation should all provide opportunities for innovative services to flourish. Yet, in a climate of political uncertainty, the future direction of welfare policy making remains unclear and there is growing concern that the advances which have been made could all too easily be undermined. As Ann Kestenbaum points out, 'In such a time of uncertainty and change, it is important to achieve as clear a picture as possible of the practices that support or impede Independent Living, and of the policies that would make it a more practical possibility for many more disabled people' (1996, p.1).

If, as those within DCDP/DCIL argue, community care implementation does indeed threaten the hard won achievements of the disabled people's movement to promote integrated living solutions, then this task is all the more important. Moreover, if research into these issues is to have relevance and validity for disabled people themselves, then it is vital that they should be involved throughout the process.

It was my intention that this study should be defined and guided by the disabled people with whom I was engaged. This book is, then, the end product of a process in which we sought to share control over the research production process. It was they who defined the central questions and guided the research. The resulting analysis, however, remains my responsibility. The data from this research highlight specific barriers to policy change and suggest that effective self-organisation within a cohesive social movement is a necessary prerequisite for the liberation of disabled people.

Some general hypotheses

The impact of social policy is measured against notions of quality which are culturally, structurally and bureaucratically defined. In the case of disability, ideas about quality are bound up with (a) cultural values about the role of disabled people in society and (b) the social relations of welfare production in a capitalist economy. This study investigates these relationships by testing three broad propositions.

First, definitions of quality derived from individual models of disability will be at variance with those derived from social models. In arguing for the latter, disabled people's organisations have often found themselves at odds with the values embodied in recent community care reforms. Second, these variances will be most apparent where disabled people's organisations are themselves the providers of contracted community care services. In such cases, services designed within a social model of disability will often be evaluated against quality standards defined within an individual model. Third, the idea of 'quality' within a social model of disability involves not only enhanced services but also enhanced civil rights and citizenship. To achieve these things would require a more fundamental redefinition of the social relations of welfare production which, in turn, would undermine powerful interest groups within welfare bureaucracies and challenge the economic imperatives of welfare state capitalism.

In testing these propositions, it would be naive to consider this (or any other) conflict of welfare ideologies in isolation from its social context. Political ideologies do not emerge or compete in a simple pluralistic way and the relative influence of competing values is contingent upon the distribution of power within a given society. Disability policy making is not played out on a level field and the policy making community is weighted against the disabled people's movement. These existing power relationships are premised upon a number of disabling assumptions and historical developments.

The rationality of policy making is bounded by bureaucratic and economic constraints. Any attempt to restructure British social policy to accommodate the agenda of the disabled people's movement would require a fundamental redefinition of the social relations of welfare production. The liberation of disabled people threatens powerful professional interest groups, it brings into question the legitimacy of the welfare state and it challenges the economic imperatives of capital accumulation. In this broader context, disabling values function ideologically – by portraying disabled people's oppression as inevitable and thereby obscuring the possibility of enabling policy alternatives. Conversely, the ability of the disabled people's movement to generate significant resistance is indicative of its potential as an agent of social change.

In order to understand why conflict has arisen over services in Derbyshire in the mid 1990s, it is necessary to pose some more basic questions. It is important to ask where these competing values came from, why some values are dominant over others and who's interests are served by the maintenance of particular discourses. It follows that the study of competing welfare ideologies needs to be located within a frame of analysis which can accommodate the social relations of welfare production. Ultimately, any study of competing policy values will have something to say about the relationship between ideology and economy in contemporary, welfare state capitalism.

Some specific questions

Bearing in mind the background outlined so far, the specific research questions addressed in this book are as follows:

- In what ways does the community care agenda perpetuate disabling discourses and relations of welfare?

- How did the disabled people's movement come to a point where it could begin to challenge these discourses and modes of welfare production?

- How do the value conflicts between community care and integrated living affect individual disabled people who use services?

- How have disabled people's organisations fared in their attempts to market the social model of disability within the policy framework of community care?

- What is the best way to measure and improve the quality of community support services to disabled people?

- What is the best way to measure and improve policy outcomes for disabled people?
- What are the barriers to implementing an agenda set by the disabled people's movement and what strategies are available for their removal?

Towards a model for disability research

The act of researching disability has become increasingly problematised as disabled people have begun to examine the relationship between themselves and those who have studied their situation. These critiques have led to the development of an 'emancipatory' paradigm for disability research which has much in common with feminist, anti-racist and anti-imperialist research methods (Stone and Priestley 1996).

The decision to undertake this study was driven by a commitment to engage directly with the research agenda of the disabled people's movement. Specifically, it arose from an attempt to place my research skills 'at the disposal' of the disabled people's organisations with whom I was engaged (Barnes 1992a, p.122). My aim in doing this was to challenge some of the established social relations of disability research production by redefining the relationship between myself and the other participants in the project (Priestley 1997b).

The social relations of research production

Paul Abberley argues that:

> ...the sociology of disability is both theoretically backward and a hindrance rather than a help to disabled people. In particular, it has ignored the advances made in the last 15 years in the study of sexual and racial equality and reproduces in the study of disability parallel deficiencies to those found in what is now seen by many as racist and sexist sociology. (1987, p.5)

Abberley describes how disabled people have been treated predominantly as 'passive research subjects'. This objectification (or subjectification) of disabled people has been premised upon disabling social relations within the research process itself. Thus, Mike Oliver reflects on the failure of much feminist and 'Third World' research to effect significant change and concludes that:

> It is to what can only be called the social relations of research production that the failures of such research can be attributed, and indeed, it is to these very social relations that attention must be focused if research, in whatever area, is to become more useful and relevant in the future than it has been in the past. (1992a, p.102)

Problematising the social relations of research production brings into question power relationships between the researcher and the other research participants. This in turn has profound implications for their respective roles in the research production process.

In her feminist analysis of disability research production, Jenny Morris (1992, p.159) quotes Adrienne Rich's assertion that 'objectivity is a word men use to describe their own subjectivity'. Similarly, claims to objectivity by non-disabled researchers have often been perceived as marginalising the experience and self-determination of disabled people. Gerry Zarb (1992) for example, is concerned that disabled participants' own research priorities are frequently subordinated by the 'objectivity' of positivist research paradigms. This process was most graphically exposed by Paul Hunt (1981) writing about his experience of being researched as a resident of the Le Court Cheshire Home. In particular, Hunt condemned the researchers' obsession with 'detachment'. For Hunt, such claims were inherently flawed because they were made within a context of oppression. Similar experiences have led many disabled writers to consider the notion of detached objectivity as a falsely premised, if not inherently oppressive, standpoint for doing disability research.

The significance of these arguments is particularly apparent in a study such as this one, which engages directly with the struggles of the disabled people's movement. In seeking to expose and redefine oppressive social relations, new social movements (including the disabled people's movement) have *de facto* challenged many of the mores of social research. Consequently, researchers of emancipatory social movements have found it increasingly difficult to work within a positivist research paradigm (Touraine 1981, 1985). In this respect, feminist critiques of 'objectivity' in social research have been among the most significant (see Smith 1988; Stanley 1990).

Touraine argues that it is difficult for the student of social movements to arrive at an understanding of them other than by identifying with them. Thus, his approach to action research states openly that the purpose of the research is to 'contribute to the development of social movements' and envisages permanent change in the movement effected by the research. For

Touraine then, research with social movements is a means of 'raising their capacity for historical action and hence increasing the strength and elevating the level of their struggles' (1981, p.145).

Touraine suggests that the researcher can adopt an 'agitator's function' in assisting the group's own self-analysis and a 'secretary's function' in recording the substance of group process (in a critical way). Thus, he concludes, while participant observation can provide 'superficial inform-ation', a more productive approach is that of 'committed research' (1981, p.198). The practice of committed research clearly raises many questions about the political position of the researcher (Finch 1990). Moreover, personal commitments do not automatically translate into 'emancipatory' research. In order to understand how this might be achieved it is important to consider the development of an emancipatory paradigm in more detail.

An 'emancipatory' research paradigm?

It is relatively uncontentious to conclude that disabled people should be more involved in disability research production. It is more difficult to deter-mine exactly what the form and content of that involvement should be. Simply increasing levels of participation does not necessarily challenge or alter the social relations of research production. For this reason, Zarb finds it necessary to distinguish between 'participatory' and 'emancipatory' research methods, 'Simply increasing participation and involvement will never by itself constitute emancipatory research unless and until it is disabled people themselves who are controlling the research and deciding who should be involved and how' (1992, p.128).

Since participation is not tantamount to emancipation, it is important to consider how participation might best be translated into control. The practicalities of participatory data collection have been sufficiently outlined in the feminist and 'Third World' research literature. However, the emancipatory model requires more. It suggests ownership of the means of research production and distribution – by the research participants rather than by the researcher.

The emancipatory research paradigm presents a substantial challenge to the established social relations of research production. Disabled writers in particular have argued that the researcher needs to engage directly in the emancipatory struggles of disabled people by laying her/his research skills 'at the disposal of disabled people' (Barnes 1992a, p.122), 'for them to use in whatever ways they choose' (Oliver 1992a, p.111).

In this way, disabled people have sought to identify new research methodologies commensurate with the emancipatory struggles of the disabled people's movement. These moves have been consolidated in recent years with the articulation of an 'emancipatory' paradigm for conducting disability research (Rioux and Bach 1994; Barnes and Mercer 1996). In a previous paper with Emma Stone (Stone and Priestley 1996) we reviewed the development of this approach in the literature and identified six core principles which we felt characterised the emancipatory paradigm:

- the adoption of a social model of disability as the basis for research production
- the surrender of falsely-premised claims to objectivity through political commitment to the struggles of the disabled people's movement
- the willingness only to undertake research where it will be of some practical benefit to the self-empowerment of disabled people and/or the removal of disabling barriers
- the devolution of control over research production to ensure full accountability to disabled people and their organisations
- the ability to give voice to the personal whilst endeavouring to collectivise the commonality of disabling experiences and barriers
- the willingness to adopt a plurality of methods for data collection and analysis in response to the changing needs of disabled people.

In presenting these arguments, it was important for us to consider how we might address the social relations of our own research production *vis à vis* the disabled people with whom we sought to work. At the same time we found it necessary to satisfy academic peers. It was often hard to conceive how this balancing act might be successfully achieved, to which end we prioritised four aspects of the emancipatory model which we felt summed up the 'tug-of-war' between academic-self and committed-self, namely:

- the contradiction between surrendering control and maintaining integrity
- the tension between accepting our expertise *as researchers* whilst accepting disabled people's expertise as *knowers*

- the problem of collectivising analysis within a social model where that model is not necessarily part of the participants' own understanding of disability

- a recognition that positive outcomes in individual lives need not be the sole criterion of 'good research' where a real contribution can be made in the wider context or the longer term.

Working it out in practice

If the principles of emancipatory research were to mean anything then it was important to establish how control could be devolved in setting up the project. Specifically, I wanted to find out whether it would be possible to produce an academically credible piece of research shaped by the priorities of the research participants. To this end it was important to think critically about setting a research agenda, undertaking the project, defining the specific research questions and obtaining funding.

My initial interest in disability research was prompted both by my previous employment (as a rehabilitation instructor with blind and partially sighted people) and by my academic interest in political theory. During the 1980s I had become increasingly aware of the contradictions between the discourse of 'care' and 'rehabilitation' within which I was professionally cultured and the ideology of self-empowerment articulated by the emerging disabled people's movement. My increasing exposure to the self-organisation of disabled people and to social model writers such as Vic Finkelstein, Mike Oliver and Jenny Morris served to further illuminate these contradictions.

The opportunity to explore some of these issues came in 1993 while studying for a Master's degree in Social and Public Policy at the University of Leeds. As a dissertation project, I was able to work closely with the Association of Blind Asians (ABA) in Leeds in order to witness, record and support their struggle to develop new modes of collective welfare production based on self-advocacy and mutual support (Priestley 1994a, 1994b, 1995a, 1996a). It was this experience above all that shaped my personal agenda for further study. In particular, I became increasingly interested in examining how the new community care purchasing framework might be exploited by disabled people's organisations to establish more participatory modes of welfare production.

Writing as a non-disabled person, I was initially concerned about whether I should be pursuing any research with disabled people's organisations, although Barnes (1992a) argues that cultural differences such as class, education, and life experience may present as many barriers to the researcher as disability.

The first stage was to come up with some specific research questions. However, it was important that these should be derived from the priorities of the research participants. To this end I wrote, in December 1993, to the then chair of the Derbyshire Coalition of Disabled People, Ken Davis, outlining my interests. A meeting was arranged between myself, Ken and the research manager at Derbyshire Centre for Integrated Living, Dave Gibbs, during which we discussed the social policy issues facing disabled people's organisations. Not surprisingly, implementation of the NHS and Community Care Act earlier that year figured prominently in this discussion.

It was clear that the unfolding purchaser-provider reforms required DCDP and DCIL to reevaluate their relationship with the local agencies of the welfare state. There was much concern that unique support services, developed by disabled people in partnership with the local authority, might now be threatened by the new contractual framework. Specifically, it was felt that new definitions of service quality might fail to recognise the 'added value' of an integrated living approach. In view of this it was suggested that we might use the research to develop an approach to quality measurement which would give due credit to the kind of services developed by the movement for independent/integrated living.

Following these initial discussions I set about the task of forming the ideas and concerns into a research proposal. This development was fed back and discussed with DCDP/DCIL over a period of two or three months and resulted in agreement on a set of hypotheses and an outline method for the project (based initially on interviews with service users). This proposal was consolidated into a funding application and submitted to the Economic and Social Research Council (ESRC) in May 1994.

To secure funding from a major government research council for a project determined by representatives of disabled people's organisations did at least demonstrate that disabled people (in collaboration with a 'committed' researcher) *could* gain access to relatively scarce funding resources. However, it did not provide any guarantees to the participants that I would continue to devolve control over the conduct or dissemination of the research (see Hunt 1981).

Having secured funding for the project, the next problem was to determine how control could be devolved to the participants. In August 1994 we discussed the proposal again and it was suggested that I could be 'commissioned' (without remuneration) to do the research for DCDP. An initial contract was drawn up and agreed to this effect. In practice, it is fair to say that the contractual nature of our relationship was not evoked at any time during the project. Its primary function was therefore in setting the tone of our relationship rather than in governing it. However, it was a more than symbolic representation of the idea that this research should 'belong' in some way to its primary participants.

Case study methods

Representatives of disabled people's organisations in Derbyshire had selected the topic for research because it was a pressing organisational issue for them at the time. Thus, it was not surprising that their activities frequently coincided with this agenda. The difficulty for me (as someone hoping to write a book) was then to forge coherent links between the sometimes disparate opportunities for data collection. I have found it helpful to consider the evolving data collection as a set of three semi-discrete projects guided by the changing needs and priorities of the research participants.

Action research on user involvement

In July 1994, DCIL's General Council considered a proposal to host a Joint Focus Group project on 'Improving User Participation in Service Monitoring' in collaboration with the Living Options Partnership (LOP). Since this initiative coincided directly with our collaborative interest in quality and user controlled services, it was suggested that I could be 'employed' to facilitate the project for DCIL.

DCIL's General Council asked its member organisations to nominate representatives for the group and an initial meeting was convened in November 1994. This meeting was attended by representatives of DCDP, the social services department and the two local NHS Trusts. LOP's Network Coordinator was also present. At this meeting, each representative was asked to prioritise a user involvement issue in Derbyshire. It was decided that these contributions should form the basis for a series of four workshops to be held at DCIL over a period of several weeks.

The workshops were chaired by me and each representative invited disabled service users from their organisation to attend. The meetings were tape recorded and notes made of the main contributions. The notes and tapes were analysed after each meeting and summaries of the main points were made. These summaries were copied and circulated to the participants for feedback. After the fourth workshop a summary report was compiled, together with a key-point checklist, in collaboration with DCIL's research officer. These were circulated to the participants for validation. A final meeting was convened at which the participants discussed the report and decided collectively on its dissemination.

The object of the workshops was twofold. First, we anticipated that each organisation would learn something about the process of user involvement in its own, and other, agencies. Second, we hoped to produce some draft guidelines for evaluating user participation in purchaser and provider organisations. To this end, the outputs of the project (a report and an evaluation tool) were widely disseminated among disabled people's organisations and service commissioners.

In March 1995, DCIL's General Council adopted the evaluation tool as a basis for assuring user involvement in disability services and agreed to promote the summary report with its constituent organisations. In September 1995, we were able to present a version of the report and recommendations to the European Symposium of Disabled People's International (Gibbs and Priestley 1996). This prompted much discussion and enabled us to validate the initial work with a wider range of disabled activists. Later, we were able to use outcomes from the project as the basis for a presentation to an NHS Management Executive seminar organised by DCIL in Derby (Priestley 1996b). This provided an opportunity to disseminate the group's work to a national constituency of service commissioners and providers.

A study of contracting

Our agreed agenda for research focused attention on the definition and mea-surement of service quality. However, it was apparent that DCIL perceived their contractual relationship with the local authority as the most immediate barrier to implementing quality services within an integrated living approach. During 1995 we discussed the possibility of using the project to facilitate further action research with the purchasing authority, aimed at resolving some of these conflicts. For this reason it was important to under-stand as much as possible about the impact of community care implementation on the organisation.

In order to achieve this, DCIL provided me with complete and unrestricted access to their organisational records. I was able to analyse internal minutes, supporting documents, reports and financial accounts for the period immediately before and after community care implementation

(1991–1996). This provided much detailed information about the impact of contracting on DCIL's ability to provide participative, integrated living services to disabled people in the locality. I was also able to talk at length with DCIL managers about the operational pressures of contracting for 'community care' services.

Ultimately, there were few tangible outcomes from this part of the study. The relationship between DCIL and the social services department was becoming increasingly strained and some of the issues targeted for research moved onto a more political plane. In view of this, the opportunities for social services participation in the research design became increasingly limited and it was necessary to refocus the study onto its primary participants. I had written up a detailed analysis as a draft 'academic' paper but much of the material was politically sensitive and it would not have been appropriate to disseminate this analysis widely at that time. This in itself was a useful lesson, illustrating the potential conflict between 'academic' self and 'committed' self (Stone and Priestley 1996). To share control over the dissemination of research findings is to accept that there may be constraints on the researcher's ability to 'publish'.

An evaluation project with service users

The need for service user input was always a priority. On a personal level, I was keen to 'get some interviews'. However, there was no point in pursuing user interviews unless these were relevant and useful to all concerned. For some months we were unable to clarify how user involvement could be best targeted. However, by early June an opportunity for relevant contact began to present itself.

Towards the end of the first year of DCIL's service contract with the local authority it became evident that some evaluation of service quality would be required. Managers at DCIL were becoming increasingly concerned that any evaluation conducted by social services might be limited in scope and therefore fail to recognise the 'added value' of an integrated living approach. In view of this it was suggested that I might conduct the evaluation as an 'independent' outsider.

We planned to adopt a similar model to Barnes' (1992a) 'three stage' interviews. Within this approach the first stage would be critical. In particular, we wanted to ensure that the participants could make informed decisions about their contribution before any interviews took place. To this end, we drafted a set of potential questions, a statement of good practice and a covering letter. In the letter, we outlined the purpose of the research, the role of the researcher, an explanation of the accompanying documents and a suggested time scale for the interviews. The statement of good practice gave a concise account of what participants should expect from contact with a researcher. The list of questions provided a speculative agenda for the interviews while giving the opportunity to amend or veto its form and content. These documents were discussed in draft with DCIL, amended, clarified and sent out to the participants.

Two people declined to be interviewed (one due to lack of time and one because he had nothing to say other than that DCIL's service was 'excellent'). In consultation with DCIL a schedule of visits was arranged for early August to meet the remaining seven people. Most people chose to be interviewed at home; one elected to use a day centre; another met me at his place of work. The meetings were arranged so as to give the participants several days notice to think about these questions. The interviews lasted for between 40 minutes and an hour and a half. Each interview was tape recorded and typed transcripts were made. The transcripts were reviewed and the major points summarised in note form.

The main points, together with supporting quotes were written up as a short report and a one page summary. These were circulated back to all the participants (including those who were not interviewed) for comment and amendment. The participants were encouraged to use the interviews not only to voice their experiences but also to influence the future development of DCIL's services. The final report (Priestley 1996c) was submitted to DCIL and the summary was tabled at their Annual General Meeting in September 1996. Additional material arising from the interviews was also written up, in consultation with DCIL, as a paper for the *British Journal of Social Work* (Priestley 1998b).

Summary of data collection and analysis

The data for the study were drawn from policy documents and records, from discussions, from action research and from interviews with individual disabled people. In addition, I was able to participate in various organisational activities, including working parties and discussions directly relevant to the study. Thus, data from the focus groups, documentation and interviews were supplemented by field notes taken during this time. During these ongoing contacts the issues raised were constantly fed back and discussed.

Central government data were drawn from legislative documents, from policy guidance and from Parliamentary debates and Committee Reports. The implementation of the community care reforms generated an enormous amount of such data and it was necessary to prioritise those documents which dealt most directly with the issues raised by participants.

The establishment of DCIL arose from the self-organisation of disabled people in Derbyshire. This conscious political action was relatively well recorded in both published and unpublished papers. In 1993 DCDP produced an historical account of its activity to mark the tenth anniversary of the organisation (Davis and Mullender 1993). DCDP also publishes a regular newsletter. Content analysis of these documents was supplemented by personal discussions and tape recorded interviews with key informants who were able to shed additional light on their relevance and accuracy.

A review of committee minutes and reports yielded much data about the changing nature of DCIL's organisational structure. It also provided important insights into the level of collective consciousness about organisational values and mission. These documentary data were supplemented by ongoing discussions with DCIL's director, research manager and the manager of the Personal Support Service.

To summarise, a large amount of qualitative data were collected for the study from a variety of sources. The data collection was shaped by the changing priorities of the primary participants, by my shifting analysis of those priorities and by the bureaucratic politics of the organisations involved. In this sense it was highly typical of dynamic grounded theory (Glaser and Strauss 1967) and coparticipatory data collection.

Dissemination issues

Coparticipatory research means sharing control over all aspects of the research production process, including the dissemination of research outputs. The research participants were able to suggest a number of opportunities for bringing the work to a wider audience (including joint presentations and publications). Their priorities were for forms of dissemination that would contribute to service development and influence the practice of purchasers and providers. My own priorities also included the need to produce a credible PhD thesis and to publish 'academic' work arising from the study.

The methodological issues were prepared as a collaborative paper with Emma Stone during early 1995 and published in the *British Journal of Sociology* (Stone and Priestley 1996). We hoped that this paper would 'benchmark' our political aspirations as disability researchers and generate useful feedback. We also established an e-mail discussion group (*disability-research@mailbase.ac.uk*). We envisaged that the list would put us in contact with others engaged in similar research and that it would contribute to the dissemination of social model thinking amongst the research community.

The case study methods were also written up as part of a book published by the Disability Research Unit on the practice of *Doing Disability Research* (Barnes and Mercer 1997). The chapter was prepared in consultation with DCIL's Research Manager and our dialogue formed the basis for a joint presentation to an international conference under the same title in September 1997. Again, the emphasis was on disseminating more widely the benefits and methodological implications of active coparticipation between disabled people's organisations and academic researchers.

The substantive issues arising from the case study were also widely disseminated. Outputs from the project on user involvement were presented jointly with DCIL to the European Symposium of Disabled People's International (Gibbs and Priestley 1996) and to a seminar hosted by the NHS Management Executive in Derby (Priestley 1996b). The central arguments about quality issues were published in a paper for *Critical Social Policy* (Priestley 1995c) and the specific quality issues arising from interviews with service users were disseminated in report form by DCIL (Priestley 1996c). The implications for community care management and assessment were published in a paper for the *British Journal of Social Work* (Priestley 1998b). This ongoing process of collaborative dissemination enabled us to reach both disabled people's organisations and service commissioners.

Structure of the book

The remainder of the book is organised in seven chapters which deal with the specific research questions outlined earlier. The first two chapters explore the political and historical background to the issues. The following two chapters draw extensively on the case study data to show how competing values impact on the assessment of 'need' and on the pattern of service commissioning. The final three chapters identify a number of barriers to integrated living, within the framework of community care, and explore some strategies for change.

Chapter 2 begins the examination of conflicting values by analysing the dominant discourses of disability policy making in Britain with specific reference to the community care agenda for change in the 1990s. This analysis shows how disabling policies have been premised upon the cultural representation of disability in terms of personal tragedy, the impaired body and otherness. Such values find their expression in British policy making through a preoccupation with 'care', individualism and segregation. This value-laden policy agenda then functions ideologically by obscuring the possibility for alternative modes of welfare production.

Chapter 3 charts the development of the disabled people's movement with specific reference to events in Derbyshire. This evidence suggests that the politicised self-organisation of disabled people can be considered as a significant form of resistance to disabling policy discourses. In particular, the development of social model thinking, through the praxis of independent/integrated living, illustrates the ability of disabled people to forge new ways of speaking and acting in response to disabling barriers. These attempts to develop a policy agenda based on participation, integration and equality stand in stark contrast to the disabling values outlined in Chapter 2.

The ideological conflicts outlined in Chapters 2 and 3 also impact directly on the experience of those individual disabled people who use services. Thus, Chapter 4 draws on personal accounts to illustrate the tensions between disabling and enabling forms of community support. In particular, the discussion contrasts the enabling philosophy 'self-assessment' and 'self-management' with the disabling practices of 'care assessment' and 'care management'.

Chapter 5 examines how disabled people's organisations have fared in their attempts to market self-managed support schemes within the purchasing framework of community care. This analysis draws on DCIL's experience of contracting in order to illustrate the mechanisms involved and the impact of marketisation. It also shows how these processes (within a climate of resource rationing) can reinforce disabling discourses of 'care', medicalisation and segregation.

Despite their underlying differences, the competing philosophies of community care and integrated living demonstrate a rhetorical convergence on many issues of service quality. For example, both agendas claim to value user participation, choice, self-determination and independent living outcomes. Yet, disabled people within the movement have been concerned that this rhetoric is rarely translated into practice. Chapter 6 assesses the scope for improving quality in community support services through training, quality assurance systems and, above all, user participation.

Chapter 7 shifts the focus from the process of service delivery to outcomes. Various outcome-oriented approaches are outlined and illustrated using the experience of service users. The discussion also considers the methodological and political issues involved in measuring 'quality of life'. This analysis suggests that outcome measurement must always relate ideas about service quality to the principles of equality and citizenship in the wider world.

The final chapter reviews the barriers to integrated living posed by community care policy implementation, together with some strategies for change. The discussion deals with implementation at a local level, legislative change at a national level, and social change in a global context. Ultimately, the liberation of disabled people threatens the legitimacy of a welfare state in crisis and undermines the economic imperatives of capital accumulation. This analysis suggests that real progress remains contingent upon the effective self-organisation of disabled people within a cohesive social movement.

CHAPTER 2

Disabling Values: Disabling Policies

As noted in the introduction, this study arose from concerns expressed by disabled people's organisations in Derbyshire about the implementation of community care policies in the 1990s. Many of these concerns arose from particular local circumstances and parochial politics. However, the form and content of community care policy making can also be seen as reinforcing disabling social relations and values in the wider world. In this sense, the concerns of the primary research participants exemplify a more fundamental conflict of values which exists between disability policy makers and the disabled people's movement.

Many of our dominant cultural values about disability are themselves disabling. The experience of disabled people is invariably presented to us in terms of personal tragedy, the impaired body or 'otherness'. In general terms, disability is constructed as individual misfortune, rather than as social exclusion or oppression. Although the rhetoric of policy making has begun to reflect more enabling values, the reality of implementation has often undermined those same policy goals. In particular, the language of 'community care' epitomises a mode of welfare production based on dependency, individualism and segregation.

Disabling values

The argument presented in this chapter suggests that recent community care policies have been premised upon a number of disabling assumptions which mirror key features in the cultural construction of disability in industrialised western societies. Specifically, cultural representations which portray the disadvantage experienced by disabled people in terms of 'tragedy', the 'impaired body' and 'otherness' are reflected in policy responses which

27

favour 'care', individualism and segregation. Moreover, these values function ideologically where they portray disabling social relations as inevitable and thereby obscure the possibility for more enabling modes of welfare production.

The role of values in oppression

Disabling values can contribute to oppression in a number of ways. On an individual level the expression of disablist attitudes and beliefs may impact directly on disabled people's experience and identity. Such attitudes or values may also be shared by groups of actors who have a great deal of power over disabled people's lives (for example, a team of service providers or a group of local policy makers). Within welfare institutions, disabling values may become highly codified as professional discourses of surveillance and discipline. On a macro-level disabling values may operate as culture or ideology.

Collective social values may be revealed in many ways – through cultural representations; through the form and content of legislation; through administrative and institutional arrangements for welfare production. Fraser (1987) argues that dominant cultural products reflect the values of dominant social groups and that these values then define the needs of subordinate groups (in Fraser's case, women). This position is reminiscent of Du Bois' (1969 [1903]) seminal work on racism in which she reflected on 'this sense of always looking at one's self through the eyes of others, of measuring one's soul by the tape of a world that looks on in amused contempt and pity' (p.45).

Lugones and Spelman (1983) theorise the role of values in oppression as 'cultural imperialism' and this concept has been extensively employed in order to explain the oppressive role of patriarchal and imperialist values. More recently, it has been employed by social model writers such as David Hevey (1993) and Tom Shakespeare (1994) to examine the oppressive nature of disabling cultural representations. In this sense, cultural imperialism provides a useful way of looking at the relationship between disabling cultural values and the oppression of disabled people.

For Iris Young (1990, p.58), cultural imperialism involves the 'universalisation of a dominant group's experience and culture, and its establishment as the norm'. Where this occurs the normalcy of the dominant group's perspective leads alternative perspectives to be judged as deviant; to be characterised as 'other'. For Young this is a 'paradoxical oppression' because the imperialised group is both made invisible (through cultural norms) and simultaneously marked out as visibly different through stereotypes (usually related to bodily characteristics such as skin colour, gender, age or impairment). Thus: 'To experience cultural imperialism means to experience how the dominant meanings of a society render the particular perspective of one's own group invisible at the same time as they stereotype one's group and mark it out as Other' (Young 1990).

Social constructionist approaches to disability have been enormously useful in detailing how this occurs. However, they do not necessarily account for why it occurs in particular historical contexts (Priestley 1998a). For example, while accepting that the 'consistent cultural bias against people with impairments' has been undervalued by materialist writers, Colin Barnes remains concerned that the idealist approach, '...reduces explanations for cultural phenomena such as perceptions of physical, sensory and intellectual difference to the level of thought processes, thus detracting attention away from economic and social considerations' (Barnes 1996a, p.49).

There are parallels here with the discourse on 'race'. Black British writers such as Ballard (1979), Lawrence (1982) and Gilroy (1987) have found it useful to employ cultural arguments. However, Bourne (1980) points out that racism resides in power rather than culture, while Cross (1982) and Solomos (1985) show how an overemphasis on cultural explanation can reinforce racist power relations. Thus, Williams (1989, p.95) argues that analyses based in culture tend to obscure the structural relations of power between white and black people. This line of argument is equally applicable to other modes of oppression – for example, the distinction between 'sexism' and 'patriarchy' (Busfield 1989; Walby 1990).

Social creationist models of disability have produced similar reasoning. For example, in reviewing his own attempts to explore the cultural variation of disability, Mike Oliver suggests that 'what evidence there was showed that the medicalised and tragic view of disability was unique to capitalist societies and other societies viewed disability in a variety of ways' (Oliver 1996b, p.28).

In this way, Oliver argues that it is the mode of production which influences cultural values and representations and not the converse. The assumption is that cultural values contribute to disability in so far as they maintain and legitimise the social relations required by a dominant mode of production. From this perspective, the notion of cultural imperialism may be better understood as ideology.

This is a familiar argument from Marxist and feminist medical sociology. For example, Waitzkin (1979, 1989) shows how 'structural patterns of domination and oppression' can be reproduced in the interaction between doctors and patients. This was also the message of those in the anti-psychiatry movement – that psychiatric diagnosis could operate as a form of social control (Foucault 1977; Scheff 1966; Szasz 1973). It is important to note that such literature falls short of making claims about the ideological function of physical impairment (Goffman 1961; Laing 1960). However, Sedgewick (1982) questions this omission and other authors have argued that medicalised definitions of physical impairment can be construed as upholding particular state or class interests (see Abberley 1992, 1995; Albrecht 1992; Stone 1984).

Marxist writers have tended to argue that the development of nineteenth century industrial capitalism and Fordist production methods required a set of social relations which excluded most people with impairments from equal participation in the labour force (Finkelstein 1980; Oliver 1990; Ryan and Thomas 1980). These factors, it is suggested, led to the growth of institutional welfare arrangements to accommodate the newly created 'care' needs of disabled people. In more general terms, Habermas (1987) has argued that welfare capitalism creates specifically new forms of domination and subordination as the 'life world' becomes increasingly 'colonised' under the control of rationalised bureaucracies. In this sense, disabled people have been much more 'colonised' than non-disabled people. From different premises, Ingstad and Reynolds-Whyte (1995, p.10) argue that, 'disability in Europe and North America exists within – and is created by – a framework of state, legal, economic, and biomedical institutions. Concepts of personhood, identity, and value, while not reducible to institutions, are nevertheless shaped by them.'

Within the industrialised capitalist economies of Europe and North America, the construction of disability as an administrative category has thus been contingent upon its commodification within the expanding production of medical and rehabilitative services (Albrecht 1992; Finkelstein 1991; Stone 1984). Within this context, discourses of personal tragedy (Hevey 1993; Oliver 1990) and functional limitation (Abberley 1992) serve to individualise disability and thus to obscure its social and economic causes. The point is simply that it is not sufficient merely to identify disablist values unless it can also be shown how they become disabling.

Values play a central role in oppression when they function ideologically. That is, when (through acquired hegemony or purposeful manipulation) they preclude or inhibit significant political change. In this way, Iris Young suggests that: 'Ideas function ideologically...when they represent the institutional context in which they arise as natural or necessary. They thereby forestall criticism of relations of domination and oppression, and obscure possible emancipatory social arrangements' (1990, p.74).

Thus, disabling cultural values would function ideologically where they could be shown to uphold existing relations of domination and subordination in a real and material way (through capital accumulation, state legitimation, private or public patriarchy, imperialism and so on). They would function ideologically where they could be shown to perpetuate existing relationships of power within the production of welfare, for example between 'providers' and 'users'. They would function ideologically where they could be shown to mask or preclude the possibility of alternative social relations (for example, a more equitable reorganisation of work, family, welfare or citizenship).

The following analysis identifies three core themes within the cultural construction of disability in western societies. Specifically, the disadvantage experienced by disabled people has been characterised in terms of personal tragedy, the impaired body and otherness. The cultural currency of these representations fosters a view of disability as an individual phenomenon (arising from impairment) and thereby obscures the alternative view, that disability is a form of collective oppression which is socially produced. Similarly, the fact that British disability policy making has been conducted almost exclusively within this individual model framework obscures the possibility of more enabling modes of welfare production based on participation, social integration and equal citizenship.

The culture of tragedy

Historically, the notion of tragedy has been a consistent theme in the cultural representation of disabled people. For example, Boal, McBride and McBride (1989), Garland (1995) and Barnes (1996a) identify a link between disability and tragedy in the imagery of classical Greek and Roman culture (but see also Haj 1970, or Dols 1987, on Middle Eastern antiquity). These and other studies suggest the widespread cultural currency of deistic fatalism as a cosmology for the production of knowledge about disability in preindustrial European societies.

David Hevey (1993) illustrates how impairment has been widely employed as a popular literary metaphor to depict impotent, helpless or childlike states such as those of Clifford Chatterly, *The Elephant Man* or Lenny in *Of Mice and Men* (these and related arguments are developed at length in the analyses offered by Darke 1994; Kriegal 1987; Longmore 1987; and Shakespeare 1994). Similarly, Davidson, Woodill and Bredberg review the portrayal of disability in nineteenth century children's literature and suggest that it was widely regarded as 'a fixed, divinely ordained state of being' which set disabled people apart from the rest of society (1994, p.33).

Contemporary studies suggest that this sort of imagery remains largely unchallenged in mass media representations. For example, Cumberbatch and Negrine (1992) show how disabled people are often portrayed as powerless, or as the victims of violence. Interestingly, they are three times more likely to be dead by the end of the programme than non-disabled characters! Cumberbatch and Negrine also show how news coverage of disability issues tends towards sentimentality and patronage.

A similar picture emerges from the analysis of press reporting. Smith and Jordan (1991) argue that newspapers (particularly the tabloid press) focus only on a limited number of disability issues. These usually relate to fund raising, charity events or 'personal interest' stories. In addition, the language used is frequently oppressive, tending to generalise, patronise and marginalise the experience of disability. On the other side of the coin, newspapers frequently carry stories of the 'special achievements' of disabled people. Ordinary life course events such as holding down a job, passing exams, having successful relationships or taking part in recreational activities become remarkable front page stories. The implicit message is that people with perceived impairments are not expected to do these things.

A further medium for the representation of disability as tragedy is evident in the recent growth of charity advertising. Many disabled writers have argued that charity campaigns tend to reinforce rather than challenge tragic images of disability (see, for example, Morris 1991a). In order to elicit donations, charities frequently project an image of disabled people as 'needy' and unable to help themselves. Scott-Parker (1989) points out that the general public are affected by these images not only as donors to charity, but also in their interactions with disabled people in the wider world. The bulk of charity advertising may thus be seen to bolster the 'tragedy principle' (Hevey 1993).

The idea that disability is essentially a manifestation of tragedy or misfortune ('there but for the grace of God...') was reflected in the growth of early charitable provision for disabled people in Britain. The church retained a near monopoly over collective provision in the middle ages and there are records of medieval religious hospitals dating from at least the tenth century (Clay 1909). Indeed no self-respecting Benedictine abbey would have been without its almshouse, infirmary or pilgrim shelter. The number of these charitable hospitals, leper-houses and almshouses rose steadily from the twelfth century with dramatic increases in charitable provision occurring in the thirteenth (Lis and Soly 1979, p.21).

During the sixteenth century the recognition of dependency as misfortune was becoming more widespread and the mood of philanthropy expressed itself in private as well as public action. For example, Jordan (1959, p.260) illustrates how voluntary gifts for the foundation of almshouses began to rise sharply from the end of the sixteenth century until the Civil War. Similarly, Coats' analysis of attitudes towards the relief of poverty after 1660, shows that 'contemporary observers usually took it for granted that the impotent poor should be supported' (1976, p.102). As with early ecclesiastical provision, the establishment of charitable foundations and the giving of alms assumed the dependency of people with impairments as given. Philanthropy did not address the social causes of this dependency or challenge the social relations of its maintenance.

Although begging had been outlawed by the eighteenth century, few authorities implemented the law (12, *Ann,* c23) with any great zeal and a licensed beggar could probably still make more than most wage-earners in a good week (Beier 1985, p.27). Contemporary accounts certainly indicate that private charity was freely given to those with perceived impairments. Indeed, there are numerous accounts of poor people acquiring impairments in order to enhance their earnings potential. For example, Shaw (1734, p.183) cites the example of 'a lusty young fellow' named Wright from Leicestershire who persuaded his companion to 'strike off his Left Hand' so as to make himself 'the better quality for Begging' (both Wright and his friend were subsequently indicted and fined for their enterprise).

Religious and private philanthropy are part of a long-standing cultured response to the dependency of people with perceived impairments; a response based on maintaining them within that state of dependency rather than challenging its social causes. More significantly, the institutions which emerged from charitable provision came increasingly to dominate the collective production of welfare for disabled people up to and beyond the establishment of the welfare state (see Drake 1996). Today, the cultural currency of the 'tragedy principle' remains evident in the public promotion of charitable initiatives like *Children in Need, Telethon* and more recently the allocation of National Lottery funds. The assumption of unavoidable dependency and impotence are then directly linked to the assumption that 'care' is required.

It would seem reasonable to conclude, even from this brief review, that the notion of disability as tragedy is a long-standing feature of western cultural value systems. The assumption of impotence is evident in both religious and scientific modes of thought. Within a deistic cosmology, the aetiology of disadvantage was god-given; within scientific cosmologies, it has become biologically-determined. The uniting feature of these constructions is that they portray disability as a state of unavoidable dependency. The argument from within the disabled people's movement is that the development of welfare policies and institutions in Britain not only failed to challenge this assumed dependency but consistently reinforced it through the production of 'care' (Finkelstein 1991; Finkelstein and Stuart 1996; Oliver 1990; Oliver and Barnes 1993).

The culture of embodiment

David Hevey (1993) argues that there are potentially two ways of representing disability: first, through a representation of the impaired body and second, through the representation of disabling barriers. The cultural construction of disability has been dominated by the former. Indeed, the legitimacy of individual models of disability is premised upon the assumption that the disadvantage experienced by disabled people is a product of the 'imperfect' body (Dutton 1996). In this respect there is a striking similarity with the way in which cultural representations of women and black people have contributed to the maintenance of their oppression.

In general terms, the cultural construction of disability has drawn disproportionately on the physicality of certain impairments. More specifically, contemporary media coverage is disproportionately preoccupied with 'medical' issues and 'cures' (Barnes 1992b; Cumberbatch and Negrine 1992; Hevey 1993; Scott-Parker 1989; Shakespeare 1994; Smith and Jordan 1991). Thus, the cultural embodiment of disability is consistent with a more generalised medicalisation of social problems (Illich 1975; Zola 1977). In this context, Jewson (1976) draws attention to the increasing dominance of a biomedical paradigm in the production of western scientific knowledge – a reductionist tendency towards the definition of social problems in biological terms.

Foucault (1970, 1977) also describes how the rationalism of the eighteenth and nineteenth centuries gave precedence to knowledge produced within the biological sciences. This view of the world, he claims, imposed a 'normalizing gaze' on the human body, defining new boundaries of the 'abnormal'. Increasingly, value-laden gaze became a mechanism for the 'scaling of bodies' against physical norms. More specifically, the physical measurement of bodies relative to biological norms became the primary mechanism through which social norms of acceptance were also defined.

Iris Young (1990, p.124) develops similar themes, arguing that the rationalist paradigm required the separation of reason from the body (and emotion). This dualism, she argues, was also pejorative – assigning superiority to the cognitive over the affective and the psycho-motor. In this way, Young suggests that the scaling of bodies within a rationalist paradigm led some groups to be identified with (superior) reason and others to be identified with the (inferior) body.

This argument is familiar from feminist and anti-racist writing. The pejorative scaling of bodies, under the normalising gaze of biological science, has persistently identified black people and women with undesirable bodily attributes. The portrayal of black bodies has made associations with ugliness, uncleanness and impurity (Slaughter 1982) while idealised (male) images of female physicality have been shown to oppress large numbers of women whose own bodies are devalued against cultural norms (Davies, Dickey and Stratford 1987). From a disability perspective, Hevey (1993) shows how impairment has been similarly used as a literary metaphor for destructive or sinister traits (as in Richard III, King Lear, Blind Pugh, Long John Silver or Captain Hook for example). As Tom Shakespeare puts it, 'If original sin, through the transgression of Eve, is concretized in the flesh of woman, then the flesh of disabled people has historically, and within Judeo-Christian theology especially, represented divine punishment for ancestral transgression' (Shakespeare 1994, p.292).

This embodiment of disability has been a consistent historical feature of western cultural values. However, its significance has been accentuated by two factors. First, the increasing medicalisation of everyday life has raised awareness about the way in which social problems become defined in medical terms. Second, the increasing currency of bodily discourse in popular culture and contemporary social science has focused attention on areas of enquiry which were previously marginalised or taboo (Featherstone, Hepworth and Turner 1991; Shilling 1993; B. Turner 1984, 1992). For the purposes of this study the significance of embodiment is twofold. First, it allows social policy responses to disability to be constructed as 'individual packages of care' rather than as collective responses to collective oppression. Second, it legitimises the ability of professional elites to maintain relationships of power and gaze over disabled people in the production of welfare.

The culture of otherness

Not only have disabled people been represented in terms of tragedy and the impaired body, they have also been constructed as *other* rather than *same*. The term 'otherness' is borrowed in this context from feminist analyses of cultural representation and values (de Beauvoir 1976; Jordanova 1989; Kristeva 1982) and from anti-racist approaches to the social construction of black people's experience in western capitalist societies (Du Bois 1969 [1903]; Fanon 1967). However, it is important to note that disabled writers have employed similar concepts to describe their experience for at least 30 years (see Hunt 1966). Otherness should perhaps also be considered within the sociological context of 'outsider' groups (see Becker 1963).

Certainly, it is fair to say that perceived impairment has been used to set apart certain groups of people from the mainstream of western society. For example, Barnes (1996a; 1996b) shows how the cultural separation of disabled people can be traced throughout the history of western society from the Ancient Greeks to the present day. This analysis is further reinforced in the work of Garland (1995) and Dutton (1996). The setting apart of people according to perceived impairment has thus been a persistent feature of western cultural representation, evidenced in Judeo-Christian theology, Shakespearean drama, 'rationalist' biological science, nineteenth-century literature and contemporary discourses of welfare.

The construction of impairment as otherness remains a popular metaphor. For example, Cumberbatch and Negrine (1992) reviewed television and film coverage and found that while disabled people do appear in factual programmes (especially in the news) they almost never appear in game shows and are under-represented in fictional programming. This analysis is clearly reminiscent of feminist and anti-racist critiques indicating that women and black people remain similarly under-represented in fictional and non-fictional media programming. Additionally, Cumberbatch and Negrine note that disabled characters in film and television are half as likely as non-disabled people to be involved in a sexual relationship and are usually solitary 'loners' (see also, Nordon 1995). Thus, disabled people have consistently been represented as excluded from society by their impairment.

Iris Young (1990) suggests that the notions of 'same' and 'other' are symptomatic of a more generalised preoccupation with conceptual dichotomies rooted in the pervading influence of western rationalist philosophy – what Adorno (1973) calls the 'logic of identity'. The tendency to classify things which are similar into a category of 'same' generates a logically opposing category of 'other'. In turn, Young argues, such dichotomies become associated with the underlying normative dichotomy 'good/bad', so that 'same' equals 'good' and 'other' equals 'bad'. This process then obscures the richness and plurality of difference within a heterogeneous public.

The scaling of bodies by the biological sciences has generated normative physical categories based on an idealised notion of the young, white, male body (Daunt 1996; Dutton 1996). Judged against this socially constructed norm, people with black skins, female genitals and physical or cognitive impairments fall by default into the residual category of 'other'. Once the characteristics of otherness become attached to an identifiable social group, a number of social responses are likely to follow. There may be a tendency for members of the group to become physically segregated, to be considered as a separate administratively category, to be avoided, to be feared.

Julia Kristeva (1982) suggests that fear and avoidance of the 'other' serves as a mechanism for the affirmation of identity amongst those considered as 'same'. This, she argues, is most marked where the other's identity impinges most closely upon our own. Where we perceive ourselves as only marginally separated from the other, we most fear losing our identity. It is under these circumstances that we will most forcibly reject the other. The fear is not so much of the other but of an insecurity of self (Allport 1954) and, ultimately, of death – not so much a fear of the *object* as the *abject*. This process Kristeva terms 'abjection'.

Young (1990, p.145) agrees with Kristeva that it is precisely 'what lies just beyond the self' that constitutes the greatest threat to identity. Thus, she suggests that abjection may be a useful way of understanding how 'other' bodies become constructed as ugly or fearsome. For Young, the examples of ageing and impairment fit well with this explanation. Ultimately, she argues: 'The aversion and nervousness that old and disabled people evoke, the sense of their being ugly, arises from the cultural connection of these groups with death' (1990, p.147).

From a disability perspective, Tom Shakespeare (1994) makes the same association with Kristeva's work and argues similarly that the abjection of impaired bodies serves to protect the identities of non-disabled people against the fear of ageing, impairment and death.

The cultural construction of disability as otherness is significant for this study because it has been mirrored in the administrative construction of disability as a separate policy category. This separation has been expressed through both the physical and the administrative segregation of welfare production for disabled people in Britain. Thus, our welfare tradition marks out the 'needs' of disabled people as qualitatively different from those of other citizens and reinforces administrative structures which keep disabled people in a state of dependency, within segregated systems of welfare production (Finkelstein 1991; Finkelstein and Stuart 1996).

The analysis presented so far suggests that the cultural construction of disability in western industrial societies has been premised upon three disabling assumptions. Specifically, the disadvantage experienced by disabled people has been characterised in terms of personal tragedy, the impaired body and otherness. The cultural currency of this value system legitimises a pattern of welfare production which addresses that disadvantage through care, medicalisation and segregation (rather than through participation, integration and equality).

An agenda for change?

From the publication of the Griffiths Report (Griffiths 1988) community care reform was promoted as a radical agenda for change. Rhetorically at least, the primary legislation and subsequent policy guidance promised a fundamental departure from established patterns of welfare delivery. In particular, the new policy agenda held out the possibility of increased choice and self-determination for disabled people in accessing needs-led support towards independent, integrated living. However, in the intervening years of implementation, critics within the disabled people's movement have increasingly argued that the resulting policy framework perpetuates many of the barriers to achieving those ends. Exploring this contention is a central theme of this book.

The legislative framework

It is not necessary to provide a detailed history of British community care policies here. Suffice to say that the current wave of reform is only the most recent expression of a policy agenda which had been evolving for at least 30 years previously. More generally, the relocation of welfare production from institutions to 'the community' has been accelerated by two factors. On a structural level, fiscal crisis and spiralling public sector borrowing heightened the economic imperative for greater efficiency in the production of welfare. On an ideological level there had been increasing challenges to traditional views of 'care' (based on critiques of dependency, medicalisation and physical segregation).

The general framework of social services departments' responsibility to provide 'welfare services' to disabled people is set out in Section 29 of the 1948 National Assistance Act (responsibilities to 'old people' are included in Section 45 of the 1968 Health Services and Public Health Act and in Schedule 9 of the 1983 Health and Social Services and Social Security Adjudiations Acts). However, the primary enabling legislation for local authority providers is contained in Section 2 of the 1970 Chronically Sick and Disabled Persons Act, which places a duty on social services authorities to provide particular kinds of support to disabled people where they have been assessed as needing them.

Many of these responsibilities are concerned with practical help, adaptations and the provision of information about services. In addition, Section 21 and Schedule 8 of the 1977 National Health Service Act give social services departments the power to provide certain other kinds of support (such as laundry services and home help). District health authorities are also empowered to provide community care services by Section 3 of the 1977 National Health Services Act. The requirement for health and social services authorities to provide care services to some people with mental health problems is specifically stressed in Section 117 of the 1983 Mental Health Act.

This post-war legislative framework tended to give local authorities discretionary, enabling powers rather than mandatory obligations to support disabled people in the community. Despite the fact that the provision of some services followed automatically from an assessment of need, there was no clear requirement to assess those needs in the first place. The 1986 Disabled Persons (Services, Consultation and Representation) Act was then significant in emphasising the duty of local authorities to assess people's needs for services under the 1970 Act. Section 47 of the 1990 NHS and Community Care Act further reinforced this duty by requiring local authorities to assess needs where it appeared that support services might be required.

In general terms then the 1990 Act did not replace or consolidate the preexisting patchwork of legislative measures so much as redefine the mechanisms for organising its implementation. Consequently, it is by no means a unitary Act and community care legislation remains a complex phenomenon. Furthermore, its implementation has been accompanied by a wealth of policy guidance from central government departments and quasi-governmental agencies.

The Griffiths Report

In December 1986 the then Secretary of State, Norman Fowler, commissioned Sir Roy Griffiths (then chief executive at Sainsbury's) to develop proposals for the reorganisation of community care. His brief was to review arrangements for public funding and to advise on how such funds could be better used 'as a contribution to more effective community care'. The report, setting out a concise but seemingly radical agenda for change, was published two years later.

Griffiths (1988) was concerned that resources should be used to foster local innovation rather than solutions prescribed by central government. The mechanisms for achieving this, he suggested, should be a system of assessment based on local and individual needs and the development of a market for 'care' that would provide greater choice and diversity in meeting such needs.

Griffiths argued that responsibility for community care should lie with the Local Authority (while Health Authorities would retain responsibility for the 'medical' aspects of care). However, the main thrust of this responsibility was simply to ensure that support was provided in accordance with need (and within available budgets). It was not, he suggested, necessarily the local authority's responsibility to provide such support directly, especially where local markets could generate a diversity of provision in the voluntary and private sectors. Under Griffiths' proposals, the social services department would be required to assess needs in their area, to set priorities and to develop a plan for meeting the assessed need. They would ultimately be responsible for arranging the necessary service provision to fulfil that plan (DoH/Price Waterhouse 1991).

The agenda for change set out in the Griffiths Report was then primarily concerned with organisational and bureaucratic restructuring. Indeed many critics have argued that the main political thrust of the proposals was to reduce the role of local authorities as providers, while increasing independent sector provision 'under the guise of a mixed economy of welfare' (Walker 1989, p.204). However, the agenda for change was also being driven, rhetorically at least, by a critique of traditional modes of welfare production.

A service-led tradition

Griffiths had pointed to a substantial reality gap between the rhetoric and the practice of community care in local authorities. Although his research highlighted the existence of numerous small-scale innovatory projects, he concluded that 'social services authority activities tend to be dominated by the direct management of services which take insufficient account of the varying needs of individuals' (Griffiths 1990, para.4.7).

In a similar way, the White Paper *Caring for People* acknowledged that domiciliary and day care arrangements tended to match clients to services, rather than vice versa. Department of Health research into services for 'younger' physically impaired people also showed that residential and respite care continued to dominate over home-based alternatives (DoH 1993a). Increasingly, government policy guidance articulated the view that traditional service delivery structures in the public sector could themselves be considered as the primary barriers to change. As the Audit Commission argued, 'The organisational framework inherent from the past places undue emphasis on the role of services, with the needs of users and carers taking second place. It has itself become a major impediment to further development, producing inflexibility and rigidity' (Audit Commission 1992a, p.1).

The rigidity of this organisational structure was evident in the attitudes of staff, in organisational values, in administrative systems, in bureaucratic structures. For example, the Department of Health noted that the attitudes of practitioners had been 'framed by the traditional service-led approach, which fits individuals into existing services' (DoH *et al.* 1991b: para.5.23) and that existing budgetary arrangements made it difficult to change priorities in response to need (DoH *et al.* 1991b, p.1). Audit Commission research (1992b) confirmed that traditional management structures, based on buildings rather than the needs of consumers, tended to exhibit a 'rigid style of operation' which was itself a barrier to the development of more responsive and innovatory alternatives.

There is, then, much common ground between these critiques of traditional service provision and those offered by the disabled people's movement (Finkelstein 1981, 1991; Finkelstein and Stuart 1996; Oliver and Barnes 1993). Rhetorically at least, both agendas for change agree in their portrayal of a service-led tradition based on rationalised bureaucracy and the administrative routinisation of support services available to disabled people. Both suggest that the attitudes, corporate values and organisational structures of traditional welfare delivery raise barriers to flexible independent living solutions. Taken at face value, they also concur in calling for the transition to a more flexible and innovative needs-led approach (although they depart radically when it comes to implementation and the definition of 'need').

A needs-led agenda?

When the community care White Paper appeared in 1989 its emphasis was on the managerial responsibilities involved in implementing Griffiths' recommendations. However, the document also contained a clear set of values for the new service arrangements. Community care was to be built around 'services that respond flexibly and sensitively to the needs of individuals and their carers'. Furthermore, the new arrangements would be characterised by 'services that intervene no more than is necessary to foster independence'. In particular, there was a recognition that community care should seek to replace service-led structures with consumer-driven alternatives, a message reiterated in the Audit Commission's report *Managing the Cascade of Change*:

> The essence of the new approach is not the procedural changes introducing contracts, competition, etc., but the establishment at the heart of the service of a direct relationship between users and their carers and commissioners who can direct resources in a flexible way to meet their needs. (Audit Commission 1992a, para.50)

The expectation was that the new administrative arrangements would enable resources to be used more creatively, to establish innovative patterns of support in direct response to individual needs. Specifically, it was envisaged that needs-led 'care assessments' and 'case management' would be the primary mechanisms for creating bespoke 'packages of care'. However, when the Audit Commission reviewed progress in more than 80 per cent of all English local authorities during the summer of 1993, they concluded that there were still many obstacles to a truly needs-led purchasing system (Audit Commission 1993a, p.5).

The promotion of a needs-led approach to assessment was not new. It had already appeared in the 1986 Disabled Persons Act and was a key feature of the much quoted *All Wales Strategy for People with Mental Handicaps*. However, its centrality in the 1990 Act stood in marked contrast to the general drift of service-led legislation in the post-war period. Indeed, in a letter to the London authorities on 1 March 1993, the Assistant Chief Inspector of the Social Services Inspectorate, pointed to, 'an area of legal ambiguity between the Chronically Sick and Disabled Persons Act 1970, which is service-led and the Disabled Persons Act 1986 and the NHS and Community Care Act, which are needs-led'.

As this brief review illustrates, the rhetorical commitment to develop needs-led assessments and creative patterns of responsive welfare delivery was built upon a critique of traditional service-led policies and welfare institutions (as well as on economic imperatives). With this in mind, it is significant to note that the agendas for change promoted by British policy makers and the disabled people's movement share some important areas of common ground – greater choice, self-determination, deinstitutionalisation, needs-led service provision and so on. Yet there has been much conflict between these approaches. In order to show where the differences lie it is necessary to look more closely and critically at the form and content of community care policy making.

Disabling values and community care

The final part of this chapter parallels the earlier analysis of disabling values in order to highlight a number of disabling assumptions in community care policy making – first, that disabled people require 'care', second, that this requirement is a product of physical impairment, and third, that care should be provided within an administratively segregated system of welfare production. Thus, the form and content of community care policies mirror the cultural construction of disability, in terms of tragedy, the impaired body and otherness. In so doing, they function ideologically (by legitimising disabling social relations and by obscuring more enabling alternatives).

The discourse of 'care'

The first assumption of community care policy is that disabled people are dependent and need 'care'. Such assumptions are frequently conveyed in the language of policy making. For example, in writing his report, Griffiths (1988, para.2.3) had 'concentrated on adults who require more than the usual care and support from others *because* they are elderly, mentally ill, mentally handicapped, or physically disabled' [my emphasis].

The White Paper, *Caring for People,* characterised community care as referring to 'people whose needs extend beyond health care to include social care and support...*which they cannot arrange for themselves*' (DoH *et al.* 1989, para.3.2.2, my emphasis). Similarly, the introduction to the Audit Commission's report *Managing the Cascade of Change* referred to 'the care of sick and dependent people' (Audit Commission 1992a, para.1). There are countless other examples. Suffice to say that the construction of disability as dependency has been a recurrent and pervasive feature of community care policy making. As Mike Oliver (1996a, 1996b) has pointed out, this way of speaking about disability implies a unidirectional and causal connection between impairment and dependency. In so doing, it obscures other ways of speaking and acting in response to disability. Specifically, it obscures the possibility that the dependency of people with perceived impairments might also be socially produced.

Thomas (1993) suggests that the notion of care has not been uniformly defined in sociological writing and that it ought to be considered as an empirical concept. However, disabled writers have tended to regard 'care' as a key ideological construct. Richard Wood (1991) for example, attacks the philosophy of *Caring for People* for emphasising 'care' over concepts like 'choice' or 'control'. Thus, he concludes: 'The fundamental problem with these proposals stems from the notion that disabled people want care. Disabled people have never demanded or asked for care!' (1991, p.199).

Similarly, Ann Kestenbaum argues that care assessments and care management are a product of 'the way that society views people with impairments as dependent'. This, she suggests is characterised by 'the assumption that they need caring for, that it is their carers who need the resources and support, and that it is their carers who will speak on their behalf' (1996, p.4).

In this way, community care policies have been much less concerned with why care is provided than with defining who should be cared for, who should do the caring and how this relationship should be organised. As a consequence, important policy debates about the role of disabled people in the community have been effectively obscured by debates about 'care' and 'carers' in the community.

Fox (1995) suggests that care (particularly professionally codified notions of care) can be construed in Foucauldian terms as discipline. For Fox this 'vigil of care' is a relationship of power and control based on knowledge generated within professional discourses (see Hugman 1991; Rose 1989).

He contrasts this disciplining, controlling notion of care with Cixous' (1986) advocation of (feminine) caring as a 'gift' based on 'generosity and the celebration of difference'. For Fox then, 'care-as-gift' can be regarded as an enabling form of resistance to 'care-as-discipline'. In a similar way, Jenny Morris differentiates between loving 'care about' and custodial 'care for' in her study of community care and independent living (1993b, p.149). Thus, 'Once personal assistance is seen as 'care' then the 'carer', whether a professional or a relative, becomes the person in charge, the person in control' (Morris 1993a, p.8).

The construction of commodified care as disciplining discourse is helpful in pointing to the codification of surveillance by professional groupings. However, the juxtaposition of loving interpersonal care as 'resistance' is problematic, primarily because it does not challenge the idea that disabled people need care in the first place (however produced). Relationships of surveillance, subordination and control may operate within the private as well as the public domain, even where they are construed by the dominant party as 'love'. Feminist work on the simultaneous significance of public and private patriarchy provides a useful analogy in this respect (see Walby 1990).

The central role of 'carers' was emphasised in *Caring for People* (as it had been earlier in *Growing Older*). This role has often been described as 'care by the community' (Glendinning 1992; Walker 1989) although, as Means and Smith (1994, p.5) point out, it is not so much the community as individuals who provide the bulk of support. Moreover, the division of unpaid caring labour is highly gendered and individual carers are predominantly women. Thus, Green (1988) and Finch (1990) summarise the argument that 'community care' means care by women within the family home. Glendinning (1992) concludes that the justification of community care as 'lower cost' has only been possible because its true cost is obscured in the exploitation of women's caring labour.

Developing the feminist analysis, Dalley (1988) suggests that community care policies contain an implicit assumption that the (idealised, nuclear) family represents the most appropriate site for care production. Thus, Dalley regards familism as the dominant ideology of community care – legitimising a private production of welfare, premised upon the exploitation of women's caring labour. From a disability perspective, Ken Davis (1995) notes that the promotion of family support, as a cost-effective substitute for state support, can also be disabling. Similarly, for Jenny Morris:

>...a reliance on assistance solely provided by family and friends is incompatible with the philosophy of independent living. Those people who have significant personal assistance requirements and who have been able to participate fully in society have done so *because* they have not had to rely solely on family and friends for the help they need. (Morris 1993b, p.153, original emphasis)

Bond (1991) argues that loving and giving relationships within the family can all too easily become relationships of possession and control. Through financial reward and 'training', relationships with friends and family become formalised, subject to expert knowledge and medicalised judgements. In this way, Bond suggests that the focus on 'informal' support masks the way in which it can be incorporated as a mechanism of surveillance and control. Similarly, Ken Davis argues that the political manipulation of family through community care policies has been a key factor in the continuing oppression of disabled people:

>In the daily round, it doesn't come easy to visualise our partners, wives, husbands, mums, dads and distant aunts that smell of mothballs, as pliable instruments of public policy. But in the Community Care League, these same people are rounded up and fielded in the shape of an homogenous heap labelled 'carers', in the 'Informal' sub-division. (K. Davis 1995, p.7)

If familism and gendered role expectations have dominated the discussion of care production in the private domain, so commodification and marketisation have dominated the analysis of public welfare production. Marketisation was emphasised in the Griffiths Report as a key mechanism for reform and actively promoted by central government as the central feature of the 1990 Act. A great deal has been written about this and I will explore the issues in much more detail later (see Chapter 5). However, it is important to note, as Ungerson (1994, p.13) does, that 'the condition of disability will increasingly have to have money attached to it, and personal care services, from whatever source, will increasingly be commodified'.

As with debates on familism and the needs of carers, the burgeoning literature on social care markets and commodification takes the dependency of people with impairments as given. Again, social policy debates have focused on the effective production of care, rather than a critical examination of its ideological significance. Suffice to say that a preoccupation with the mechanisms of care production obscures an unquestioning acceptance that disabled people require 'care'. The discourse of care (in its commodified and professionally-codified form) is premised upon the assumption that disabled people are unavoidably dependent upon non-disabled people, and that the relationships of power and domination which exist between them are therefore unproblematic.

The assumption that disabled people require 'care' results in a preoccupation with the mechanics, economics and labour divisions of care production which obscures the discussion of more enabling alternatives. The agenda for community care policy making has thus been premised upon the view that those who 'cannot help themselves' require 'care' (or control). This view is part of a more general cultural construction of disability as 'personal tragedy'. The construction of disability as personal tragedy conveys the idea that the dependency experienced by disabled people is both unavoidable and irrevocable. In this context, tragedy conveys much more than simple misfortune; it conveys the idea of powerlessness – of impotency.

The discourse of individualism

If the primary assumption of community care policy is that disabled people need care, then the second assumption is that this need arises as a result of personal inadequacy. It is the individual, rather than the collective needs of disabled people, that are made an issue. This kind of individualism is closely linked to personal tragedy theories of disability and thus to biological determinism. The construction of disability as 'personal tragedy' emphasises not only the 'tragic' but also the 'personal'. As Dalley (1991, p.3) points out, this involves a process:

> ...whereby the experience of disability is fragmented into a series of individualised episodes devoid of sociological significance. Accordingly, disability becomes unique for each individual; the disabled person must make his/her own adjustment to the circumstances of disablement and negotiate a means of 'coping' as best s/he can.

As numerous others have noted, the definitions of disability employed in British welfare policy have been framed exclusively within an individual, rather than a social, model approach. For example, the regulations governing Section 47(2) of the 1990 NHS and Community Care Act define disabled people as those who are 'blind, deaf or dumb, or who suffer from mental disorder of any description, and other persons aged 18 or over who are substantially and permanently handicapped by illness, injury or congenital deformity'.

This incorporation of personal aetiology into disability policy making reinforces individual models of disability. The emphasis on medical or functional criteria is consistent with a broad flow of policy making which confuses disability with impairment, and with illness (Barnes and Mercer 1996). For example, the 1948 National Assistance Act took sickness and impairment as a combined category (namely, persons 'substantially or permanently handicapped by illness, injury or congenital deformity'). This association was later reinforced in the 1970 Chronically Sick and Disabled Persons' Act and the 1972 Local Government Act.

There are numerous other examples. In 1991, despite protest from disabled people's organisations, the OPCS perpetuated the link between illness and disability in their wording of the National Census form. In setting targets for *The Health of the Nation,* the government's only reference to people with physical impairments was to call for a reduction in the number of pressure sores. Similarly, the introduction of Incapacity Benefit in the 1995 Social Security (Incapacity for Work) Act illustrated a continuing reliance on medical testing as the gateway to disability benefits. Yet, many disabled people are not ill. Obstacles to work have as much to do with inaccessible workplace environments, or employers' refusals to accommodate their needs, as with the person's personal 'capacity' for work. As Dave Gibbs observes, 'What many of us feel, as disabled people, is that we are being dragged along by a system which insists on regarding our bodies as the source of the problem' (*Observer,* 7 May 1995).

Alden Chadwick (1996) argues that this persistent use of medicalised definitions in British social policy can be regarded, in Foucauldian terms, as a discursive power/knowledge nexus. Thus:

> By creating and subsequently existing within a medical knowledge of disability, the medical professions and their associates cannot (or choose not to) concern themselves with the unthought, ungoverned social barriers which cause disability – a causality they monopolise and demonstrate to society at large, a society which in turn empowers (through legislation, myth or finance) the institutions, the knowledge and the professions therein. (Chadwick 1996, p.33)

Marxist approaches to the sociology of medicine (Mishler 1981; Waitzkin 1979, 1989) have shown how medicalisation reinforces the ideologies of particular state or class interests. Similarly, Paul Abberley argues that medicalised definitions of disability serve a greater purpose, 'Functional definitions are essentially state definitions, in that they relate to the major concerns of the state…production, capacity to work…welfare, demands that have to be met from revenue if they cannot be offloaded on some other party…' (Abberley 1992, p.141).

More generally, the medicalisation of social issues tends to depoliticise them. Thus, the embodiment of disability depoliticises discrimination and obscures the lack of state intervention for its amelioration. At the same time, functional definitions legitimise professional interest groups concerned with maintaining the dependency of disabled people through 'cure' or 'care'.

Similarly, Ryan and Thomas (1980) argue that it is no 'accident of history' that the NHS assumes so much responsibility for people with learning difficulties. Rather, they suggest, it is indicative of the way in which our society deals with people it cannot accommodate – by defining them as medical problems. This medicalisation of social problems functions ideologically, they argue, by masking the social aspects of their exclusion. Importantly, Ryan and Thomas assert that medical dominance extends beyond the walls of institutions into a generalised social response, 'Medical model thinking tends to support the status quo. The subnormality of the individual rather than the subnormality of the environment, tends to be blamed for any inadequacies' (1980, p.27)

The formulation of community care policy, and the discourse which surrounds its implementation, is framed within an individualist view of disability. These ideas function ideologically by obscuring other policy agendas. Community care policy making has assumed the 'problem' of disability to be an individual rather than a social phenomenon. That individualism has functioned ideologically by masking the collective oppression of disabled people. In particular, speaking about disability and disadvantage as an individual problem prevents us from discussing the removal of disabling barriers in the wider social world.

The discourse of segregation

The third and final theme in this analysis concerns the assumption that the needs of disabled people should be addressed (in the public sphere at least) through separate institutions of welfare production. On first inspection this seems incongruous, given that the stated objective of community care policies has been to break down segregative welfare arrangements and to relocate care production within 'the community'. Ostensibly, the community care reforms were intended to establish a means of 'providing the services and support which people…need to be able to live as independently as possible in their own homes, or in 'homely' settings in the community' (DoH *et al.* 1989, para.1.1). Rhetorically at least, the policy agenda promoted decarceration and the social integration of disabled people.

Certainly, the primary site of welfare production has shifted from large residential institutions to 'community settings' and the home. However, it is important to ask whether the significance of this move is anything more than geographic. Segregation may be physical (in the case of residential, health, education and day care services) but it may also be administrative (in the creation of distinct bureaucratic systems and administrative structures). Moreover, administrative segregation can be as powerful a form of surveillance and control as physical incarceration, if more insidious. In order to understand this point it is important to remember that British policy making continues to demonstrate an almost complete segregation of services for disabled people. Indeed, there are 'special' policies or statutes covering health, education, housing, transport, employment, social services, welfare benefits, sexuality, reproduction and civil rights (Barnes 1991).

The concept of administrative segregation hinges on the maintenance of an administrative disability category which allows the segregation of disabled people to function not only physically but also bureaucratically. Thus, Stone (1984) argues that disability is a socially (or bureaucratically) constructed category. This flexible category, she argues, functions ideologically by defining those 'not able' to work. It is a negative category because it does not define disabled people so much as non-disabled people (i.e. those who are required to work). Thus, 'The disability concept was essential to the development of a workforce in early capitalism and remains indispensable as an instrument of the state in controlling labor supply' (Stone 1984, p.179).

There is not room here to explore this argument in detail and other authors have examined the issues extensively elsewhere (Oliver 1990 and Finkelstein 1991). The legislative origins of such a category in England can be traced back at least to the sixteenth century (Priestley 1997a). The relevance of the point is simply that community care policy making remains located within a welfare heritage which takes disability as a separate administrative category. In so doing it perpetuates a tradition in which the needs of disabled people are accommodated within a segregated system of welfare production.

To summarise, the preceding discussion highlights three key assumptions within the formation and implementation of British community care policies

– first, that disabled people require 'care', second, that this need for care is a product of impairment and, third, that care should be provided within an administratively segregated system of welfare production. Consequently, the policy agenda for community care reinforces individual models of disability and obscures the consideration of other modes of welfare production based on participation, integration and equality.

Conclusions

Dominant cultural values are reflected in the self-portrayal of a society and negative representations of disability abound. The imagery of impairment has consistently been employed as metaphor for tragedy, imperfection and isolation. This imagery has been mirrored in a welfare system which responds to the social exclusion of disabled people through individual care, medicalisation and segregation. The implication is that where disabled people are unable to participate in production and reproduction it is because of their impairment. More importantly, because this is no-one's fault it is also *unavoidable.* Consequently, they should be cared for in their 'misfortune'.

Discussions about 'care' have been much less concerned with *why* care is provided than with defining who should be cared for, who should do the caring and how this relationship should be organised. In the private domain, the assumption of care by women within the family has remained unchallenged since pre-Christian times. In the public domain there have been more developments. However, the idea that people with impairments need 'care' was as central to the Cistercian or Benedictine abbots as it was to the philanthropic asylum builders of the early nineteenth century, to Leonard Cheshire or to Sir Roy Griffiths.

In considering the cultural representation of disability as tragedy, it is important to remember that most other forms of structural oppression have, at one time or another, also been constructed as misfortune and impotence. For example, membership of the working classes was often considered by English welfare philanthropists as an unfortunate accident of birth (rather than as a form of structural oppression). The idea of poverty as personal misfortune and powerlessness gave rise to corresponding policy responses. Thus, many early initiatives for the amelioration of urban poverty and the improvement of factory conditions were conducted within a culture of philanthropy or paternalism rather than political struggle.

In a similar way, the social disadvantage experienced by women, black people, elders, children, lesbians and gay men in Britain has frequently been viewed as biological destiny or ill fortune (rather than as the product of a capitalist economy within a patriarchal or imperialist legacy). Suffice to say that where forms of social division or stratification are thought to be the consequences of misfortune then policy responses have often reflected that same value structure.

This idealist narrative suggests that the value base which determines how the 'problem' of disability is perceived may influence the policy response. For example, where the perceived problem is impairment, the likely response might be medical treatment; where the perceived problem is public attitudes, the response might be public education; where disability is perceived as discrimination, the response might be anti-discriminatory legislation and so on. Using this approach, the likely policy implications of various individual and social model approaches to disability are summarised in Table 2.1.

British disability policy has consistently reflected the values of an individual model approach, by favouring charity over civil rights, individual care over collective needs and segregation over inclusion. The result has been individual model services in which quality is judged by the standard of physical care, treatment or commodities afforded to individuals. The 'success' of such services has then been judged by their ability to maintain disabled people in the most cost-effective way, while keeping them within the distributive (rather than the productive) system of welfare and justice.

Table 2.1 Policy responses to individual and social model values

Location	Perceived Problem	Likely Response
INDIVIDUAL	misfortune impairment otherness loss limitation welfare	charity medical treatment segregation adjustment remedial therapy care
SOCIAL	prejudice poverty physical barriers discrimination oppression	public education disability income access civil rights political struggle

Policy responses to the disadvantage experienced by disabled people have been largely concerned with individual 'care', medical 'cures', rehabilitation, loss adjustment, counselling and so on. As Lakey (1994, p.132) argues, 'if anything, welfarism has helped to reinforce our experience of dependency'. Similarly, Oliver and Barnes (1993, p.269) suggest that we have witnessed a disabling shift from 'rights based' to 'needs based' policy responses during the post-war period. The significance of this transition, they argue, has been masked by a focus on community care.

Conversely, organisations within the growing disabled people's movement have been the primary advocates for new, enabling policy responses based on social models of disability. Their critiques of 'care', treatment and segregation have been accompanied by the promotion of alternative models of service delivery which challenge the established social relations of welfare production. The self organisation of disabled people has thus created opportunities for the emergence of new policy debates about participation, integration and equality.

In outlining the disabling assumptions of community care I have adopted a broadly idealist narrative which draws heavily on social constructionist writings. I have chosen this approach because the initial focus for the study was prompted by the participants' emphasis on 'value' conflicts. However, there are some important deficiencies in this line of argument. Abrams (1982) for example, is concerned that idealist approaches to welfare policy leave some vital questions unanswered: 'where for example do currents of opinion come from? Why is one, rather than another dominant at any particular time? And how precisely do such currents become embodied in legislation?' (p.11)

It would be naive in the extreme to consider any conflict of welfare ideologies in isolation from its socio-economic and historical context. Welfare ideologies do not emerge or compete in a simple pluralistic way and the relative influence of opposing values systems is contingent upon the distribution of power within a given society. Moreover, there is considerable evidence that these existing power relationships are not only culturally constructed but also socially produced (Barnes 1996a; Finkelstein 1980, 1991; Oliver 1990; Ryan and Thomas 1980).

It would be impossible to consider the differential incorporation of disabled people without recourse to a social model of disability. However, there are dangers here too. In particular, there is certain 'poverty' in crude historicism and it is easy to obscure or marginalise the agency of disabled people through this kind of discourse. Although the notion of personal tragedy provides the basis for individual models of disability (Oliver 1996, p.31), social model approaches also run the risk of tragedy-speak. Where the 'cripple' has been portrayed as impotent in the face of deistic or biological omnipotence, so the 'disabled person' may all too easily seem impotent in the face of historical materialism.

Narratives of biology, culture, professional power and political economy all tend to suggest a non-reciprocal process in which disabled people have been more acted upon than acting. They are often stories of passivity, treatment, surveillance, control or confinement. Disabled people have not only been excluded from many of these narratives but also from the telling of them. The process has been one of objectification (or subjectification) in which non-disabled people have acquired the power to define the identities and experiences of disabled people. Yet this is only one side of the story and there are other less often told versions – narratives in which disabled people, as much as philanthropists, physicians, professional elites, legislators or ruling classes are the central actors.

The very act of observation connotes a power relationship between observer and observed. Feminist analyses have shown how gaze itself can be construed as a form of mastery (Berger 1972) and how the ability to scrutinise is premised upon power (Coward 1984). Thus, the ability of non-disabled people to dominate the discourse of disability indicates an underlying power-knowledge relationship. Conversely, the ability of the disabled people's movement to 'gaze back' at a disabling society is an important indicator of its potential as an agent of social change (Morrison and Finkelstein 1993). Thus, the following chapter charts the evolution of the disabled people's movement and its role in developing a counter-hegemonic value system and an alternative set of policy options. This alternative narrative deals as much with the personal as with the political and is illustrated with reference to the case study in Derbyshire.

CHAPTER 3

An Enabling Counter-Culture

Where community care policy making has been framed within an individual model of disability, so the development of the disabled people's movement is inextricably bound up with a social model of disability. Within this context, the self-organisation of disabled people highlights the existence of a significant counter-culture, and a coherent ideology for change. In particular, the philosophy of independent/integrated living offers new policy alternatives to the philosophy of 'community care'.

The discussion in this chapter begins with a review of the literature on social movements and its relevance to the emergence of the disabled people's movement (with particular reference to events in Derbyshire). The second part of the chapter examines the theory and practice of independent/ integrated living, paying particular attention to the history of Centres for Independent/Integrated Living (CILs). Finally, this history is related to the establishment of the Derbyshire Centre for Integrated Living (DCIL).

Social movements

It is not necessary to provide a comprehensive review of the literature on social movements here and several authors give good historical overviews (Boggs 1986; Eyerman and Jamison 1991; Herbele 1951; Roberts and Kloss 1974). However, it is important to understand something about social movement theory in order to contextualise the development of the disabled people's movement. The literature is both extensive and diverse. Most of it is either liberal-pluralist, post-Marxist or postmodernist in its analysis. New social movements are widely recognised as agents of significant social change within either a reformist or a radical socialist tradition.

Social movements, old and 'new'

Early writing on social movements is closely identified with class struggle. Much of it deals with the emergence of proletarian or socialist movements. Herbele (1951), for example, notes Von Stein's (1850) use of the term (*Socialen Bewegung*) to describe socialist or communist movements after the French revolution. Similarly, Herbele points to Sombart's (1909) view, that social movements can be thought of as practical attempts to realise socialist goals (see Roberts and Kloss 1974). The identification of social movements with a single class actor has led other non-class movements to be described as examples of 'false consciousness', or indeed, as 'non-movements' (Blumer 1946). Consequently, a great deal of the writing in recent years has been concerned with explaining the rise of 'new' social movements, like those associated with black civil rights, feminism, peace, sexuality and ecology (see Eyerman and Jamison 1991).

Hobsbawm (1963, ch. IX) argues that modern social movements are more concerned with content than with form (compared to their 'archaic' predecessors). Offe (1980) develops the form-content distinction and notes that new social movements tend to articulate 'post-materialist' demands and that they have involved 'social alliances' rather than a single class (Offe 1985). Mauss (1975) bases his study of new social movements on a social constructionist analysis, defining them in terms of 'social problems'. Thus, Mauss sees 'publics' forming around particular economic, political, moral, occupational, psychological and scientific interests. Similarly, Touraine (1985, p.777) identifies new social movements with heterogeneity and with 'ethnic and moral pluralism', rather than with a commonality of class interest.

These sort of definitions pose some difficulties for the Marxist, class-based analyses which characterise writing about earlier social movements. Boggs (1986, p.3) for example, distinguishes 'new' social movements as those movements 'not primarily grounded in labor struggles' and suggests that a 'post-industrialist' society requires a 'post-Marxist' response. For Boggs, 'the very appearance of the new social movements has effectively overturned the Marxian assumption…that the industrial working class is the decisive revolutionary protagonist within capitalist society' (1986, p.17).

Such arguments have, then, led many writers to consider new social movements within a postmodern (or late modern) analysis of society (Boyne and Rattansi 1990; Harvey 1989; Murray 1991; Turner 1990). As this brief review indicates, the literature on new social movements is both extensive and diverse. It would certainly be impossible to provide a comprehensive review here. However, I have chosen to prioritise two issues which have a direct bearing on the disabled people's movement. First, it is important to review the way in which new social movements can bring about social change. Second, it is helpful to think about how new social movements come into being.

Social movements and social change

In explaining how new social movements can act as agents of social change, in other than purely class terms, several authors draw on Gramsci's work. Gramsci (1971, p.12) was able to transcend purely economistic ideas about social revolution by admitting that socially constructed 'blocs' of people could bring about significant social change within 'civil' and 'political' society. Laclau and Mouffe (1985) argue that such blocs can indeed be mobilised from sections of society exploited in other than purely economic terms (for example, women, gay men and lesbians, people from ethnic minorities and so on). Thus, they refute the idea of a unified or total hegemony and break with the Marxist tradition of economistic historicism. Similarly, Boggs (1986) draws on Gramsci to assert that new social movements possess counter-hegemonic potential, as agents in a 'war of position' leading to decisive political change.

There is also much debate about the kind of social change envisaged by social movements. While there is a clear distinction between new social movements and 'pressure groups', reformism rather than revolution is the recurrent theme. Touraine (1981) identifies self-limitation as a key feature of new social movements while Cohen (1985, p.664) talks of their 'self limiting radicalism'. Melucci (1989, p.39) notes that social movements have tended to seek inclusion rather than overthrow and concludes that they 'contain no antagonistic dimension'. It would be inappropriate to consider all contemporary protest movements in this light (for example, the anti-road building movement). However, it is certainly true that the agenda for action within many movements has been focused on issues of incorporation and welfare (Williams 1991, p.18).

Significantly for this study, the experience of differential incorporation and abnormal levels of state surveillance have been important catalysts for the self-organisation of disabled people in Britain. For example, referring to their work with mental health user groups, Barnes and Shardlow (1996, p.115) suggest that 'it is the use or survival of services, rather than the experience of mental distress *per se* which usually provides the starting point for involvement in the movement'.

In a more general sense, such experiences are reminiscent of Habermas' (1981, 1987) contention that new social movements often act to challenge colonisation of the 'life world' by bureaucracy and micro-authority (see also Wolfensberger 1989, p.34). Walzer (1982) also develops this theme, arguing that bureaucracy is the primary target for 'insurgent' movements. Similarly, Zola (1987) suggests that these movements are often concerned with decolonising service provision through 'politicised self-help'. In this context it is important to remember that disabled people have been more 'colonised' by service provision than non-disabled people, and that the movement for independent/integrated living has been particularly concerned with issues of decolonisation.

Having said this, it is also important to remember that the agenda of the disabled people's movement extends far beyond specific welfare issues and consumer demands. In redefining disability, the disabled people's movement has challenged much more than just professional interest groups or institutions of welfare delivery. It has also brought into question the social relations of production and reproduction which create disability in the first place. In this sense, the disabled people's movement is perhaps less like a 'new' social movement than some other current forms of collective action. Indeed, the disabled people's movement is perhaps more susceptible to a class-based analysis than some other contemporary social movements (Priestley 1995b).

The emergence of social movements

Probably the biggest debate in the recent literature concerns the emergence of new social movements. How and why do they come about? Two broad schools of thought are evident. These are sometimes described as 'break-down' (or 'resource-mobilisation') models and 'solidarity' (or 'identity-oriented') models (Cohen 1985; Melucci 1985; Useem 1980). The following review briefly outlines these approaches and some recent attempts at synthesis between the two.

Broadly speaking, breakdown models suggest that social disintegration, coupled with discontent, is central to the mobilisation of support for social movements. Smelser (1963), like Durkheim, argued that portions of society experiencing economic, political or social loss (as a result of cultural modernisation) are more likely to turn to 'deviant' social action. For example,

Crawford and Naditch (1970) explain urban rioting in the 1960s in terms of 'deprivation' and 'powerlessness', while Piven and Cloward (1977) connect the American poor people's movements of the 1930s with the preceding depression. Cohen (1985) points out that most breakdown model explanations have focused on resource-mobilisation. That is, they have focused on the development of organisation and communication within the movement. Consequently, they may sometimes tend to marginalise the study of feelings or grievances amongst those who are mobilising.

While breakdown approaches suggest that those with a weak sense of community identification are more susceptible to 'deviant' social movements, solidarity models suggest that isolated individuals are actually less likely to protest. For example, Tilly, Tilly and Tilly (1975) provide empirical studies of collective action up to the 1930s which support a solidarity model. Similarly, Freeman (1973) prefers a solidarity explanation in her analysis of the 1960s 'women's liberation movement'. Pursuing this line of argument, Cohen (1985) notes how neo-Marxist interpretations tend to emphasise the importance of consciousness, ideology, social struggle and solidarity. Thus, they represent an identity-oriented approach to collective action.

Touraine (1985) associates these two models with conflicting schools of sociological thought (functionalism and 'structuro-marxism'). Klandermans and Tarrow (1988) and Kriesi (1988) identify the dichotomy with American and European approaches respectively. There are empirical studies which support both solidarity and breakdown models. Indeed, both models have proved effective in explaining the emergence of new social movements (see Useem 1980). Equally, both are open to criticism. Melucci (1985, p.792) for example, argues that resource-mobilisation approaches fail to explain why social movements emerge (in terms of meaning) while identity-oriented approaches fail to explain how movements are established and maintained (in terms of organisation).

Bearing in mind the tensions in the literature, it is important to develop an account which recognises both the ideological and organisational features of the disabled people's movement. As the remainder of this chapter shows, the analysis of disabled people's self-organisation suggests that identity and resource-mobilisation have been interdependent. Widespread discontent and a clear set of values helped to facilitate organisational cohesion within the movement. At the same time, the establishment of formal and informal structures helped to create new spaces in which alternative debates and positive identities could be forged.

The disabled people's movement

Disabled people have increasingly demonstrated the potential of politicised self-organisation. Indeed many contemporary disabled writers argue that the growth of a broadly based social movement is central to the liberation of disabled people. Oliver for example, rejects that idea that disabled people can look to the welfare state or traditional political activity for significant improvement in their experience. For him, 'The only hope, therefore, is that the disabled people's movement will continue to grow in strength and consequently have a substantial impact on the politics of welfare provision' (1990, p.112).

The following discussion illustrates how such a movement has been brought into being through the personal and collective struggles of disabled people. I have adopted a broadly historical narrative which draws on the experiences and accounts of disabled people who were involved. In particular I have sought to link the personal struggles of disabled people in Derbyshire to the development of the wider movement.

A brief history

I do not propose to provide a comprehensive history of the disabled people's movement here and several authors give good overviews (e.g. Campbell and Oliver 1996; K. Davis 1993; De Yong 1981; Driedger 1989; Finkelstein 1991; Hasler 1993; Oliver 1990). As with other notable new social movements, the disabled people's movement grew from a wide variety of personal and collective struggles; only in retrospect were many of these personal experiences recognised as political. Thus, in examining the emergence of the movement, it is important to give credence to first-hand accounts and individual struggles as well as to macro-level analyses.

Pagel (1988) reviews the self-organisation of disabled people and links its emergence to the early labour movement (rather than to the post-war era of 'new' social movements). Pagel cites the formation of the British Deaf Association in 1890 (see Grant 1990) and the National League of the Blind and Disabled – which was constituted as a trade union in 1899 (see NLBD 1988). Ken Davis (1993, p.287) notes that such organisations were generally 'single interest' groups representing only their own members, and often restricted to people with a common form of impairment. Although these organisations may not have constituted a broadly based social movement they do demonstrate how disabled people in Britain have been organising themselves to act politically for almost a century.

Throughout the twentieth century the numbers of organisations of disabled people have increased and their activities have developed. Finkelstein (1991) identifies the growing activism of the Association of Disabled Professionals, the Association of Blind and Partially Sighted Teachers and Students, the Spinal Injuries Association (see Oliver and Hasler 1987) and the National Federation of the Blind (NFB). Hasler (1993, p.279) notes the importance of the Disablement Income Group (DIG), formed in 1965 as a campaigning organisation, and Campbell and Oliver (1996, p.44) draw attention to the Disabled Drivers' Association. However, Oliver (1990, p.114) suggests that these campaigning organisations remained 'single issue groups'. Disability was still defined in terms of impairment and there was little cohesion between groups. Moreover, in the emerging welfare state, it was welfare charities and professions controlled by non-disabled people that dominated the disability policy community.

As in other parts of Britain, the disabled people's movement in Derbyshire grew from the struggles of individual disabled people against oppressive environments – in families, in educational establishments, in employment and in residential institutions (particularly at the Cressy Fields Cheshire Home). On an organisational level, an active branch of the NFB had been running in Sherwood Peak since the 1950s. In 1967 a branch of DIG was established in Derby, followed shortly by an NFB Derby branch and a second DIG branch in Erewash. Davis and Mullender (1993) also draw attention to the Portland Training College Old Students Association and (from 1974) the UPIAS (Union of Physically Impaired Against Segregation) meetings at Cressy Fields. These organisations, they argue, facilitated contact between groups and individuals. These early meetings brought people together and opened up new spaces for discussion in which previously isolated experiences became linked to ideas and strategies for building a mass movement. As Davis and Mullender put it: 'This gradual process of coming together was accompanied by a slow build up of confidence in the validity of personal experience of disability as being the only reliable basis for practical action. The personal had started to become political' (1993, p.7).

Most accounts of the disabled people's movement point to the late 1960s and early 1970s as a period of change. Gerber (1990, p.4) links the strategies of the movement to a 'generalised questioning of the legitimacy of official and institutional cultural authorities' evident in feminist, 'Third World' and black movements. For De Yong (1983, p.12) the US civil rights movement had a strong influence in legitimising non-traditional forms of protest.

Hasler (1993, p.283) however, points out that the NLB had used direct action and lobbying in Britain as long ago as 1933. Pagel (1988) suggests that participation within a wider climate of social protest enabled disabled activists to acquire the skills and confidence for their own political self-organisation. Specifically, Scotch (1985, p.ii) argues:

> Demands for full access by disabled people occurred in the wake of the widespread and highly visible social conflicts of the 1960s... A number of disabled people had been active participants in these movements, and they came to see their disability in the same political sense as blacks viewed their race or women their gender.

The turning point

The beginning of the 1980s heralded a major turning point in the development of the disabled people's movement locally, nationally and internationally. Prompted by a rising global awareness of disability, the United Nations established plans for an 'International Year for Disabled People' (IYDP). However, in a climate of growing consumerism and politicisation, the demand from disabled people was that the International Year should be 'of' rather than 'for' Disabled People. At its World Congress in 1980, disabled representatives called on the Rehabilitation International to share control with disabled people. Driedger (1989) describes how the defeat of this motion, together with the issues raised by IYDP, provided a dramatic catalyst for the foundation, in 1981, of Disabled Peoples' International (DPI) as the global expression of disabled people's self-organisation.

Similar processes were apparent at a local level in Derbyshire. Traditional charitable organisations controlled by non-disabled people were approaching IYDP in a manner which highlighted a fundamental conflict of values between themselves and local disabled people. Davis and Mullender (1993) describe how the most prominent of these organisations, the Derbyshire Association for the Disabled, proposed to mark the coming international year with a 'craft competition and coffee morning' at Chatsworth House. Local disability activists were both bewildered and outraged at the prospect of an event so far removed from the spirit of IYDP and set about organising an alternative strategy.

Approaches to Derbyshire County Council's social services department resulted in an agreement to organise a Derbyshire IYDP Conference in collaboration with the Derbyshire Information Advice Line (DIAL) under the slogan 'full participation and equality'. The conference took place in

February 1981 and the formation of the Derbyshire Coalition of Disabled People (DCDP) followed as a direct result. A steering group for the embryonic coalition had been recruited from the floor of the IYDP conference and this small collective set about organising meetings in different locations throughout the county (to facilitate attendance by people with limited access to transport). A grant of £20,000 was obtained from the County Council and the inaugural meeting of DCDP took place at Matlock on 12 December 1981.

The initial Coalition meetings involved a relatively small group of people. In the main they were active disabled people with some experience of discussing similar issues in the UPIAS 'cells'. Consequently, the steering committee for the new Coalition was composed largely of people who had been exposed to the main political arguments at an earlier stage. As a consequence, these meetings, like those of UPIAS, ran the risk of alienating other, less politicised disabled people. Consequently, a good deal of effort was required to 'ground' the work of the Coalition in tangible local issues with which people could identify. As one founder member put it:

> ...the Union may have itself narrowed down to a rather small number of highly intellectually active people, but I could see at a local level that you couldn't move in that way...I mean to get a mass movement you had to be much more open, able to engage people where they were in their own situation and somehow give them a feeling, a reason, you know, to want to come together. All sorts of people came into contact with the Coalition, took part in the early discussion groups and teach-ins as we called them. And releasing things for the first time and having the opportunity to do this on common ground, and growing in understanding as they went along. It wasn't about imposing your own political ideas on people, because you couldn't do that. People were isolated anyway...and yet we did move on in ideas fairly rapidly. (Interview transcript)

The Coalition was able to draw not only on the contributions of those disabled people who became actively involved but also on the wealth of accumulated knowledge and experiences derived from the Derbyshire Information Advice Line. DIAL had been established as an information service at Cressy Fields in the mid 1970s and the growing number of telephone queries helped to establish a broad picture of the needs and problems of disabled people in the county.

At the same time there had been a growing cohesion amongst disabled activists in other parts of the country and abroad. In the United States, disabled people were forming the American Coalition of Citizens with Disabilities and preliminary work was being undertaken towards the establishment of a similar national coalition in Britain. Sixteen organisations controlled by disabled people were identified and the formation of the British Council of Organisations of Disabled People (BCODP, now the British Council of Disabled People) was arranged to coincide with that of DPI in November 1981. The Derbyshire group were instrumental in the foundation of BCODP and its national offices were located within the county. BCODP in turn played a key role in determining the eventual structure of DPI. Consequently, the self-organisation of disabled people in Derbyshire was not only influenced by the wider movement, it also acted reciprocally in shaping the development of that same movement both nationally and globally.

Back at the local level, the formative Derbyshire Coalition sought to influence policy making with the County Council. The political climate in Derbyshire was shifting and the local elections in 1981 brought in a new Labour administration committed, in principle at least, to equality issues for minority groups. Striking while the iron was hot, DCDP challenged the local authority to make a public commitment to the principles of the International Year of Disabled People. Although the Coalition's initial demands posed a direct challenge to local authority service provision, they also appealed to the political climate of 'equal opportunities' prevailing in Labour authorities during the early 1980s. A draft statement was prepared by the Coalition and subsequently adopted, with only minor alteration, by the newly elected Labour Council.

This *Statement of Intent* recognised the principles of the IYDP and the United Nations' aims and accepted the rights of disabled people to full participation and equality of opportunity. In the statement, the County Council reaffirmed its existing policies and pledged to participate with disabled people in a number of key areas (consultation, access, housing, transport, education and information). The full text of the statement is reproduced in Davis and Mullender (1993, p.19).

Thus, in the space of just a year, the individual and long-standing struggles of disabled people in Derbyshire had found practical and political expression. Not only had they formed the first broadly based coalition of disabled people in Britain, they had also secured public commitment from the primary welfare state agent to their goals and values. At an organisational level, it was the formation of local, national and supranational coalitions which helped the modern disabled people's movement to become a cohesive political force for change. From its dramatic beginnings, DPI has developed a global network of more than 70 national assemblies. It has also achieved a significant 'seat at the table' with consultative status at the United Nations, UNESCO and the International Labour Organisation (see Driedger 1989). BCODP's membership has grown to more than 100 constituent organisations and, from 1996, numerous individual members.

The preceding analysis emphasises organisational structures (a resource-mobilisation model). However, it is important to recognise that many of the coalescing influences were associated with the discovery of new identities and shared values (a solidarity model). On an ideological level, the self-organisation of disabled people in Britain became united to some extent around the issue of poverty during the 1970s. DIG played a significant role in this respect by focusing coordination on the campaign for increased disability benefit levels. However, in the end, it was the development of 'social models' of disability within the movement which formed the basis for an ideology of political action.

For Hasler (1993) 'The Big Idea' for the disabled people's movement was developed principally through the creation of the Union of Physically Impaired Against Segregation (UPIAS) in 1974. UPIAS' (1976) major contribution was in articulating a social definition of disability, later amended by BCODP to include all disabled people (see the introduction to this book). The importance of a 'big idea' in mobilising activism is indicative of an identity-oriented process. For example, Turner (1969) is keen to stress that the emergence of new social movements is generally characterised by the promotion of 'normative revision'. Specifically he argues that such movements are primarily concerned with new conceptions of social justice. Thus: 'A movement becomes possible when a group of people cease to petition the goodwill of others for relief of their misery and demand as their right, that others ensure the correction of their condition' (1969, p.391).

This shift from notions of 'charity' to notions of 'what people have a right to expect' (Turner 1969) has been a key factor in the ability of disabled people to challenge the culturally-constructed and administratively maintained association between disability and tragedy.

Tom Shakespeare (1996a, p.99) suggests that positive identity narratives are not only reinforced by self-organisation but are also a precondition for it.

The emerging recognition that disability could be reconstructed within a social model provided the basis for an entirely new discourse of rights, citizenship and inclusion. The sharing of experiences and ideas created opportunities for more and more disabled people to uncover new perceptions of commonality, based on their experiences of discrimination and exclusion. This discourse of commonality was thus a central feature of disabled people's emerging resistance to the culture of tragedy, individualism and segregation described in Chapter 2. However, it would be wrong to consider this development as entirely unproblematic. The unifying concepts of social model analysis have been central to the mobilisation of disabled people within the movement but they have also been prone to criticism, for marginalising diversity in the lives of disabled people.

Commonality and difference

For Vic Finkelstein (1993) and Jenny Morris (1991a) the 'commonality of disability' is a central feature of the disabled people's movement. However, Sally French expresses concern that some may become alienated from the movement if personal experiences of impairment are not taken seriously. Thus, 'The aim of the disability movement is to change the way society operates so that disabled people are accommodated on equal terms, but our credibility is undermined, among the membership at least, if we cannot respond to each others needs and rights' (French 1993, p.23).

In a more general sense, any social movement based upon a commonality of interest runs the risk of alienating those with unique personal experiences. Experiences of specificity and difference are evident in all social movements. For an emergent movement, the recognition of difference may give rise to fears of fragmentation. As the experience of the women's movement or the black civil rights movement shows, such fears are easily manifested in a reluctance to acknowledge separatism or specific interest groups. Consequently, there may be much for the disabled people's movement to learn from issues of difference within other social movements (Priestley 1995a).

As mentioned earlier, identification with specific forms of impairment was a feature of early self-organisation amongst disabled people in Britain. For example, the development of UPIAS was clearly focused on the common interests of people with physical impairments. Their political organisation around issues of physical access and institutionalised welfare provision gave grounding to social definitions of disability and offered tangible opportunities for campaigning. However, this strategy also ran the risk, in its early stages, of defining people with differing experiences of impairment as 'other' rather than 'same'. As one UPIAS member put it:

> ...the Union was really set up as an organisation of physically impaired people, and other people with allegedly mental health problems and people with learning difficulties were conceived and actually written into our policy statement as 'other oppressed groups', quote unquote. You know, we should develop supporting contact but, seen as other groups. (Interview transcript)

It has also been suggested that the early self-organisation of disabled people in Britain was dominated by men (Morris 1993c, 1995). It would perhaps be more accurate to say that the published accounts of that organisation were dominated by male writers (but see Hunt's 1966 collection or Campling 1981, for some notable exceptions). Certainly, disabled women have increasingly seized the initiative in telling their own stories (Deegan and Brooks 1995; Driedger and Gray 1992; Lloyd 1992; Lonsdale 1990; Morris 1991b, 1993c, 1995; Saxton and Howe 1987; Wendell 1996). One woman described the situation as follows:

> I think also a lot of us women, sort of tended to...follow you men. It was, the men were sort of intellectual and us women hadn't had a lot of training which was, difficult...and it was you men that sort of, taking the debate forward. I mean we were involved but we weren't the ones who were doing all the writing... But I think if the debate were to start again...I think this time, I mean I feel a bit stronger about you know, participating in that debate. The confidence of going through the experience.... (Interview transcript)

In a more general sense, the emphasis on commonality raises difficulties for various groups who consider that they have separate interests, to which the mainstream of the movement are not as yet responding. Groups whose personal and collective experiences emphasise difference over commonality present important challenges to disability alliances and to the disability movement as a whole.

There is some concern amongst such groups that special interests like race, ethnicity, gender, sexuality or age may be perceived as 'optional extras' to the common experience of disability. Such arguments are reminiscent of feminist literature on single interests within the women's movement. Spelman (1990, p.6) for example, argues that the western feminist movement tends to 'add on' groups such as black women or disabled women. Applying a similar line of argument to the disability movement, Jenny Morris (1991a, p.12) asserts that 'black disabled people and disabled gay men and lesbians express their particular concerns in particular contexts…such groups should not be treated as an 'added on' optional extra to a more general analysis of disability'.

Morris' apparent call for unity in the movement is tempered by Sally French's (1993, p.22) pragmatic reasoning that 'unifying disabled people is problematic…because they are geographically dispersed and socially and culturally dissimilar'. Ossie Stuart (1992, p.181) highlights the 'absence of black faces' in the disability movement and (1993, p.195) notes that disabled people's organisations have consistently failed to attract membership from minority communities. Similarly, Morris (1991a, p.178) makes the point that 'Disabled people and their organisations are no more exempt from racism, sexism and heterosexism than non-disabled people and their organisations'.

Such arguments have been well rehearsed in the literature arising from other new social movements. Parmar (1988) for example, notes the lack of attention given in feminist literature to the lives of black women and argues that to speak of 'all women categorically' is to perpetuate white supremacy in the movement (1988, p.236). Lorde (1988) concludes that there is a tendency for white women within the women's movement to focus only on their oppression as women at the expense of differences in race, sexual preference, class or age. Thus, Lorde argues that the umbrella term 'sisterhood' is questionable and that 'Ignoring the differences of race between women and the implications of those differences presents the most serious threat to the mobilization of women's joint power' (1988, p.271).

For similar reasons, Jeewa (1991) argues that black disabled people need to organise separately from white disabled people at present. By contrast Stuart (1993) expresses concern that black disabled people may become estranged, because neither the disability movement nor the anti-racist movement is fully able to accommodate their experience. Thus Stuart argues that separatism is 'a very dangerous option' (1993, p.187). As this brief review shows, issues of commonality and difference within the disabled people's movement are complex and contentious. Suffice to say that where perceptions of difference are perceived as important by local disabled people then mass mobilisation around issues of commonality can become more difficult.

The preceding analysis highlights some of the main factors in the development of disabled people's self-organisation. The successful development of a new social movement was contingent upon new forms of self-organisation amongst disabled people and upon the development of new identities and narratives, based on the commonality of disability. Issues of difference and experiences of simultaneous oppression present difficulties for the mobilisation of a movement which speaks equally to the diverse personal histories of disabled people. However, the success of the movement has been in locating levels of analysis, and forms of organisation, which can accommodate such differences within a common experience of disability.

The movement for independent living

By the mid 1980s the disabled people's movement had firmly established both its organisational structure and its ideological identity. The remainder of this chapter shows how these two themes have been reflected through the concept of independent/integrated living. As an intellectual paradigm, independent/integrated living is a development of social model thinking; as an operational strategy it links the diverse support structures which have been promoted by disabled people's organisations. In general terms independent living has been defined by the disabled people's movement as...

> ...a process of consciousness raising and empowerment. This process enables disabled persons of all ages and with all types of disabilities to achieve equalisation of opportunities and full participation in all aspects of society. Disabled people must be in control of this process. Meaningful choices must be available in order to exercise control... (Definition adopted by the Assembly of DPI's Independent Living Committee and Symposium, Helsinki, May 1990)

The development of this concept in the struggles of disabled people is sometimes described as a social movement in its own right. De Yong (1981, p.242) links the growth of the independent living movement to other new social movements based on 'consumerism', 'self-help', 'demedicalisation' and 'self-care'. However, it is probably more accurate to think of the movement for independent/integrated living as a central strand within the wider disabled people's movement (but see Williams 1983, for a critique).

The concept of independent living

In its narrowest sense, independent living is sometimes viewed simply as self-determination and control over housing and personal assistance.

However, it is more commonly articulated as a generalised and holistic response to disability. As John Evans (1993, p.63) puts it:

> Life is more than just a house and getting up and going to bed. Independent Living is about the whole of life and it encompasses everything. We want equal opportunities. We want citizenship. These are the issues that drive the independent living movement. It is philosophical, it is political, it is about integration and disabled people becoming a part of this world and not separate, segregated and second class. That is what we are actually after and that is why independent living is so important.

Ann Kestenbaum (1996) also notes how independent living is often used in a restricted sense (referring to a move from institution to community, to the provision of equipment and adaptations or to the employment of personal assistants). However, she is concerned that such interpretations can,

> conceal the fact that there are some fundamental differences of view between disabled people and those who seek to 'care' for them. The substitution of the term Independent Living for the term Homecare may give the appearance, but not necessarily the reality, of a transfer of power. (Kestenbaum 1996, p.2)

For Kestenbaum, the philosophy of independent living involves three core components. First, independence is taken to refer to the ability of disabled people 'to achieve their goals and control their own lives, whatever assistance they need to do so' (see Morris 1993a or French 1993). Second, independent living strategies are based on social models of disability and conducted within the context of demands for human and civil rights. Third, the notion of independent living is generally considered to embrace the concept of 'integrated' living. As I will show later, this distinction has been particularly important in the development of services by disabled people in Derbyshire. Finally, Kestenbaum notes that the implementation of independent living solutions may have variable significance for disabled people in a variety of situations. So:

> While accepting that the core feature is the ability of a person to have choice and control within a context of equal opportunity and citizenship, it is important to recognise that Independent Living has different shades of meaning for people with different ages, cultural backgrounds and personalities. (Kestenbaum 1996, p.3)

In Derbyshire, the philosophy of integrated living was developed around seven core areas of need – information, counselling, housing, technical aids, personal assistance, transport and access. The prioritisation of these areas of need arose directly from the experience of disabled people involved with the Grove Road independent living project (see Ken Davis 1981, for a first-hand account) and from the accumulated knowledge acquired through the DIAL initiative at Cressy Fields. As one of the participants in this study put it:

> The seven needs were always put in our minds in this order...the order of the seven needs in terms of information, counselling, housing, technical aids, personal assistance, transport and access was very, was really an escape route, how to escape from an institution into an ordinary house... At the heart of it there was, you know, that interaction between housing, technical aids and personal assistance really, coming out of Grove Road. (Interview transcript)

The 'seven needs' provided an agenda for redefining the supports required by disabled people who wished to live independently in their communities. In order to understand how this agenda became translated into action it is important to emphasise the significance of Centres for Independent/Integrated Living.

Centres for Independent/Integrated Living

The first recognised Centre for Independent Living (CIL) was established in Berkeley, California in 1973. The university in Berkeley had previously taken the unprecedented step of providing personal assistants for three disabled students to enable them to study. On graduating, the three worked to persuade the local authorities to set up a radically new personal assistance scheme so that they could live independently in the community. This scheme operated under the control of its users and was founded on five core areas of concern – housing, personal assistance, accessible transport, access and peer counselling (these five areas were similar to DCDP's 'seven needs' which in turn have become central to the British movement). The Berkeley CIL was soon making its services available to other local disabled people and, within ten years, more than 200 CILs had been established across the United States.

At the same time, related projects were emerging in mainland Europe. Most notable among these were the Swedish *Fokus* projects for integrated community living (Brattgard 1972), the *Collectivhaus* initiatives in Denmark and *Het Dorp* in the Netherlands (Klapwijk 1981; Zola 1982). In Britain, early attempts at deinstitutionalisation met with only limited success and were rarely under the control of disabled people themselves. The Spastics Society (now SCOPE) tried a version of *Fokus* at Neath Hill in Milton Keynes and the Habinteg Housing Association set up support services attached to community houses. The Leonard Cheshire Foundation also made some moves towards self-managed personal assistance schemes from their flats in Tulse Hill.

Real change began to be achieved through the struggles of disabled people themselves in specific small-scale projects. For example, Ken Davis (1981) describes the experience of deinstitutionalisation at the Grove Road independent living project in the Midlands (Ken Davis was later to become the first coordinator of DCDP and a key figure in the establishment of DCIL). At 22 Main Street in Newton disabled people acted collectively, hiring personal assistants to facilitate integrated living under their own control. Similar collective living projects were started by disabled people in Edinburgh, Rochdale and Gillingham. During this time, a number of other struggles against oppressive institutional regimes were also taking place – for example, at the Ludwig Guttman Hostel in Stoke Mandeville, at Pearce House in Essex and at Cressy Fields in Derbyshire. As these examples illustrate, 'It is important to remember that the idea of Independent Living for disabled people evolved from within the disability rights movement – and not from within able-bodied society' (Bracking 1993, p.11).

For the participants, these early projects provided tangible lived experiences of barrier removal. They also demonstrated, on a small scale, the potential for an alternative mode of self-organised welfare production. As the social model ideology provided an agenda for discussion and campaigning, so integrated living projects created the physical spaces and opportunities in which that ideology could be played out. As one person described it:

> ...you could talk...for ever and a day...and you never knew whether you were getting anywhere. Nothing ever seemed to change. But once we got stuck into Grove Road and trying our own solution it was a very different matter. You know it was about engaging with people and arguing through strictly practical outcomes... And we found that really that was more influential on people's attitudes after the place was built than any of the thousands of words that had been...[said before]. (Interview transcript)

The accounts of those involved in the early British projects suggest that there was a considerable degree of scepticism (if not open hostility) from professionals and policy makers within the mainstream. The success of these

projects was often achieved in spite of, rather than because of, the involvement of social workers and other 'caring' professionals. By contrast with the
American experience, disabled people's struggles in Britain were often com-
plicated by administrative, professional and bureaucratic dominance over
existing welfare provision. Maggie Davis (1993) draws out this distinction:

> There was in both cases of course the shared struggle for practical
> resources and attitudinal support in the community. However, in Britain,
> as in some other countries, disabled people have had in addition to
> overcome the obstructions, anomalies and vested interests of a
> well-established welfare state. (M. Davis 1993, p.15)

DCDP's attempt to establish a Centre in Derbyshire had been motivated in
part by the independent living movement in the United States. However,
they were also heavily influenced by a British social policy context in which
professionals and local authorities occupied pivotal roles, as the gatekeepers
and administrators. Bearing in mind the earlier review of social movements
literature, this experience offers some support for Walzer's (1982, p.152)
assertion that the 'insurgency' of radical movements often 'seeks to make the
'helpfulness' of the welfare bureaucracy into the starting point of a new politics of resistance and self-determination'.

It is also consistent with Habermas' (1981) argument that new social
movements often seek to challenge the colonisation of social life by public or
private bureaucracies, rather than to expand state welfare provision. As the
following analysis shows, these issues are particularly well illustrated in the
attempt by members of the Derbyshire Coalition to establish a Centre for
Integrated Living.

The establishment of DCIL

Following the establishment of the Coalition and the publication of the
Council's *Statement of Intent,* DCDP and the County Council (DCC) set up a
Joint Working Party in February 1982. The creation of a new forum for dialogue provided local disabled people with the opportunity to challenge
traditional assumptions about disability held by local authority planners.
Their policy of direct engagement with the local authority met with a degree
of success, at least initially. There is, for example, some evidence that,
through involvement in joint planning groups, the Coalition were able to
influence service development towards a social model approach (Gibbs
1995). The apparent success of this early collaborative work was bolstered
by the subsequent publication of 'Joint Strategies' for service development.

Ultimately, joint working was to result in the investment of considerable stat-utory resources in non-traditional forms of service development under joint control with local disabled people. However, such developments were not without conflict.

Plans for a CIL were a priority for the core membership of the new Coalition and they persuaded the Council to include a commitment in principle in their 1983–86 Strategic Framework. However, there were clear differences of opinion about the way in which it should work. The Coalition saw the Centre as a way to replace existing services with new arrangements under shared control. Members and officers of the Council on the other hand saw it primarily as an additional service. In particular, DCDP's specific proposal to establish a CIL in place of institutional arrangements at Cressy Fields met with considerable resistance from the social services committee (Kay 1984). One DCDP member described the situation as follows:

> …I think…the Council thought that, you know, the Coalition was going to make proposals for new services, not to get rid of existing ones. This was a proposal that the Council had never anticipated and for this reason it wouldn't get any support. That if the Coalition wanted to come back with an idea of a Centre for the Independent Living or, you know, somewhere else in the County that was providing a service that disabled people clearly wanted then it would get the maximum support of the authority…I mean in many ways there were political reservations about CIL as a whole Mark… You know, how far it was a Trojan horse being, used by right wing influences against the authority and when [the Council leader] said in Statement of Intent he only wanted to give it qualified support, that's what he meant. (Interview transcript)

In the 'war of position' this battle was ultimately lost, and the Coalition set-tled for alternative arrangements (see Davis and Mullender 1993, for a more detailed account). The plan for a CIL in Derbyshire was finally agreed in Feb-ruary 1984 and the centre opened its doors at Long Close in Ripley in March 1985. DCIL was registered as a company later the same year and as a charity in 1988. By 1993 DCIL employed 24 staff (many part-time) and 124 volun-teers (all disabled people). By this time it had both extended and consolidated its activities under a number of core functions.

The increasing number of information enquiries and training requests meant that, by 1993, DCIL was dealing with up to 400 enquiries per month from disabled people and service agencies (DCIL Director's report, July 1993). Information was being produced in a variety of formats (including

Braille, large print and tape) and increasing emphasis was placed on peer information support. 'Counselling' services (see Lenny 1993) were made available to an average of 40 people per month, again with an emphasis on peer support provided by trained disabled people (working as volunteers). The development of peer support was also being extended through DCIL's role in facilitating self-help groups focused on local issues (such as access, consultation with statutory providers and campaigning).

At this time DCIL was also becoming more active in research and training (again involving disabled people in the collection and dissemination of information). Other activities included the proposed development of home equipment, housing and employment services. DCIL was also beginning to provide intensive support and assistance to individual disabled people in order to establish integrated living packages (for example through applications to the Independent Living Fund), as well as payroll and administrative support in maintaining those packages.

It is hard to overestimate the significance of these developments, arising as they did from the personal and political struggles of local disabled people within a growing movement, and in direct engagement with the agencies of the local state. The form and content of DCIL's strategy offered a break with the established pattern of welfare production for disabled people in two ways. First, it sought to engage the statutory authorities in a social model approach, completely at odds with the dominant policy discourse of 'care', medicalisation and segregation. Second, it sought to engage disabled people themselves as the primary actors – as self-determining users of support services and as the providers of support to others. In this way, it challenged, at a micro level, the established social relations of welfare production and blurred the distinction between 'providers' and 'users'. It is no coincidence then that this mode of welfare production should have arisen from the self-empowerment of disabled people within a broader social movement.

An integrated living approach

As mentioned earlier, DCDP was the first coalition of disabled people in Britain and DCIL was the first British centre for independent/integrated living. There were thus few reliable models to draw on in establishing a new structure for the delivery of disability services in Derbyshire. The Coalition were certainly unstinting in their ambitions: 'The Centre for Integrated Living was to be the spearhead of the way into a new future for disabled people in the county... It was to set the pace in breaking down the barriers which prevented disabled people living a full and equal life.' (*INFO: the Voice of Disabled People in Derbyshire,* Issue 1, June 1992, p.1)

The Coalition's vision for DCIL was twofold. On the one hand, it would begin to redefine the form and content of welfare delivery, going beyond the provision of 'care' and concerning itself instead with the removal of barriers to integrated living. On the other hand, it would begin to alter the social relations of welfare production by establishing mechanisms of joint control between the local state and disabled people themselves.

DCIL's establishment in Derbyshire was followed quickly by the Hampshire Centre for Independent Living (HCIL). CILs have varied in their response to local needs and it is interesting to compare the histories of the first British centres. In Derbyshire, moves towards the establishment of DCIL evolved through the conscious political action of an existing organisation (DCDP) within the disabled people's movement, representing a wide variety of personal and collective experiences. In Hampshire, by contrast, the idea for a CIL arose directly from Project 81 – an initiative by a small group of disabled people moving out of one residential institution (the 'Le Court' Cheshire Home). Thus, it reflected more closely the close-knit experience of the Berkeley CIL founders. The Hampshire group were able, with some difficulty, to persuade the local authorities who funded their institutional care to finance community support for them. As in Berkeley, the success of this scheme resulted in it being made available to other disabled people locally.

Perhaps because of its specific and individual beginnings, HCIL's services have centred on the issue of individual personal assistance while DCIL has adopted a more holistic approach, based on the Coalition's 'seven needs'. DCIL regards its policy of viewing personal care in the context of other life needs as a central value. As Maggie Davis (1993, p.18) notes:

> In this way, it tries to ensure that the personal assistance issue is not used as a political device simply to replace care with cash – and as a means to conveniently dodge the wider social responsibility to remove the many other social barriers which prevent disabled people as a group to secure equal rights and opportunities.

This holistic approach to personal support raises a potential conflict of values between DCIL and the agenda for 'community care'. It also highlights differences in approach between DCIL and other British CILs, many of which favour a more individualised approach to 'cash for care' and do not necessarily subscribe to a collective basis of service provision. The implications of these differing approaches are explored more fully in subsequent chapters.

Conclusions

The analysis presented in this chapter locates the self-organisation of disabled people in Derbyshire within the wider context of a growing disabled people's movement. This analysis demonstrates how both ideology and organisational structure have interacted. On the one hand, 'big ideas' based on social models of disability were important where they spoke to the lived experience of local people. On the other hand, new organisational structures (cells, teach-ins, discussion groups, the Coalition, Joint Planning groups and so on) created new spaces in which disabled people could forge new collective identities and challenge old assumptions.

A conflict of values

The initial agenda for this study was prompted by the concerns of disabled people in Derbyshire who perceived a conflict between their own organisational values and those of community care policy makers. The analysis presented in this chapter shows how the positive identities and values forged within the emergent Coalition, and later expressed in the establishment of DCIL, stand in stark contrast to the core values of British disability policy making (discussed in Chapter 2).

The key value differences between the competing policy agendas of British disability policy and the disabled people's movement are both numerous and complex. Where the policy making process has been preoccupied with care, medicalisation and segregation so the disabled people's movement has promoted participation, integration and equality. Where the implementation of community care policies has reinforced professional dominance, familism and commodification so the disabled people's movement has advanced the values of self-help, communalism and citizenship. These differences are summarised in Table 3.1.

For politicised and campaigning organisations, like the early Coalition in Derbyshire, such value conflicts are hardly surprising. However, the significance of DCDP's strategy lies in the organisation's direct engagement with the state. This relationship was inherently conflictual since the promotion of integrated living at DCIL was necessarily based upon a critique

Table 3.1 Some key value differences

Traditional policy values	Integrated living values
care	participation
medicalisation	policisation
segregation	integration
professionalisation	self-help
familism	communalism
eugenics	diversity
normalisation	self-determination
individualism	collectivism
charity	civil rights
commodification	citizenship

of the existing public sector services. Thus, in a recent management report on DCIL's organisational structure, Crosby (1994, Appendix 1) notes that:

> DCIL is part of the international Disabled People's Movement. This wider movement retains an interest in the first disabled people's organisation in Britain to receive significant public funding, which remains the only one to characterise its major funding organisation as its oppressor, yet seeks to involve them in its own development.

This anomalous relationship presented equal contradictions for the local authority. Although committed in principle to a service philosophy based on supporting disabled people towards self-determination, the County Council remained 'keen on its own services' as a means to this end (minutes of meeting between DCIL, DCDP and DCC, March 1993).

Heightened tensions

I suggested in the introduction that the implementation of community care reforms served to heighten the organisational contradictions and value conflicts within DCIL. In particular, the 1990 Act reinforced the priority given to individualised services based on care, medicalisation and administrative segregation. On an organisational level, the imposition of new purchasing arrangements, coupled with cuts in local authority funding, began to undermine DCIL's ability to provide less orthodox modes of support to its users.

Events took a dramatic turn when the County Council's budget for 1990–91 was capped by central government. Along with other 'voluntary' organisations, the second half of DCDP's annual grant funding was withdrawn and DCIL was forced to consider a major restructuring of its operational management. Although DCIL's new Operational Plan retained a commitment to the 'seven needs' approach, the proposed purchasing arrangements required a new focus on those 'services' which could be contracted for. These processes are discussed in more detail in subsequent chapters. Suffice to say that, in the years to come, they would threaten the scope and philosophy of DCIL's activity in a variety of ways.

In particular, DCIL embarked on the design and implementation of a new Personal Support Scheme for which it hoped to tender with the local authority. The proposed scheme sought to carry forward the established principles of integrated living, but to deliver them in accordance with the contractual requirements for individual 'packages' of support. The over-arching concept was one of 'Self-Assessment and Self-Management' (SASM) in which the end users of support services would exercise participation and control. Personal assistance with daily living would be combined with peer advocacy and simultaneous community development work as part of a total package.

The intention was to offer the purchasing authorities a 'complete service for people who wish to live independently and to manage their own care in ordinary domestic surroundings in their own communities' (letter from DCIL's Director to the purchasing authorities, January 1993). The operation of such a scheme offered a qualitatively different kind of support to that available within the mainstream. For DCIL, there were 'no direct parallels to be found in statutory public services to the sort of personal support role which is proposed under this initiative' (DCIL Director's report, August 1993).

The following chapter explores how self-assessment and self-management have been put into practice. There is a growing body of evidence from within the disabled people's movement that self-managed personal support schemes provide many benefits for their users when compared to other, more traditional, forms of support. Indeed, it is at the level of lived experience that the enabling philosophy of self-assessment and self-management often comes up against the disabling values of 'care assessment' and 'case management'.

CHAPTER 4

From Principles to Practice

This chapter draws on data from the case study in Derbyshire in order to show how the value conflicts explored so far are played out at a micro level. The first part of the chapter outlines the development of self-managed personal assistance schemes in Britain and compares them with other forms of support (such as unpaid help, statutory services and private 'care' agencies). The second part focuses on the distinction between 'care assessment' and 'self-assessment' in defining service users' needs. The final section addresses the implications of self-management within a resource-rationed 'package of care'. This analysis illustrates how the framework for community care purchasing can impede the development of enabling support schemes, and maintain disabling relationships of dependency.

Personal assistance and independent living

Caring for People argued that 'Social care and practical assistance with daily living are the key components of good quality community care' (DoH *et al.* 1989, para.2.4). For the majority of disabled people, this kind of personal support comes from friends and family, from statutory 'home care' services or from independent 'care' providers. However, there has been increasing concern about the ability of such support structures to foster independent living outcomes. Within the movement for independent/integrated living the emphasis has been on developing self-managed personal support schemes which empower disabled people to exercise greater choice and control over the assistance they receive.

Self-managed personal assistance schemes

Although personal assistance is only one among the 'seven needs' it has become an essential prerequisite to independent/integrated living for many disabled people. As Simpson and Campbell argue:

> ...independent living is being in control of your life and being able to make decisions and choices about your daily living arrangements. It is about having the same opportunities as your non-disabled peers and to participate fully in the community. Having control over your own personal assistance is fundamental to this. (Simpson and Campbell 1996, p.4)

Since the early 1980s a wide variety of personal assistance schemes have been developed by disabled people. Some, like Project 81 in Hampshire or the Kingston Independent Living Service, resulted from the personal struggles of disabled people to gain control over their own affairs. Others have been led by established organisations of disabled people or centres for independent/integrated (such as those in Avon, Southampton, Derbyshire and Greenwich). Often they have involved local social services departments or voluntary organisations – for example, the Wiltshire Independent Living Fund (WILF), Voluntary Action Sheffield, The Pendrels Trust in Coventry, Fairdeal in Leicestershire, the Norfolk Independent Living Group (ILG) and Merton Social Services Department.

The goal of self-managed support is to bring choice and control closer to the end user. However, the way in which this is achieved varies considerably. Some are 'direct payment' schemes (where money is paid directly to the individual person to enable them to purchase the help they need). However, the majority have used 'third party' organisations or trusts to broker funds (see Zarb and Nadash 1994). For example, in Barnet and Hackney, Choice offered a care brokerage scheme run by disabled case managers. In Merton, personal assistants have been employed directly by the social services department (pending the implementation of direct payments legislation). In Derbyshire, DCIL employs personal support workers (under the direction and control of the end service user).

The central objective of all these arrangements is the same – to bring the employment of personal assistants under the control of the individual disabled person (whether or not actual money is devolved). However, simply making payments accountable to the end user is not a sufficient condition for a successful self-managed support scheme. As Oliver and Zarb's evaluation of the Greenwich scheme shows, 'simply transferring funds to users and expecting that the majority will be able to operate their own Personal Assistance Schemes without any advice, information or support is completely unrealistic' (Oliver and Zarb 1992, p.5).

Consequently, all of the quoted examples rely for their success on the provision of supplementary back-up services, or Personal Assistance Support (PAS) schemes. Additional support varies. It might include help with self-assessment, writing job descriptions, advertising, interviewing, administering payroll and tax, arranging emergency cover or mediating between users and their support staff (DIG 1996; Oliver and Zarb 1992; Simpson 1995; Simpson and Campbell 1996). In general terms, PAS schemes offer information, peer support, advocacy and administration services to enable personal assistance users to exercise self-assessment and self-management.

Inevitably, the provision of additional support has been dependent upon available funds. The Avon scheme (now West of England CIL) adds 30 per cent to the basic cost of personal assistance wages. In Hampshire, the addition is 20 per cent and in Norfolk, 15 per cent. The Hampshire Self Operated Care Scheme (SOCS) is able to fund development and support workers using this revenue. WILF offers similar back-up and was also able to employ an advisory worker for one year to develop service take-up amongst black disabled people. The Greenwich Scheme employs a 'Personal Assistance Advisor' to provide information and advocacy. Norwich ILG offer support with self-assessment and provide regular visits from a scheme coordinator.

No single scheme has yet developed a complete package and there have been many battles in persuading commissioning authorities to come even this far along the road. Self-managed schemes can all too easily be seen as a cost effective way to off-load responsibility for service provision, rather than as an opportunity to devolve sufficient resources for enabling support under the control of disabled people (DIG 1996, p.8). Additionally, commissioning authorities and individual care managers are often unconvinced of the benefits of this way of working.

Background to the evaluation project

DCIL were particularly concerned that the research for this study should focus on the 'added value' of their self-managed personal support services. To this end I was 'commissioned' by DCIL (without remuneration) to talk to some of their users as part of a service review. Some of these data were published in a report commissioned by DCIL (Priestley 1996b) and in a sub-sequent paper for the *British Journal of Social Work* (Priestley 1998b). Parts of the analysis which follows are therefore a development of that collaborative work, although in a substantially altered form.

The sample of Personal Support Service users included four women and four men of varying ages and social backgrounds; some who lived alone and some with significant others. The range of their previous support included help from friends, family, neighbours, partners, volunteers, personal employees, private care agencies, hospitals, day centres and the home help service. Unless stated otherwise, all the quotations are derived from transcripts of semi-structured interviews conducted with these people during August 1996, although fictional names are used to protect the identity of the respondents. Some brief vignettes of the eight people who took part are included below.

No specific information is included about the nature or degree of impairment experienced by the participants, since this was irrelevant to the issues in hand (we chose not to ask for this information and only one person mentioned their impairment during the interviews). Suffice to say that all the people involved would no doubt be considered as 'disabled' within the definition governing Section 47(2) of the 1990 NHS and Community Care Act. Reference to the age of the participants has also been omitted. Age, as much as disability has been socially constructed within an administrative category, reflecting the bureaucratic and economic imperatives of welfare state capitalism (Barnes 1997; Townsend 1981; Zarb and Oliver 1993). However, the majority of the sample would probably be regarded by local authority and NHS commissioners as 'adults' or 'younger disabled people' rather than 'elderly'.

Joe had previously derived all his support from his parents. He felt constrained by not being able to make decisions or speak for himself and, as his father approached retirement age, it became clear that change was needed. Despite a brief spell of support from the home help service, his parents felt that he would not be able to live on his own and began to suggest that a nursing home would be the only option. Joe had spoken to a social worker who arranged for him to attend a nearby resource centre run by the Cheshire Foundation. After spending a short time in the 'independent living unit' there, Joe began attending one day a week but after a few months, when his father fell ill, he was persuaded to come full time. Eventually, Joe was able to move into a shared tenancy with his partner although as time went on strains in their relationship prompted him to think about looking for other accommodation in which he could support himself.

For many years Richard had received most of his support from his wife. However, their subsequent divorce created an urgent need to develop a new way of managing his own affairs. Seeking to organise an alternative support system, he began using staff from a private agency while simultaneously talking to DCIL about the possibility of alternative arrangements. Richard experienced enormous difficulties with the agency due to the high turnover of staff and felt that he was losing more and more control over his life.

Hugh and Margaret had supported each other for many years with additional domestic help which they arranged privately. Because of changes in Hugh's employment they had moved from a nearby county where they had recently established a package of support under their own control. On arriving in Derbyshire they hoped to negotiate a similar package but experienced great difficulty in obtaining what they wanted through the statutory agencies. They felt that the social services department did not know how to cope with their individual needs and were worried for the future stability of their support.

Terry had been living with his ex-wife in the absence of any alternative support and needed to move as a matter of urgency. In the absence of any family support, Terry drew much help from friends and neighbours. He had received some private nursing care but was unhappy about the staff provided and about the way in which the service was organised. Initially he had been offered a place in a residential home for elderly people (he was 42 years old at the time). Although Terry did not feel able to look after himself, he was keen to take the first suitable house that came up and eventually, with assistance from social services, he moved into a bungalow and set about constructing a package of support that could be put in place as quickly as possible.

Carol had always lived with her parents and derived most of her support from them until the death of her mother. Her father became increasingly unable to provide all the support she needed and she began to use the home help service. However, there were problems, particularly in getting the help that she wanted at the times she wanted it. She was also worried about confidentiality. Increasingly, she felt constrained by the home help management regime which did not easily accommodate the demands of her varied employment and daily living routine.

Liz lived on her own and had drawn combined support from social services and a neighbour in managing her own affairs. Social services cut backs meant that she was not able to get help with many basic tasks and she was becoming concerned about making increasing demands on her neighbour as he was getting older. Liz had experienced problems with the home help service who were not able to provide the kind of support she needed at the times she wanted. Despite her increasing needs she was unable to obtain any extra help from social services.

Dorothy had been drawing on a package of 24 hour support put together and paid for by her son since she had became unable to manage by herself. This support involved assistance from private agencies and from the home help service. However, when her son retired he was unable to continue funding this level of support and turned to social services for financial assistance.

As an initial indicator of quality we asked the participants to compare their experiences of using DCIL's Personal Support Service (PSS) with other kinds of support they had received in the past. In general terms their responses suggest that self-assessment and self-management offer higher levels of choice, reliability and respect than help from friends and family, statutory services or the private sector. In this sense the initial data supports the findings of similar studies – notably Jenny Morris' (1993a, b) work on community care and independent living (involving 50 people in four areas) and Zarb and Nadash's (1994) comparative study for BCODP (involving 70 disabled people in ten local authorities).

Some initial comparisons

Most of the PSS users reported that their need for additional support had arisen from a change in the ability, or willingness, of family and friends to cope. For example, Carol had relied on her parents for help until the death of her mother. Her father continued to provide most of her assistance but became increasingly unable to manage because of illness. Similarly, Richard had gained most of his assistance from his wife until their divorce. Terry had moved away from his family and felt that he simply did not have anybody 'close' who would want to assist him. By contrast, Joe had struggled hard to escape from the constraining 'care' of his parents. Although he now lived with his partner, their relationship did not extend to personal assistance.

Morris' (1993a) study showed that although personal assistance can be accommodated within loving relationships it can also create unwanted dependency and pressure for both parties. Several people in our sample were acutely aware of tensions between their own needs and those of the people closest to them. Those who did make use of family and friends as unpaid helpers were concerned that the demands of the job sometimes interfered with their personal relationships. Where the bulk of assistance was provided within a close relationship this raised real concerns as the following two comments illustrate:

> I think, looking back, I've made, and in fact until quite recently, I've made unreasonable demands...asked [her] to do more than was reasonable (Hugh).

> ...I knew I needed extra help or extra hours because you know, it's getting too much for [him]. You know, he is a friend, a good friend... I'm so afraid...I don't want to lose his friendship... (Liz).

However, where a 'burden of gratitude' existed (Begum 1990), it was perceived to be the product of insufficient public support rather than personal inadequacy or intrinsic dependency. For these people at least, there was a degree of resistance to policy debates which focus on the needs of 'carers in the community' rather than on the needs of disabled people themselves (Morris 1993a). Indeed, such debates must be considered as part of a disabling ideology that portrays dependency within the family as inevitable, and thereby masks the fact that many people are perfectly capable of managing their own affairs given appropriate levels of external support.

The literature on 'informal carers' correctly emphasises the gendered analysis of women's unpaid labour (Finch 1990; Glendinning 1992; Green 1988). However, the majority of unpaid help identified by the participants in our study was provided by men. The sample is not large enough to draw much conclusion from this detail but it is important to question whether the allocation of public funding (through care assessment) might be more forthcoming for people perceived as dependent upon men than upon women. Ann Rae (1993) notes that disabled women are often discriminated against because need is more readily recognised for men than for women. Thus, 'If you can walk then God help you, because if you can walk you can push a Hoover, and you don't need a home help' (Rae 1993, p.47).

In addition to support from friends and family, four of the participants had used home help services. Two more had made individual arrangements with the local authority for assistance to be provided in their home and one attended a day centre. All of these people reported cutbacks in their support. All had experienced difficulty in getting the kind of help that they wanted at the times when they needed it. Apart from one or two very specific criticisms, the overriding feeling was that existing local authority services could not provide a flexible enough package of personal support. As Margaret put it:

> They didn't really know how to cope with us. They really didn't know how to give us a personal package. They got us slotted all in... (Margaret)

These experiences are similar to those of disabled service users recorded in comparable studies. For example, Jenny Morris' study of community care and independent living (1993a, 1993b) found that most service users experienced unacceptable levels of inflexibility. Similar concerns were expressed by the Audit Commission (1992b) immediately prior to community care implementation. Although they identified some innovative pilot projects, attempts at flexibility had 'rarely been translated into mainline services for the majority of users' (1992b, p.31). More recently, a PSI study for BCODP (Zarb et al. 1996) identified lack of flexibility and choice as a major disadvantage of service provision when compared with self-managed personal support schemes (see also Zarb and Nadash 1994).

The third form of support in our sample was help from private agencies. The community care policy agenda emphasised the 'mixed economy of care' and market incentives have increased the profile of private sector agencies in many parts of the country. Just prior to implementation, Ann Kestenbaum (1993b) carried out a specific study of agency services in the East Midlands area (which includes Derbyshire) for the Independent Living Fund. She identified a total of 41 agencies working in the region (80 per cent of them in the private sector). Her report concluded that private provision was very patchy, especially in rural areas, and that there was a high turnover amongst small local providers.

Kestenbaum's research drew on interviews with 38 disabled people in receipt of ILF payments who were known to have used agency services to assist them with 'personal and domestic care'. Many had chosen to use agencies because they could not find suitable staff themselves or because they were simply unaware of any alternative. For some, agencies were seen as a positive choice – offering reliability and safety. However, there was also considerable criticism of agencies with high staff turnover, inflexible service criteria and excessive charges.

Two of the DCIL sample had previously used private care agencies at home and one had used them when staying away from home. For these three people (all of them men) adopting a consumer relationship with the private sector had not noticeably enhanced the quality of support they received. Indeed, Terry and Richard, who had used local agencies, reported exactly the same kinds of restrictions and inflexibility associated with local authority domiciliary services. In addition, they were concerned about high staff turnover rates and about receiving assistance from private agencies that were 'uncaring' and profit-oriented. In common with Kestenbaum's study, such feelings were particularly linked to perceptions of low agency wages and high commission costs (see Kestenbaum 1993a, p.13):

> I realised with the agency that the main problem was money…it's all down to money. The better you pay people the more loyalty you get… The agency were paying the workers two pounds an hour…so in the end you just get what you pay for really. (Richard)

> …they get paid about twenty quid a night, you know, for a whole session, for about twelve hours. So, obviously they're not all that interested. They don't pay the rates…the people they send down don't get paid enough to be interested in your life. (Terry)

In contrast to the support received from unpaid helpers, statutory services and private agencies, the interviewees' experience of self-managed support demonstrated very high levels of satisfaction, choice and control. Again, this finding supports the more general analysis presented by Zarb and Nadash (1994). Everyone in the sample felt that self-managed personal assistance was considerably better than the other forms of support they had used in the past, particularly when compared to direct service provision. As Richard put it:

> I can't really fault it…I feel that I'm more in charge, more in control. My life's not organised by social services which it was getting to be. (Richard)

Two factors seemed to be particularly important. First, people valued the service most when they felt a high degree of participation and choice in the way it was provided. Second, satisfaction was explained in terms of positive outcomes in people's lives. For some, this meant being able to do specific things which had not been possible before – such as shopping, having a hot meal during the day, going out for lunch or attending meetings. For others, personal support meant freedom from dependency on family, friends or institutionalised services. In this sense the degree of choice offered by self-managed personal support amounted to a major change in quality of life for most of the people who were interviewed.

In more general terms, the style and philosophy of the service provision was considered to be very different from that experienced in mainstream services as the following comments indicate:

The first thing they did was get the trust right. (Richard)

...it just makes you feel an equal. Whereas with the other [services] your not, you're not an equal at all when someone comes in to do for you...it's completely different. (Carol)

It's not clinical... The support was for me as a person not as an object of care. (Terry)

To summarise, this initial analysis of the views expressed by users of DCIL's Personal Support Service raises many concerns about other kinds of support and echoes the findings of other recent studies. There was much concern about enforced dependency on family and friends, about lack of flexibility in mainstream service designs and about the organisational values of 'for profit' providers. All the participants identified something of additional value in the support they received from DCIL. They valued the increased flexibility, choice and respect which this way of working afforded them and they valued the organisational ethos within which it was provided (these issues are discussed more fully in Chapter 6).

'Care' assessments and self-assessment

For organisations within the movement for independent/integrated living, the establishment of a truly needs-led package of personal support begins with a process of self-assessment. In this respect, it is important to emphasise the distinction between the competing philosophies of self-assessment and 'care assessment'. Professional control over the practice of community care assessment disempowers disabled people (Ridout 1995, p.2) and reinforces the dependency-laden assumption that they cannot define their own needs. Conversely, properly supported self-assessment offers opportunities for resistance to this discourse and creates opportunities for disabled people to reclaim control over their daily lives.

The experience of 'care' assessments

We did not plan to ask the Personal Support Service users about their experiences of 'care assessment', since the focus of the project was on the quality of DCIL's own service provision. However, all but one of the participants raised issues of concern during the interviews and it was therefore important to address them directly. This material was beyond the remit of the internal report for DCIL so a separate paper was prepared, in consultation with DCIL's research officer, for submission to the *British Journal of Social Work*

(Priestley 1998b). This, we hoped, would have more impact on those with an influence over care assessments. The following section draws on the arguments developed for that paper.

Amongst the key objectives set out in *Caring for People* was a commitment to make 'proper assessment of need and good case management the cornerstone of high quality care' (DoH *et al.* 1989, para.1.11). Indeed, the Audit Commission argued that assessment was so central to community care implementation that 'Authorities will rightly be judged by the quality of this process above all else' (Audit Commission 1993a, p.9). However, subsequent studies have indicated continuing dissatisfaction with the process of care assessment amongst disabled people (e.g. Lamb and Layzell 1995).

Wilding (1982, p.16) argues that professional power is most obviously manifested in the definition of 'needs' and 'problems' (see also, Oliver 1996a, p.75) and nowhere is this power more obvious than in the practice of community care assessment. In this light, it is significant that the Department of Health's initial guidance on care management took the concept of 'need' to mean: 'a shorthand for the requirements of individuals to enable them to achieve, maintain or restore an acceptable level of social independence or quality of life, *as defined by the particular care agency or authority*' (DoH *et al.* 1991a, para.11, my emphasis).

In its *Sixth Report,* the Commons Health Committee recommended that assessments should be objective statements of need, established 'without regard to the availability of particular services or resources' (HC 482–I 1993, para.26). In practice, it has now established that assessments of need are constrained by the requirement to balance finite budgets. Consequently, the rationing of scarce resources, according to professionally and bureaucratically codified definitions of need, is at the heart of the assessment process (Zarb 1995b, p.12).

Several of the service users in Derbyshire found that their self-assessment of need required a quantity of staff hours that exceeded the 'glass ceiling' of budgetary constraints. For example, in one case the care manager sought to reduce an initial package by five hours a week; in another the package awarded amounted to four hours less than the individual's self assessment of need. Richard and Terry's applications for 24 hour support were both rejected on financial grounds and Liz was refused even an extra quarter of an hour of 'home care' despite a considerable change of personal circumstances. Terry was simply told by his care manager that he 'cost too much'.

There were also occasions when considerations of quantity and quality became conflictual. Terry was only able to obtain more total hours support by losing a qualified social worker and replacing him with unqualified staff. Although this provided more hours of support it left him feeling that his expressed needs were not being met by appropriate staffing. Margaret described her dilemma in similar terms:

> I would rather have twenty quality hours than forty non-quality hours, but you see that's a downhill slope… You have got to say I want the budget making up to quality hours, right? Because once you start on that slippery slope you ain't ever going to get those hours back. (Margaret)

There was thus much anxiety amongst the service users in Derbyshire about budgetary constraints, and a feeling that assessments had become more budget-led than needs-led. This amounted to real fear and resentment for some people. For example, Terry said that he felt under pressure to 'get better' as quickly as possible in order to 'keep up with the budget':

> …there's just constant pressure all the time. They want to cut it…and it's frightening…because they hold a threat over you all the time. They could take it away. (Terry)

Only one person felt happy about the conduct of community care assessment (although she was very unhappy about the outcome). There were clearly some 'teething problems' and some people did not feel that their care assessors were sufficiently versed in (or committed to) the new policy framework. Carol put the difficulties down to her care manager's lack of familiarity with the system while Margaret and Hugh felt that their newly appointed care manager was 'completely out of his depth'. Terry was more forthright in his analysis:

> What I think is they put some incompetent people as care managers…some of them are all right but I know the departments involved don't let good social workers go as care managers and fought to keep them as staff and some of the flotsam and so on has been put in as care managers. (Terry)

Initial policy guidance stressed that users should 'feel that the process is aimed at meeting their wishes' (DoH/DSS 1990, para.3.16). However, early research findings indicated that people were 'substantially excluded from the decision-making process' and that some people were not even aware that they were being assessed (Social Services Inspectorate, SSI 1991, pp.39–40). Six years on, the continuing incidence of such practices provides evidence that properly supported self-assessment is an essential prerequisite to needs-led purchasing, as the following comments illustrate:

> ...one of the social workers came to see me and we had a talk like and she went away, came back. Then she says the only place who would take me is [local resource centre]. (Joe)

> The social worker tried to do one for me, so I believe, tried to con me and not tell me what it was, which I wouldn't accept. Luckily I'd got the nous to sus that out anyway, but they do that sort of thing because it suits them. (Terry)

Although some people felt that social services had been very helpful in supporting them initially, there were also examples of misunderstandings and mistrust. Terry perceived a lack of genuine interest and concern on the part of the assessors, who he felt had 'become removed from what they're there for' by the administrative pressures of the new system. For Hugh and Margaret, relationships with their care manager had broken down to such a degree that they would not allow him to visit them at home (preferring periodic telephone contact). Some people felt patronised. For example, Margaret reported that her care manager had said that he could 'understand' how she felt because his elderly mother also used a wheelchair. Carol was frustrated:

> You can't have a good argument with them because they won't argue with you...they're so nice all the time. (Carol)

There were specific complaints about assessors who were preoccupied with their own needs, as the following two comments illustrate:

> They're always trying to explain to you what their problem is and I don't want to know what their problem is... They can't do this and can't do that because we haven't got the money, which I can understand, but I don't want keep telling. I mean I can understand all of it, I'm not stupid, I know they've got limitations. (Carol)

> I heard more about their problems than my problems which I thought was quite unfair because my problem was a little bit greater than theirs, you know. (Terry)

The community care reforms established the principle of joint working between health and social services authorities as a priority for effective care assessment and management (with social services taking the 'lead role'). Although joint commissioning of services and the development of partnerships remain high priorities, a lack of inter-organisational collaboration was evident in service users' experience of care assessment. As one person put it:

> They [social services and health] don't work together at all... They just don't work together, it's as simple as that. We've had meetings and there's been a clash. (Terry)

To summarise, the people involved with this study had experienced a number of difficulties in obtaining appropriate assessments. Delays, lack of information, poor communication, patronising attitudes, and an absence of collaborative working were all evident in their experiences. The fact that we did not include any specific questions on community care assessment in the original interview schedule simply emphasises the strength of feeling evident in the participants' criticisms.

The fact that disabled people and community care assessors come to the encounter with different agendas and expectations is not surprising. Such conflicts are an established feature of the sociological literature on lay/professional encounters. For example, Freidson (1975, p.285) argued that 'The separate worlds of experience and reference of the layman [sic] and the professional worker are always in potential conflict with each other'.

The encounters between disabled people and their assessors provide a microcosm of such conflicts. Thus, Chadwick (1996, p.35) suggests that care assessment can be considered as a 'framework of opposing knowledges' (see also Hugman 1991; Tuckett 1985). However, the existence of conflict between individual experience and the representation of that experience by the purveyors of dominant power/knowledge also creates opportunities for new discourses of resistance to emerge (McNay 1992, p.153). It is in this context that support from organisations like DCIL is often most significant – creating opportunities for 'self-assessment' through the provision of peer support and advocacy.

Self-assessment

Speaking at a conference organised by Coventry Independent Living Group (CILG), John Evans (chair of BCODP's Independent Living Committee and a representative of Hampshire CIL) argued that, 'There ought to be no compromise regarding self-assessment; it is fundamental to the empowerment of disabled people. It is critical in terms of the assessment process that self-assessment is the starting point in enabling disabled people to determine their lifestyles' (quoted in Barnes, McCarthy and Comerford 1995, p.3).

However, other disabled people contributing to the same debate reported varying degrees of success in promoting self-assessment. WILF, Norwich ILG, and the West of England CIL have been able to promote self-assessment with some success, but in Hampshire and Derbyshire the situation is more patchy. In North London, Choice have been able to broker self-assessment using 'professional' disabled people as case managers. CILG found that self-assessments in Coventry were relatively straightforward for confident people but not an option for those with less experience or few communication skills. In Shropshire the Disability Consortium's initial success in establishing self-assessment as the norm had been partially undermined by a lack of user involvement in designing assessment forms. In Lothian established practices of self-assessment have been threatened by local government reorganisation (see Craig and Manthorpe 1996).

As with other personal support schemes, DCIL's approach to self-assessment and self-management (SASM) depends on supporting users in making informed choices about their needs. From DCIL's perspective, 'SA/SM clearly implies and expects an individual to choose this option on the basis of a conscious awareness of what is involved and by comparison with other options' (DCIL Director's report, November 1993).

However, this is no simple process. Many disabled people have been historically disempowered by dependency-creating welfare services and may lack the confidence or the knowledge to make informed choices about the support they need. In this respect DCIL have emphasised a particular need for intensive support work with younger people who are leaving residential care (similar concerns are evident in Leicestershire, Coventry and Norfolk). Historic disempowerment and lack of experience mean that simply asking people what they want is no guarantee of a satisfactory outcome. The following comment from one of the participants in this study illustrates the point:

> Well they [care assessors] just sort of ask you what times you want them. Well that gets me a bit because you don't really know what times. It's like organising your life for a year in advance... It's difficult to know how many hours you're going to want. You can't just organise that, how many hours you want. I mean how can you? (Carol)

Kestenbaum (1993b, p.38) notes that unsupported self-assessment can lead to an understatement of real needs. Thus, the Disablement Income Group

(DIG 1996, p.10) argue that Personal Assistance Support (PAS) schemes are crucial in preparing potential personal assistance users for their community care assessments and supporting them through the process itself. Zarb and Nadash (1994, p.vi) conclude that the effective use of personal assistance depends on the quality of support that people receive when organising their package. Similarly, Simpson and Campbell (1996, p.5) note that where PAS workers were involved prior to a community care assessment the outcome was more likely to be successful for the disabled person.

Support for self-assessment can include meeting other disabled people and learning about their experiences, developing self-assessment skills and drawing up a personal assistance plan. DCIL's approach stresses that an 'integrated living plan' – as opposed to a 'care plan' – worked out with the person is 'the only legitimate precursor to an assessment of need for Community Care' (DCIL Director's report, July 1994). For DCIL, such a plan must take into account all the barriers to integrated living and not simply the need for personal assistance. This kind of planning provides 'an opportunity for people to work out the mix of Personal Assistance, Adaptations, Technical Aids and personal transport which most suits them and the budgets provided for their community living' (DCIL July 1994).

Proper planning prior to a formal community care assessment is in the interests of both the consumer and the purchasing authority, since it cuts down on unnecessary social worker involvement and is more likely to lead to an effective and enabling use of resources (Simpson and Campbell 1996). However, the provision of intensive individual support can be time consuming and potentially costly. PAS schemes need to draw on capable and experienced support workers committed to working intensively with potential users. Some schemes rely on the goodwill of existing PA users for this function; others are able to utilise well-developed organisations with premises and paid staff.

Developing peer support in self-assessment is important because it provides positive role modelling for inexperienced personal assistance users and creates an empathic environment for the exploration of integrated living options. For DCIL, peer support workers have a key role to play in helping prospective users to develop confidence, access information and resolve practical issues to do with managing the package. Thus:

> DCIL's experience is that, initially, few younger disabled people have a positive vision of the future and a developed sense of provision. However, the opportunity provided by DCIL to talk through

possibilities, especially with people who have shared the experience and provide role-models in themselves, has helped to replace their negative outlook with a more positive objective, and a firm base on which to plan independent, integrated living... Once a personal sense of direction is established, a realistic understanding of the support, services and resources required can be achieved. Arriving at this point is the end product of 'self-assessment' as we see it. (DCIL Director's report, August 1993)

DCIL's position as an established service provider, with close links to the Coalition, has allowed it to involve local disabled people not only as consumers but as the producers of support services. The form of this involvement has been diverse. Disabled people have been mobilised to campaign on access issues, to form local self-help groups, to provide information and 'counselling', to visit other people in their own homes and so on. Consequently, the provision of peer support towards self-assessment was seen as a key feature of the Personal Support Service. However, DCIL were unable to persuade the commissioning authority to fund this vital work during the contract negotiations and the task fell to their existing bank of volunteers.

Although it has been difficult to win financial support for such initiatives, the provision of support for self-assessment is entirely consistent with the general drift of government policy. For example, initial policy guidance to care practitioners stressed that service users should 'receive every help to speak and act for themselves' (DoH *et al.* 1991c, para.3.23). Thus: 'Just as managers and practitioners will require training to understand and implement the new arrangements, so will users and carers, if they are to take full advantage of them. Such training might focus on the development of self-advocacy skills...' (DoH 1991b, para 5.44).

This kind of training has been an important feature of effective self-assessment initiatives within the movement for independent/integrated living, yet it often remained unfunded (or underfunded). The Greenwich scheme does have a properly funded training programme, although this depends on money from a charitable trust rather than the local authority (Oliver and Zarb 1992). For its part, DCIL has been able to price training programmes for professionals so as to subsidise work with users and peer support workers. In both Greenwich and Derbyshire training is now a revenue generating activity. Their experiences suggest that established organisations of disabled people, and particularly CILs, are well placed to develop peer support and back-up services for disabled people who want to manage their own affairs.

'Care' management and self-management

The essence of self-managed personal assistance schemes is that disabled people gain more independence by exercising greater control over the day to day help that they receive. As Bracking (1993, p.13) argues:

> Nobody – whether they have an impairment or not – can do everything themselves. When disabled people use P.A.s it does not mean they are dependent on others…it should be seen as enhancing the disabled person's ability to live independently. The important point is whether the disabled person has the right to say 'no', to hire and fire at will, and to control payments.

Although the policy framework for 'care management' is entirely consistent with a philosophy of self-management there are also many constraints. For the users of DCIL's Personal Support Service self-management provided new opportunities for self-determination and empowerment. However, it also meant that many of the 'difficult decisions' about rationing were devolved back to them.

Who's managing who?

The framework proposed in *Caring for People* suggested that case management would be required whenever a person's 'needs are complex or significant levels of resources are involved'. While acknowledging that the case manager would often be employed by the lead social services authority, the White Paper noted that 'this need not always be so' (DoH *et al.* 1989, para.3.3.2). For example, it was suggested that staff in voluntary agencies might sometimes be best placed to take on this role. However, the White Paper also noted that:

> It may be possible for some service users to play a more active part in their own care management, for example assuming responsibility for the day to day management of their carers may help to meet the aspirations of severely physically disabled people to be as independent as possible. (DoH/DSS 1990, para.3.17)

Initial policy guidance stressed that users and carers should 'play as active a part in the implementation of their care plan as their abilities and motivation allow' (DoH *et al.* 1991c, para.5.8). Similarly, research by the Audit

Commission (1992b, para.20) suggested that many younger physically impaired people would be 'well able to exercise choice and take charge of their affairs if support is available to enable them to do so'. Research by the Social Services Inspectorate into the first year of community care implementation (DoH 1994c, para.27) provided evidence that 'users welcomed the opportunity to self-assess and to organise and manage their own care packages'. Subsequent research into the operation of the Independent Living Fund (ILF) has lent much support to this view (cf. Kestenbaum 1992; Lakey 1994).

Within the movement for independent/integrated living much emphasis has been placed on securing the resources with which disabled people might manage their own affairs through direct/indirect payments (Morris 1993a, 1993b; Zarb and Nadash 1994; Zarb *et al.* 1996). Kestenbaum (1992) found that, given the resources, 75 per cent of ILF claimants chose to recruit and employ their own personal assistants. The success of the ILF and local self-managed support schemes prompted a sustained campaign by disabled people's organisations for direct payments legislation and the recent introduction of the 1996 Community Care (Direct Payments) Act means that this option may become available to many more disabled people. However, the permissive nature of the legislation means that local authorities can still choose not to exercise their new powers and there is evidence of political resistance to the principle in some areas (Zarb 1995b, p.11).

Hiring and firing

Some self-managed independent living schemes, like those in Hampshire, have stressed the importance of a direct 'hire and fire' relationship between personal assistance users and their staff. Others, like DCIL's Personal Support Scheme employ personal support workers on behalf of the end user. However, in both models the guiding principle is that the individual disabled person should exercise control over who is employed to provide their personal assistance.

All the PSS users were involved in the selection of their own staff, although this was done in conjunction with representatives from DCIL (usually a peer advocate and/or the service manager) and sometimes a family member. Some people, like Richard, felt very comfortable with this arrangement:

> I quite enjoyed it...me and [the community worker] and my son, he was involved as well because we thought, well, he'd to be involved with the

> people. He comes most weekends. So he'd have to get on with them.
> There was no dispute at all. We had to have a few mind you and they were
> very thorough. (Richard)

Others found interviewing to be a new and difficult experience, although
most commented that it became easier by the second or third time. Familiarity with the process and the benefit of hindsight meant that people could
identify different strategies which they might adopt in future interviews. For
example, Carol and Liz identified important questions which they had for-
gotten to ask or had lacked the confidence to raise at the time:

> ...you see with not being used to it, that's what's made you a little unsure
> what to ask them to do and don't. (Liz)

> I mean [the service manager] and [my advocate] gave me the choice, they
> wrote the questions down and I could say if I didn't like them or not. But
> with the first time I'd ever done it, I sort of did what they wanted. I mean
> they know more about it than I do. But now, now looking back... (Carol)

Both Liz and Carol also felt uncomfortable about the mechanics of the interview process and their role in it. In particular, they felt concerned about the
level of formality in the interview situation. Only Liz felt that she had not
had a controlling influence over the final decision about who should be
appointed. She would have preferred not to appoint any of the applicants and
felt 'pressurised' into making an inappropriate choice from the available
candidates.

By contrast, at least two of the men in the group (Terry and Hugh) had
previous experience of interviewing for staff in their current or past
employment. This helped them to feel much more confident than those
without that background. For them, DCIL's role was considerably
diminished. For example, Terry simply picked people who he already knew,
including local people and two nurses from an agency he had used
previously.

Ford and Shaw (1993, p.19) point out that the employment and
self-management of personal assistants brings with it not only more control
but more responsibility. There was certainly some concern amongst the PSS
users about the responsibility associated with hiring and firing staff directly.
For example, Margaret felt reluctant about dismissing an unsatisfactory PA
because she recognised that unemployment might lead to the women losing
her house (although she was eventually dismissed). Carol's expressed similar
worries:

> I find it a bit daunting, the fact that their wages depend on what hours I give them. So I try to be as fair as I can but it's difficult. Because, I think, I have a lie down at lunch time, which makes it an hour. If I don't have a lie down it's half an hour. In school holidays I don't tend to do it so much and the wages is less so I feel a bit guilty. Then I think well, I shouldn't feel guilty so I try not to. (Carol)

Most people experienced problems with managing their staff at one time or another and all but one had found occasion to end a contract of employment. Some people were able to take this aspect of self-management in their stride while others found it a daunting prospect:

> ...it had to be done, but she understood the personal side. What it was, she got a full time job. So I put up with it for so long but I had to get rid of her, which I think I was in my rights. (Joe)

> It would have to be really bad wouldn't it. Oh, I don't think I could do that. Well it depends how bad it got, doesn't it. (Richard)

> I told my complaint to [the service manager], he's going to have a word with this carer but not mention that I've said it you see... And then I feel really guilty because [the service manager], I know he's got a lot of work on with you know, looking after other people. (Liz)

It was not always easy for people to grasp the fact that they had a controlling say in who was employed. For example, at least one person could not quite believe that DCIL had backed his decision to end a PA's contract:

> And DCIL dismissed her, to my amazement...there must have been more behind that decision to dismiss than was revealed to us. (Hugh)

These experiences present a mixed picture of third-party support schemes and show just how fine the balance can be in their management. On the one hand, there was a real need for help and support with the practicalities of recruitment, interviewing and employment relations. Some people would clearly have felt very isolated in an unmediated employer-employee relationship. This is a worry for many disabled people contemplating the prospect of direct payments (Barnes 1997). On the other hand, the buffer of a third-party employer can sometimes mask the central role of the service user. Lack of confidence, and past experiences of disabling service provision, may lead people to defer to peer support workers and scheme managers as 'authority figures' unless the principle of accountability is consistently reinforced.

Personal assistance users need confidence and considerable self-advocacy skills in order to effectively engage with the self-management of personal support staff. Such skills may not come easily to people who have been historically disempowered by negative experiences of institutional or routinised support in the past. For such people the provision of peer support and advocacy is an essential part of the total package but it needs to be provided within an organisational culture in which control by 'professionals' is not replaced by that of 'professional disabled people', however unwittingly.

Managing tasks

Department of Health guidance (DoH/SSI 1993, p.iii) suggested that home support services should provide 'help with tasks associated with ordinary living that an individual might usually perform for him/herself', including personal assistance, domestic help and social or emotional support. However, recent changes in the move from 'home help' to 'home care' have focused local authority service provision on limited 'personal care' tasks, while district nursing visits are now restricted solely to 'nursing tasks'. Jenny Morris (1993a, p.18) points out that statutory domiciliary services are not generally available for assistance with activities outside the home and that they often fail to support participation in personal and family relationships. Similarly, Ann Kestenbaum (1993a, p.19) shows how ILF eligibility criteria impose parallel restrictions. By contrast, self-managed personal assistance schemes offer the means to obtain help with a wider variety of tasks than can be provided through existing service provision.

All the PSS users made use of their hours for assistance with 'personal care' tasks such as getting up, going to bed, dressing, showering, washing and using the toilet. For some this involved considerable physical assistance (e.g. lifting); for others it amounted to partial help with discrete tasks (such as putting on shoes or fastening buttons). Physical help with personal care was sometimes supplemented by the use of adapted environments, additional assistance or special equipment (e.g. hoists in the bathroom). The amount of time devoted to these tasks varied considerably from person to person but was generally between two and four hours a day.

The use of personal support for domestic chores was equally diverse. Everyone used their personal support workers to assist with some aspect of domestic management (e.g. cooking, cleaning, washing, ironing, gardening, shopping, walking the dog, doing paper work, making a coal fire). Some people did most of their own housework, some shared the chores with their personal assistants, some relied more heavily on their support staff. Terry's experience illustrates the kind of flexibility that was involved:

> When we do the housework, I can't do all of it but I do some of it... If we're cooking I can't watch all the pans at once and they do that with me, either that or they watch. When we wash up and put away we do it together. I can't reach up to the cupboards and they do that. I do part of it. So they're assisting, not 'doing for' which is very important to me. (Terry)

In addition to 'personal care' and domestic assistance, everyone was able to make some use of personal assistants for social support (such as shopping, eating out, going to the pub, pursuing a hobby or attending meetings). The following collection of comments demonstrate some of this diversity and emphasise the importance attached to social support by the research participants:

> I can't travel without them. So they come with me. I couldn't get there physically. (Terry)

> I go fishing every Saturday in the summer...and one of my ladies comes and picks me up, goes with me, drops me off, goes home, comes back and picks me up. (Richard)

> when I'm out the only time that I need them is if I want to go to the toilet and stuff like that...and they have left us in a pub or restaurant and they've come back later. (Joe)

> ...there's not been anything more difficult than having to say to a personal assistant I want to watch a film, I know there's some iffy bits in it, I want you to come and sit by my side and hold my hand. And we've actually watched films like that. That's something you've got a lot of trust in, and that they've found difficult as well sometimes. (Terry)

> I do local history research, and we went to [the local] record office. Well my father took me a couple of times over the past few years but he was getting fed up of walking around [town] while I was in doing that. That was OK because it's [PA]'s job and she didn't mind walking round [town]... So I shan't feel awkward about asking to go again... (Carol)

> I don't know what's going off around this area and I rely on them to tell me... (Liz)

If self-managed personal assistance is to contribute towards the goals of participation, social integration and equality then this kind of support is essential. Without support to travel, to pursue social contacts and to take part in the life of their communities, many disabled people face a bleak future of isolation and segregation within the home. As Jenny Morris (1993b) argues, services which are limited to medicalised personal care and 'essential' domestic assistance form part of an 'ideology of caring' which undermines the citizenship and civil rights of disabled people. For Morris, 'The ideology of caring which is at the heart of current community care policies can only result in institutionalisation within the community unless politicians and professionals understand and identify with the philosophy and the aims of the independent living movement' (Morris 1993a, p.45).

For DCIL's service users, there appeared to be little if any dispute with purchasers about the allocation of adequate resources for support with 'personal care' and limited domestic help. By contrast, it was much harder to agree about the 'need' for social integration. For example, Liz reported that her care manager would not give her any hours to support social activities (such as preparing a meal for visitors, going out to eat or going on holiday). Terry received funding for overnight support but was initially denied any assistance during the day because his need for company was not accepted by the care manager. Where the overall level of funding fell short of self-assessed need it was invariably social support that had to be sacrificed (or paid for from personal resources).

In general terms, the PSS users found it easier to obtain funded hours for help which fitted traditional patterns of domiciliary 'care' than for support within an integrated living model. Where individualised assistance within the home was readily accepted as a 'need', support for integrated community living was more likely to be characterised as a 'want'. Similar experiences have been identified in other studies. For example, Morris (1993a, p.20) demonstrates how 'personal care' was given precedence over domestic assistance and social support in her sample. Thus: 'A failure of statutory bodies to provide services which enable people to carry on their daily lives and engage in ordinary personal relationships creates very poor quality of life and undermines human and civil rights' (Morris 1993a, p.26).

Disabled people within the movement for independent/integrated living have consistently argued that support services should extend beyond the confines of 'care' and enable them to 'take part in work, leisure, travel and family life if they choose' (resolution passed at the Strasbourg independent living conference, reviewed by Rachel Hurst 1989). From this perspective, current confusions between 'needs' and 'wants' are misplaced. As Mike

Ridout points out, 'The implication is that basic needs can be satisfied but wants cannot. In terms of assessments and support packages to enable disabled people to live independently there is no difference; independent living is not a luxury but a right' (Ridout 1995, p.2).

There is emerging evidence that the practice of community care assessment and management continues to produce packages of support which reflect traditional assumptions about the 'needs' of disabled people. Consequently, care assessment and management must be seen not only as a simple 'gate keeping' mechanism but as a powerful discursive activity. By focusing the allocation of resources on personal care at the expense of social integration, the assessment process maintains a view of disability which characterise the needs of disabled people in terms of dependency and 'care' rather than citizenship and social integration.

Managing flexibility

One of the main attractions of self-managed personal assistance schemes is that they allow for more flexibility in the timing and content of support compared to service provision (Kestenbaum 1992, 1993a; Lakey 1994; Oliver and Zarb 1992; Zarb and Nadash 1994). Like other self-managed schemes, DCIL's Personal Support Service aims to create a structure in which people can choose when and how their assistance is provided. However, flexibility brings with it many new responsibilities and dilemmas.

DCIL's approach to self-management operates within a total budget allocation but allows service users to transfer or 'bank' surplus hours from month to month to provide more or less support as required. For example, going on holiday with a PA would use up a large number of hours while going on holiday without the PA would enable the user to 'bank' the hours not used. Most of the PSS users attempted to use their hours in a flexible way. For example, Joe started his package with a fairly fixed routine of 31 hours per week spread between three personal assistants. However, with experience, he was able to consolidate his regular personal and domestic help into a 21 hour schedule. This meant that he had an additional ten hours per week which could be 'banked' for more flexible support with social activities or unexpected situations. Only Richard felt more comfortable with an established routine:

> I've got a regular time, itinerary…same day, same time. I know where I am and I know who's coming and I know what's what… You just get used to it, you know, I plan my life and I like to have everything mapped

out you know, a timetable kind of thing that I've planned...I've only changed the schedule once, and that was just for one day. (Richard)

Carol had been able to 'bank' some additional hours for social activities while she was on holiday, and again when one of her PAs was ill. However, in practice she had been unable to transfer this saving because there were simply not enough total hours in her package of support to allow for flexibility:

> ...every week I'm over nineteen hours, whether I've been out or not, just personal care is over nineteen hours. So I keep thinking when I've used these hours up, I've got none spare. I've got none to bank to use to go out...I've got about six hours left but when I've used them up I shan't have any... (Carol)

An important part of self-management was then to determine how the total number of hours should be apportioned between different tasks. This was particularly important for those people without additional personal resources. For example, Carol was often unable to go shopping because she had run out of hours while Liz found that she did not have time for supervision with her physiotherapy exercises. Resource rationing meant that the PSS users were often required to make difficult decisions about which tasks got done and which did not. The following two examples illustrate the point:

> When I want to pay people to do my garden I can't afford to have my support services take me out on social time. If I didn't have to pay for my garden and my borders the money that I have to pay out would contribute for the personal support services to take me out to other places. (Joe)

> I said [to my PA] in the winter time, would you do more cooking instead of house work?... Well, if I cut down my cleaning...if I had the money I would make sure they could take me out socially. (Liz)

Many disabled people have been historically denied the opportunity to make the sort of everyday life decisions which confer adult status in our society. Institutional care, 'special' schooling, 'protective' families, physical 'treatments' and chemical restraints have all contributed to this disempowerment. In one sense, the fact that the PSS users were able to make such choices at all is a measure of success. However, the examples from Derbyshire also illustrate how daily life choices acquire a particular significance for people whose resources are rationed through care assessment. For PA users 'ordinary' choices about the use of their time (cooking, cleaning, gardening, walking the dog) become commodified choices about the use of scarce financial resources.

In this context it is worth reiterating that those people with access to additional personal resources (savings and earnings) or alternative sources of support (family, friends, volunteers) were usually able to avoid such difficult decisions. As Jenny Morris concluded from her study: 'Those people who had the money to pay for personal assistance were generally able to have the kind of control over their lives which was not possible for those solely reliant on either services or on family and friends' (Morris 1993a, p.37).

The following two examples from Derbyshire emphasise the point:

> ...I think it's because of the extra money I put into the package, because it's allowed me to have the extra flexibility...I've been able to pay for it myself to a certain extent. I've got enough money to have people with me. I can go to the bank and get money. Without it I'd be struggling. (Terry)

> I just said, if they find out as I'm over my time, I've come to the agreement with my own staff without [the service manager]'s knowledge that I can pay them out of my own pocket within reason. (Joe)

It is not surprising that people with additional resources are able to make additional choices in the way they run their lives. This is the case for non-disabled people as well as disabled people. However, disabled people in Britain are more likely to live in low income households and are significantly less likely to be able to draw on additional resources (Barnes 1991; Berthoud, Lakey and McKay 1993; Disability Alliance 1987; Martin and White 1988; Thompson, Lavery and Curtice 1990). Consequently, significant numbers of disabled people without personal resources remain dependent upon the decisions made by community care assessors. Flexibility is clearly enhanced by self-managed personal support but real self-determination and life choices are still a function of personal income and familial capital for most people.

The significance of this conclusion is reinforced by the increasing incidence of charging and budget-linked rationing within social services departments (Baldwin and Lunt 1996; Chetwynd and Ritchie 1996). Lamb and Layzell's (1995) study of more than 1500 SCOPE clients showed that 17 per cent had refused a service because they could not afford it and that 18 per cent were paying for a service that was previously free at the point of delivery (see also Lamb and Layzell 1994). Similarly, 18 out of 50 people in Morris' sample were paying for some or all of their assistance (1993a, p.26).

There is now considerable pressure on local authorities to charge for services or to withdraw them. Central government allocates community care funds on the assumption that 9 per cent of domiciliary services revenue will be met through charges to service users. In the case of a shortfall, LA Circular 1994(1) advises that the service should be withdrawn. This principle has been hotly contested in recent years. However, in March 1997 the Law Lords ruled finally that Gloucestershire County Council were justified in removing 'home care' services from 1500 disabled people on financial grounds. Thus, there would seem to be legal precedent for the view that a local authority's 'duty of care' is indeed limited by available resources.

Conclusions

There is an increasing weight of evidence which suggests that self-managed support schemes bring many advantages to their users. Advocacy and peer support for self-assessment allow disabled people to challenge disabling assumptions of dependency and to explore new alternatives. Self-management involves difficult decisions but it also provides opportunities for greater choice, control and self-determination. Above all, it engages disabled people as active agents in the production of their own welfare, rather than as the passive recipients of professionally dominated services.

Personal assistance users draw on a variety of resources to construct their personalised packages. They may use their own financial resources to purchase assistance or draw on informal networks of support (e.g. friends, family, neighbours). Most rely on substantial public resources in the form of services or direct/indirect payments (such payments may come directly from the statutory authorities or from one of the Independent Living Funds).

The majority of such resources continue to depend upon professional assessments of 'need' (from which disabled people and their organisations have frequently been excluded). Consequently, personal assistance users often find themselves caught between the self-empowering values of independent/integrated living (arising from the politicised disabled people's movement) and the disabling values of a purchasing system which maintains the traditional values of 'care', individualism and social segregation. Thus, as Jenny Morris (1993a, p.38) concludes: 'The aim of independent living is held back by an ideology at the heart of community care policies, which does not recognise the civil rights of disabled people but instead considers them to be dependent people and in need of care.'

In challenging this 'ideology of care', the movement for independent living has focused attention on the development of self-managed personal assistance schemes which bring financial resources under the control of disabled people themselves. Such schemes offer vital support to those who wish to manage their own affairs. In particular, they bring greater choice, control and freedom to the people who use them. However self-managed schemes on their own cannot resolve all the problems. Without adequate resources for peer support, advocacy and organisational back-up the effect is simply to devolve the 'difficult decisions' of rationing to the end user of the service. Those without additional personal resources are then placed in a position of self-regulation and surveillance, forced to impose upon themselves the values of a welfare system which prioritises 'care' and 'treatment' over social integration and participatory citizenship.

The future of self-managed support schemes depends largely upon the purchasing decisions of commissioning authorities and community care assessors. The fear, for organisations like DCIL, is that the benefits of an integrated living approach may be undervalued (and thereby unremunerated) within a purchasing framework derived from traditional discourses of disability and welfare. Thus: 'Appropriate outcomes for disabled people in Derbyshire will depend on the degree to which the principle of user-determination is compromised by the contractual framework within which Self-assessment and Self Management is permitted to operate' (DCIL Director's report, March 1993).

The challenge for organisations within the movement for independent/ integrated living is then to demonstrate the 'added value' of this way of working, within the contractual framework of community care implementation. The analysis presented in the following chapter shows just how difficult a task this can be.

CHAPTER 5

Marketing the Social Model

This chapter examines how the marketisation of community care affects the development of independent/integrated living. The first part of the discussion focuses on the development of welfare pluralism and markets. The second section draws on DCIL's experience of negotiating contractual agreements in order to illustrate the processes involved. The final section then analyses the impact of contracting on service design and organisational structure. The case study data raises many general questions about the efficacy of marketisation as an implementation tool. Specifically, DCIL's experience suggests that the imposition of contracting for community care services threatens to undermine the goal of integrated living for disabled people.

A market for integrated living

Griffiths (1988) argued that the public sector's primary role was to ensure that 'care' was provided. How it should be provided was to be a 'secondary consideration'. Taking this lead, the community care White Paper emphasised that local authorities should seek to stimulate a variety of service provision in the voluntary, 'not for profit' and private sectors through contractual funding arrangements. This it was hoped would help to extend user choice within the 'mixed economy' of care.

Demographic change, earlier hospital discharges, increasing consumerism and acute fiscal restrictions on local authorities have added incentives towards the creation of markets in social care. The trend has also been accelerated by changes to Income Support rules, the conditions for Special Transitional Grant funding and incentives provided by the *Caring for People Who Live at Home* initiative (DoH 1994a, para.4). The development of contractual markets is of course not unique to community care and reflects a more general shift in local government policy away from public sector provision and towards the creation of 'enabling' authorities (Cochrane 1991, p.282; Gyford 1991; Glennerster, Power and Travers 1991).

Markets and 'quasi-markets'

The idea of 'competition' is a mainstay of free market economics. Yet the study of markets in health and 'social care' indicates that such competition is generally constrained and may, on occasion, be wholly absent (Pirie and Butler 1989). Indeed, early research commissioned by the Department of Health suggested that none of the sample authorities were anticipating sufficient independent sector supply of non-residential services to generate any meaningful level of market competition (DoH 1994a, para.8.13). The existence of market constraints has led many analysts to adopt the term *quasi-market* (Williamson 1975) to describe the context for contracting in social care (Hoyes and Means 1993; Le Grand 1991; Le Grand and Bartlett 1993).

In general terms, market competition may be constrained on both the demand side and the supply side. For example, a *monopoly* may exist where there is effectively only one supplier of a commodity or service. The corollary of this situation is *monopsony*, where a market contains only one customer. Both are relatively common in markets for social care where the local authority may often be the only significant purchaser (Common and Flynn 1992) or where a single provider comes to dominate the production of care services (Propper 1993). Indeed, there may sometimes be a *dual monopoly* market in which there is effectively only one purchaser and one provider. This basic typology of quasi-market structures is illustrated in Figure 5.1).

Quasi-markets in the British health and social care sectors also differ from classical markets in another important respect. The buying power of individual customers is mediated by state purchasing agencies. While National Health Service reforms have centred on the creation of 'internal markets' (based around existing statutory providers), the imposition of markets in social care has sought to generate 'a mixed economy' (emphasising the increased role of independent sector providers). However, in both cases most services remain publicly funded and are not purchased by the end user but on their behalf by statutory authorities. For the majority of service users, it is still care managers who act as the market's 'customers'.

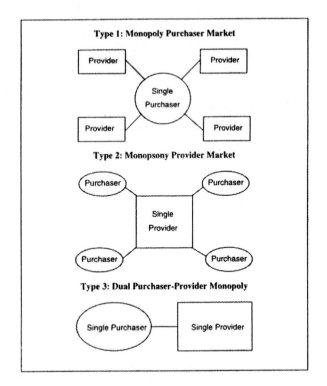

Figure 5.1 The structure of quasi-markets

The combined influence of quasi-market constraints and mediated purchasing means that many local markets are still closer to Type 3 than to the other models. However, it is important to note that any substantial increase in local 'for-profit' providers (Kestenbaum 1993a) might restructure the market into something more closely resembling Type 1. Conversely, any substantial increase in the purchasing power of individual disabled people (for example, through direct payments) might tend towards a Type 2 market. The emergence of a 'classical' free-market environment would require both these processes to occur simultaneously.

It is worth noting that, at the time of writing, there is some evidence that both these processes are indeed beginning to impact on the functioning of the market. It is too early to predict how the implementation of the new direct payments legislation will impact on the demand side of the equation.

However, it is clear that increased competition on the supply side means that organisations like DCIL are under greater pressure to differentiate their services from those of other voluntary and private sector providers on quality grounds.

Freedom and choice

For monetarist economists, like Hayek (1960) or Friedman and Friedman (1980), any reduction of individual choice is a reduction in freedom and therefore a step towards tyranny. Consequently, their promotion of market economics in welfare production is characterised by an ideological attachment to individual freedom. Similarly, Harden places a premium on consumer choice and bases his analysis of *The Contracting State* on the premise that 'Consumer sovereignty links the economic aspects of the market with a set of moral commitments. The market provides a model of economic efficiency. It also embodies values of equality and freedom... Consumer sovereignty thus amounts to a version of democratic equality' (1992, p.2).

It is then a central principle of neo-classical liberal economy that individuals should be free to bargain in the market place (De Jasay 1992). They should be free to enter into, and refrain from entering into, contracts of exchange with one another. Only in this situation can contracts be imbued with legal validity. Only in a state of contractual freedom can the contracting parties acquire the power to legally enforce private and voluntary agreements. Harden (1992, p.3) summarises the principle:

> The right not to enter a contract is thus an essential aspect of the rule of law. Without it, the weak would be exposed to the arbitrary and compulsory imposition of obligations by the strong, who would then receive the backing of the state to enforce them.

Yet, freedom of contract is not a reality in the market for social care, particularly where the number of purchasers and providers is limited, or where there are relationships of domination and subordination between them. For example, a disabled person faced with the choice between 'day care' or no care may have little opportunity for 'exit' or 'voice' (Hirschman 1970). Similarly, in the case of NHS purchasing it is not possible for a patient to appeal against the decision to provide 'continuing care' (only against a decision not to provide it). Hoyes and Means (1993, p.96) note that many people are in fact disempowered in the social care market because they are dependent on the assessment of a care manager. Thus, Common and Flynn (1992) conclude that contracting for social care has not so far increased user choice or control.

Conversely, local authorities are not free to 'exit' from social care responsibilities when the market becomes unfavourable. In fact they may have to 'opt in' at just those times when economic conditions make independent providers unable or unwilling to contract (Stewart and Ranson 1988). At the provider level too there are constraints on freedom of contract. In a monopoly purchaser market, independent organisations have little choice but to enter into contracts with the local authority. Reductions in grant aid funding mean that there are few, if any, sources of alternative revenue (these issues are discussed in more detail later).

Efficiency and values

There is considerable evidence that market relationships are rarely based on economics alone (Hansmann 1980; James and Rose-Ackerman 1986; Propper 1993; Williamson 1975, 1978). This is particularly the case in the purchase of services. Kettner and Martin (1987) argue that human services contracting is not like buying a manufactured product. It is not always in the purchaser's interest to secure the lowest price. Indeed, if statutory purchasers do exert their monopoly buying power in this way then it is the end users who may suffer from an under-funded service. Thus, Morgan and England (1988, p.986) argue that efficiency should not be pursued by purchasers to the exclusion of values such as equity, citizenship and community.

Common and Flynn (1992) studied a variety of contracting situations and found that financial considerations were often not the main motivating force in the award of contracts. Similarly, Kramer and Grossman (1987, p.38) indicate that the final decision to award contracts is rarely made on the basis of price alone and that 'all allocational decisions involve value judgements and power considerations'. Indeed, the government's initial guidance on community care purchasing stressed that 'contracts and service specifications are not, and should not, simply be a means of purchasing the cheapest care available, they must be the means of identifying and ensuring that the best quality care is obtained' (DoH/DSS 1990, para.1.16).

In Derbyshire the local authority were certainly concerned that DCIL should tender at 'a reasonable price' although the director of social services made it clear that 'We're not into tendering for lowest price issues' (quoted in *Disability Now*, April 1994, p.12). The admission that price and efficiency are not everything in the award of contracts for community care raises the question – what does matter? If politics and values *are* important influences on purchaser decision making then we need to know more about the value judgements involved and more about the power relationships that exist between contracting parties.

All contracts and contracting procedures for local authority services are governed by Local Authority Standing Orders unless specifically exempted. Part II of the Local Government Act (1988) stipulates that local authorities may not specify non-commercial considerations in contracts, although the Act does not prevent them from taking into account the bidder's management record together with any genuine occupational requirements (where these can be commercially justified). However, the Association of Metropolitan Authorities' guidance to purchasers advises that 'The values of the organisation and the way it conducts itself will be an important indicator of whether it is likely to achieve quality provision. This should be taken into account when making an assessment of whether to contract or continue to contract within an organisation' (AMA 1990, p.11).

In this context, the AMA made specific reference to an organisation's attitude and commitment to user involvement. Similarly, Department of Health policy guidance indicates that purchasers should look for evidence not only that providers are reliable and commercially viable but also that they share the values of the purchasing authority (see for example, DoH/DSS 1990, para.4.26). Yet, organisations within the movement for independent/integrated living have often been founded on the basis of opposition to those same values (through the promotion of social model thinking). More generally, voluntary sector providers tend to reflect very different service values to organisations in the public sector (Moe 1988).

In comparison with public sector services, independent providers have been credited with initiative, diversity of provision, preservation of the 'gift relationship', closeness to communities, critical voice and responsiveness to individual need (Munday 1985; Weisbrod 1977). They are also open to criticism. Thus, Salamon (1987, pp.111–112) show how the 'philanthropic' nature of the voluntary sector can give rise to insufficiency, particularism, paternalism and amateurism. Manser (1974, p.427) argues that voluntary organisations often exhibit high levels of bureaucracy and that the ideal of pluralism may conceal control by a homogeneous, class-based, 'establishment' elite.

In more general terms, Lipsky and Smith (1989) suggest that government's public accountability gives precedence to equity of service while the voluntary sector's autonomy gives precedence to responsiveness. Such value differences may then lead to conflict and mistrust in the contractual relationship (Wistow *et al.* 1994). Lipsky and Smith conclude that different kinds of voluntary agencies will be affected by government contracting in different ways but that the greatest conflicts are likely to arise amongst agencies whose structures and values differ most from those of their government purchasers. Given the fundamental value differences which exist between the disabled people's movement and agencies of the British welfare state it is not surprising that conflict has arisen over the purchasing of integrated living services.

The discourse of 'community care' and the alternative counter-culture of the disabled people's movement share many common features. However, in the practice of policy implementation they often compete. Thus:

> ...the present trends are the product of two separate currents of change – a current arising centrally from the implementation of government policies, and a current arising peripherally from a 'grassroots' social movement. These currents are not necessarily opposing ones, but the origins, goals and motive force of each have little or no reference to the other. (Gibbs 1994, p.1)

For an organisation like DCIL such differences are a very real concern, not least because the implementation of integrated living solutions depends upon successful collaboration with the commissioning and purchasing authorities. Such value differences permeate to the very heart of an organisation which engages directly in partnership with those same authorities. As Crosby (1994, p.1) notes, 'DCIL is a very small organisation, with an explicit mission, to change society, so that disabled people are full participants. Conflict is always present, most often between the organisation and its chief funders'.

The politics of contracting

The following discussion examines how organisations committed to independent/integrated living have fared in the market for community care services. In particular, the analysis draws on a review of DCIL's experience in negotiating both a General Service Level Agreement and a specific contract for the Personal Support Service. Contractual relationships bring organisations like DCIL (which adopt a social model of disability) into close proximity with the individualising values of community care purchasing. Where the commissioning authority also perceives demands for user control as part of a wider assault on public service accountability such value differences are accentuated.

Welfare pluralism and integrated living

In principle, welfare pluralism enjoys widespread political appeal. For the right, it offers a reduced state role, competition, choice and self-reliance; for the left, it offers more participation, responsive services and a challenge to bureaucratic centralism. In practice however, the mixed economy of care raises much controversy within local authorities. Johnson (1987) argues that it is not decentralisation or pluralism *per se* which have been most contentious but rather the use of markets to achieve those ends. In particular, there has been much resistance from those local authorities (mainly northern, mainly 'old' Labour) that see self-managed disability services and direct payments as a further assault on the traditions of public sector accountability and management (Zarb and Nadash 1994).

Early research by the Audit Commission (1992b, para.35) identified a considerable reluctance amongst social services departments to develop the 'mixed economy of care' at all, particularly in the private sector. However, subsequent work by the Department of Health suggested that local authorities were more amenable to contracting with voluntary and 'not-for-profit' organisations (DoH 1994a, para.4.3). In this context, it is important to remember that disabled people within the movement have been as critical of charities and organisations 'for' disabled people within the voluntary sector as they have been of disabling service provision within the public sector (see Drake 1996). Increased welfare pluralism alone is therefore no guarantee of more enabling welfare provision unless it is implemented within a social model of disability.

Within this uneven political landscape, organisations committed to independent/integrated living tread a fine line between competing ideologies of welfare. Indeed, as Barnes (1991) points out, disabled people may have something to gain from both the left and the right. The movement for independent/integrated living has a strong collectivist tradition which emphasises equal opportunities, civil rights and citizenship. For the Labour-led authority in Derbyshire, it was these aspects of the integrated living philosophy which offered most appeal in the early 1980s. Conversely, it was the promotion of consumer markets and individual 'choice' by the Conservative-led authority in Hampshire which opened the door for disabled people to establish pioneering direct payments schemes there during the same period.

It is not surprising, then, that the uneven regional development of independent/integrated living schemes has often reflected the political agendas of those authorities in which they operate. In Derbyshire, the ruling Labour group were publicly committed to the social model principles of integrated living as far back as 1981. However, they were openly resistant to the Derbyshire Coalition's proposals for replacing existing public sector provision with integrated living supports under the control of disabled people. Ironically DCDP activists received a warmer response from individual Conservative members who were able to accommodate the idea of self-managed support within their own agenda for increased plurality, competition and consumerism.

Throughout the 1990s, disabled people within the movement have struggled to influence local community care purchasing decisions towards the provision of more enabling supports (self-managed personal assistance schemes, PAS schemes, direct payments, CILs and so on). In so doing they have necessarily focused the debate on conflicts between individual model and social model thinking (Morris 1993a, 1993b). However, as the preceding analysis shows, there is a second dimension of competing values which cuts across this debate – between individual and collective traditions of welfare production. The intersection of these two dimensions is illustrated in Figure 5.2.

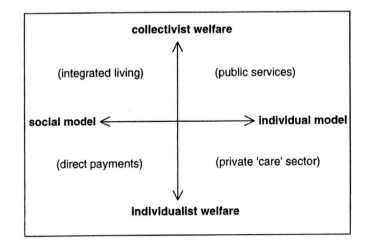

Figure 5.2 Models of disability and welfare traditions

On the one hand, self-managed personal assistance schemes and direct payments can be readily accommodated within individualist models of welfare (although they evolved from the collective struggles of disabled people working within a social model of disability). On the other hand, collective advocacy, community development work, Personal Assistance Support (PAS) schemes and Centres for Independent/Integrated Living (CILs) are collective responses to welfare production (especially when they are accountable to representative organisations of disabled people). Consequently, they have more in common with the collectivist traditions of municipal socialism or 'communitarian' politics (Etzioni 1995) than they have with *laissez-faire* individualism. As Jon Dunnicliffe (from West of England CIL) notes: 'It is important to remember that Independent Living was developed by groups of disabled people pushing for direct/indirect payments and that this is about civil rights and collectivity; not about privatisation' (quoted in Barnes *et al.* 1995, p.17).

Local authorities with a particularly strong attachment to collective service provision face a dual assault. First, they are under increasing pressure from politicised organisations of disabled people to change the services that they provide. Second, their ability to provide those services at all is increasingly undermined by central government regulation and the imposition of purchaser-provider splits. The recent introduction of direct payments legislation (although discretionary) adds pressure in both these directions – towards the creation of social model supports and towards privatised provision. These combined pressures are illustrated in Figure 5.3.

Collective approaches to self-managed support require strong partnerships between social services departments and local disabled people (Simpson 1995, p.21) and in Derbyshire, the Coalition had fought hard to establish DCIL under joint control with the statutory authorities. In so doing they hoped to redefine public sector service provision and redirect the use of public resources in a more general way. In contrast to many other independent living projects (for example, in Hampshire) there was a conscious *resistance* to the idea that DCIL might become an 'independent' service provider. However, the implementation framework for community care purchasing has created disincentives to this strategy.

In addition to the purchaser-provider splits created by the 1990 Act, subsequent policy directives increased to 85 per cent the proportion of transitional purchasing funds which were to be spent on independent sector provision. For example, the *Special Grant Reports* (nos. 6 and 7), required

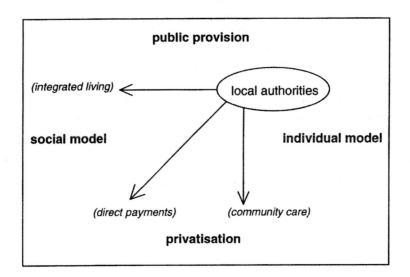

Figure 5.3 Pressures on local authority service provision

authorities to spend at least 85 per cent of the social security transfer element on 'community care services which they arrange to be provided by individuals who are not employed by any local authority under a contract of service, or by organisations which are not owned, controlled or managed by any local authority or more than one authority' (Association of Directors of Social Services, ADSS 1993).

This clearly raises difficulties for organisations which seek close partnerships with their local purchasing authorities. For an organisation like DCIL, which has actively sought to maintain a collaborative management structure, the purchasing incentive to be 'independent' raises internal contradictions. Indeed, the criteria create direct pressures to sever the very partnerships which were central to the unique establishment of DCIL during the early 1980s.

Thus, the movement for independent/integrated living faces a dual challenge in the community care market. In many areas, local commissioners still need to be brought away from the discourse of 'care' and towards a degree of social model thinking before resources can be channelled into more enabling forms of support (Northern Officer Group 1996). In other places, local politicians need to be convinced that user control over community care resources is not simply an attack on collective welfare or public accountability. The following examples of contract negotiation in Derbyshire illustrate how these battles are played out in practice.

A general service level agreement

The impending implementation of community care purchasing forced DCIL, along with many other voluntary sector providers, to radically reevaluate its role. DCIL's constitution had established its functions in the broadest possible terms (based on the Coalition's 'seven needs'). Information provision, collective advocacy, community development work, awareness raising, research, campaigning and barrier removal ran alongside supportive work with individual 'service users'. In short, DCIL's mission was to make changes in society and to radically alter the pattern of public welfare production. However, the new policy framework now required them to specify this strategy in terms of specific 'services' that the purchasing authority could contract for.

Owing to the scale of DCIL's existing grant aid from the local authority there was increasing pressure to define what was being delivered for the money. It was also becoming clear that, in view of the level of funding involved, they would need to negotiate a full partnership agreement. This, then, became the focus of negotiations over the coming months. However, both parties felt that any fundamental restructuring of their organisational partnership would only be necessary in a context of competitive tendering and that this could wait, for the time being at least.

In a climate of economic retrenchment, relationships with the local authority were coming under strain and DCIL managers soon expressed a feeling of 'back to square one' in their attempts to secure user representation in the negotiations. In November 1992, DCIL and DCDP made a joint submission to the major funding agencies expressing their concern that early proposals for a service level agreement were failing to build on the partnership which they had sustained throughout the 1980s. In particular, they were beginning to feel that the terms of such an agreement might ultimately undermine the ability of many disabled people to organise their own lives.

DCIL were concerned to ensure that purchasers should be 'informed by the direct experience of disabled people over what services to commission' and specifically that disabled people's organisations should be 'directly involved in determining the objectives for services to be commissioned'

(DCIL Director's report, December 1993). However, it was becoming increasingly clear that the principle of user determination might be compromised. Discussions with the social services department indicated that service agreements based on the expressed needs of disabled people for self-assessment and self-management were likely to be the exception rather than the rule in the new order. Furthermore, the key function of 'needs' assessment would not be contracted out.

Social services had indicated that they recognised the value of DCIL's range of supports. However, this did not appear to be acknowledged in strategic planning and, by the beginning of community care implementation in April 1993, DCIL became worried that the authority's first Community Care Plan contained little reference to any joint strategy. By mid 1995, concerns had risen to a point where DCIL managers felt it necessary to report that:

> The involvement of disabled people's organisations in decisions about their services has declined to a lower point than at any time since 1981...DCIL may now be in a position of having to form policy on the basis that faith has been broken with the Disabled People's Movement in this County. (DCIL Liaison Group Minutes, May/June 1995)

DCIL's organisational partnership with the local authority was thus coming under increasing strain – not only because of the cumulative impact of progressive funding cuts (see later) but also as a direct consequence of negotiating for community care contracts. Increasingly, the administrative boundaries within which negotiations were taking place threatened to marginalise the core values on which DCIL's mission had been founded. Increasing value conflicts in the contracting process now threatened to undermine their unique partnership with the local authority. Thus:

> Debate on DCIL's ties with the County Council is urgent, as it becomes increasingly clear that present policy, in the context of the restraints of recent years, is wholly incompatible with the aims of disabled people's organisations in the County. (DCIL Liaison Group Minutes, June/July 1995)

It would be unwise to draw too many generalised conclusions from this experience. Local politics, personalities and unique organisational pressures will always be important in contractual negotiations. However, it is important to reiterate that the imposition of purchaser-provider reforms brought organisational chaos to both the purchaser and the provider during the transitional period. It accentuated core value differences between disabled people's organisations and the statutory agencies. It undermined an innovative and productive organisational partnership. It detracted energy and resources from collaborative work towards social integration for local disabled people.

A specific service contract

In January 1993, DCIL's Director wrote to the chief executives of the primary purchasing authorities (social services and health) indicating a willingness to bid for community care contracts based on the provision of assessment and support services for people who choose to manage their own personal assistance. Initial reactions were favourable and gave further impetus to an increasing organisational focus on this aspect of service provision. By September 1993, it was agreed that the new venture should be called a 'Personal Support Service' and introductory papers were prepared with a view to contracting for support services to people who wanted to manage their own personal assistance.

In the same month an opportunity arose for DCIL to pilot the proposed scheme when a request was received for assistance from a service user and his care manager. By October the 'mini-pilot' had a total of six service users at various stages of self-assessment and self-management. DCIL's first Personal Assistant was appointed in December 1993 and managers felt confident to report that 'SA/SM has effectively come into operation' (DCIL Liaison Group minutes, December 1993). However, concerns were already being expressed that a social services agenda of 'care' still dominated the conduct of this work. Both service users and DCIL workers remained unsure what freedom they would have in the use of resources and what decisions they were empowered to make.

Meanwhile, the contracting process was proving arduous. Important value conflicts were apparent in discussions about the form and content of the service itself. In particular, social services began to express concerns about the scope of the proposal for a personal support service. While there was some recognition of the value of self-management, the purchasers did not accept the added value (cost) of providing peer support and community development work within the package. In addition, it became clear that the agreement would not finance all the 'infrastructure' costs of planning and managing the project. The initial contract offered in May 1994 was thus perceived by DCIL as nothing more than 'a basic domiciliary service incompatible with DCIL aims' (DCIL Liaison Group minutes, May 1994).

Faced with a *fait accompli,* DCIL resubmitted their tender for the personal support service with a recalculated (lower) price. The revised contract went to Social Services Committee in September 1994 and was agreed. At this point three people were employing eight PAs through DCIL's payroll and funded by social services 'care packages'. Five other people were at an initial stage as personal support service users and two were in discussions with social services. In addition, DCIL was using the payroll scheme to assist ten people in managing Independent Living Fund payments while DCIL community workers were supporting at least five more with ILF applications.

This left DCIL with a considerable problem. They had tendered for (and were providing) a complete integrated living support service including peer advocacy and community development work. However, the contract recognised and remunerated only the individualised aspects of direct personal assistance. Attempts were made to make up for the key functions of support work which had been excluded from the service contract by placing a bid to the Department of Health for 'Section 64' funding. However, this was unsuccessful and DCIL found themselves managing a contract which could not fully resource a personal support service wholly consistent with their philosophy of integrated living.

The new service proved a considerable success and brought about real life changes for the people who used it. A service manager was appointed in December 1993 and enquiries began to come from outside the county. In addition, the Social Services Inspectorate asked if they could cite the new service as an example of good practice. By July 1995, six people were using PAs employed by DCIL (with a further nine making enquiries). The demand for self-assessment, and the commitment to provide ongoing support to service users, over and above contract compliance, placed an increasing strain on the existing outreach team and peer support workers.

To summarise, the introduction of service contracting forced DCIL to redirect its resources on those aspects of service provision which could most easily be contracted for by the purchasing authorities. In particular, it was necessary to develop a new focus on the direct provision of personal support services to individual disabled people with 'complex' (i.e. expensive) needs. Resisting the temptation to replicate traditional models of domiciliary care, DCIL established their support service within a broader model of integrated living. However, in the end they were unable to contract for anything more than individualised packages of personal assistance. The 'additional' aspects of support (such as peer support and community development) remained unpurchased and thus unremunerated within the terms of the contract.

The social relations of contracting

As DCIL's experience shows, market exchanges are rarely (if ever) discrete from other social relationships. Indeed, the 'embeddedness' of the market is an established feature of the literature on contracting (see Williamson 1975, 1978). For Williamson, the development of 'trust' (rather than individual utility-maximisation) is the determinant factor in contractual decision making. For similar reasons, Granovetter (1985) argues that the primary influence on economic cooperation is its embeddedness in networks of existing social relationships. Thus, Macaulay (1963) concludes that it is necessary to explore not just the contract but the whole system of social relations involved in an exchange.

Common and Flynn (1992) found that, with few exceptions, the community care contracts they studied had grown out of existing relationships between people who already knew one another. For this reason they concluded that the way in which contracts are produced is primarily shaped by the relationship between purchaser and provider. In itself this is not surprising. Indeed, early government guidance to care managers suggested that 'Most local authorities will wish to continue building on the agreements and partnerships already established with agencies in the independent sector' (DoH *et al.* 1991b, para.4.85). Such practices work to the advantage of organisations with an established track record in local service provision. For DCIL this created a market advantage. However, it may present barriers to the development of independent/integrated living initiatives in other areas where the established providers are organisations 'for' rather than 'of' disabled people.

The existence of social and political relationships between contracting parties means that decision makers must take into account not only discrete economic considerations but also the likely impact on those relationships (Campbell and Harris 1993). In the British social care market, where there may be only a limited number of purchasers and providers, continuity of service provision will often be dependent upon the maintenance of established social relationships. In this case, considerations of 'future gain' are likely to override short-term utility maximisation in operational decision making (MacNeil 1978). Where classical or neo-classical liberal economy favours short-termism, contemporary markets in social care are necessarily influenced by considerations of future gain.

This analysis corresponds with the emerging experience of contracting in Derbyshire. Considerable conflicts were evident between DCIL and local authority purchasers about the style and operational management of the personal support service. However, the process of conflict resolution has been heavily influenced by their intimate historical and organisational partnership. It is unlikely that either party would employ legal redress within the terms of the service contract, and the approach tends to be an ongoing administrative one in which the maintenance of future relations is a priority. However, it is important to note that economic dependency makes the maintenance of organisational partnership a more pressing concern for DCIL than it is for the local authority.

The fear for value-driven organisations like DCIL is that the financial imperative to contract may force more radical service providers back towards traditional modes of welfare production. In particular, there is evidence that the process of service specification within a relationship of dependency exerts pressure on providers to produce individualised responses to impairment (rather than collective responses to disability). The result of such a drift would be to further reinforce disabling discourses of welfare and impede the development of enabling alternatives. As DiMaggio and Powell (1983, p.154) suggest: 'The greater the dependence of an organisation on another organisation, the more similar it will become to that organisation in structure, climate and behavioural focus'.

Consequently, a proper understand of contractual relationships requires the consideration of 'relative bargaining position' and 'relative power' (Evan 1963, p.67).

Bauer and Cohen (1983) suggest that the market is influenced by four types of social relation in which power plays a major part. In the extreme position there may be a relationship of *domination* in which one group is able to impose a social system on another (backed by the threat of violence and with the other's acceptance of its legitimacy). Second, a more complex relationship of *influence* may exist where one group is able to ensure that the outcome of negotiations with another group is favourable to them (primarily where such negotiation takes place within a wider framework of domination). Alternatively, power structures may arise through the ascription of social *authority* roles or through a process of *production*.

Using Bauer and Cohen's typology, it could be argued that the contracting power of the state amounts to 'domination'. However, it is perhaps more appropriate to construct the relationship between local authorities and community care providers as one of 'influence', albeit an influence which occurs within the wider social context of disabled people's domination as an oppressed group (Abberley 1987; Oliver 1990). The power of state contracting lies in an ability to shape the pattern of welfare production. The consideration of power in community care contracting is particularly important because it highlights the way in which organisational dependency can shape the form and content of service provision.

As the preceding analysis shows, it is impossible to gain a proper understanding of community care contracting without a consideration of power, politics and values. In order to understand the position of the movement for independent/integrated living within the British social care market, it is necessary to shift the emphasis of current policy debates. We need to reject the notion of an 'external' market and focus instead on the political, social and organisational processes which mediate its operation. We also need to recognise that such processes are themselves embedded within wider social relations and cultural norms which extend far beyond the purely technical processes of market exchange.

The impact of contracting

While the rhetorical agenda of community care policy making emphasises the importance of choice, innovation and responsiveness there is evidence of a counter trend. It has long been recognised that marketisation has profound implications for provider organisations – changing the structure, style and values of the services which they provide (Manser 1972). Increased fee payments from government to voluntary agencies require increased accountability for public funds which, in turn, requires increased surveillance and control over the welfare production process. For this reason, Ritchie (1994a) suggests that the purchaser-provider split in social care reflects wider industrial trends towards 'control by contract'. Lipsky and Smith (1989) and De Hoog (1985) argue that contractual funding for the independent sector should be viewed as increased government influence over provider agencies. Stewart (1993, p.10) concludes that the current system creates a situation of 'government by contract'.

Organisational impact

Prior to the implementation of the purchaser-provider reforms and the imposition of service contracting, most social services funding for voluntary sector
providers came in the form of grant aid. The terms of such support were quite
broad and provided not only for the provision of specific services but also for
the maintenance and administration of a wide range of organisational functions. By contrast, the criteria for contractual funding are much more
narrowly defined.

Although the community care legislation does not alter an authority's
ability to make grant aid payments there has been a marked shift away from
this form of funding. Indeed, research by the National Council for Voluntary
Organisations (NCVO 1993) indicated that direct grant aid from local
authorities to the voluntary sector had declined by £70 million in the period
1991–1994. In DCIL's case, financial and policy pressure from central
government on the local authority resulted in decisions to reduce discretionary direct grant aid by £100,000 in 1990 and by a further £115,000 in
1991.

Even where grant aid is replaced by income from service contracting, as in
DCIL's case, there may be delays in payment, coupled with increased
transaction and start-up costs. For many small providers, without large
financial reserves or administrative back-up, the result has been severe cash
flow problems in the transitional period. In a climate of financial
impoverishment and reduced autonomy some voluntary sector providers
face a real struggle for survival. Hudson (1994, p.71) summarises these fears:
'Voluntary agencies will find it hard to survive a climate in which purchasers
are only willing to pay for what they perceive to be the direct costs of
services'.

In Derbyshire, transaction costs were partly ameliorated by the
secondment of a local authority worker to assist with the preparation of a
contract bid. Despite this, the scale and suddenness of the cutback in grant
funding forced DCIL into a wholesale restructuring of its Operational Plan
and staffing profile from February 1991.

Faced with impending financial crisis, DCIL were forced to contemplate
the genuine threat of closure. Although DCIL survived this transitional
period the impact on its role and functions was dramatic. As early as
November 1992 DCIL's staff were advised 'to prioritise work on the basis of
revenue and potential/minimum new costs', and by March 1993 the search
for 'revenue earning activities' was firmly established as the organisation's

top priority. With continuing budget shortfalls projected for future years, DCIL faced an increasingly tight time scale for agreement on a core service agreement with the local authority.

From its establishment in the early 1980s, DCIL sought to establish a diverse funding policy, drawing income from local authority grants, district health authority joint financing arrangements, fund raising, sponsorship, revenue generating activity and bids to a variety of campaigns, trusts and commercial bodies. However, the changing nature of this funding profile during the implementation of the 1990 Act demonstrates an increasing reliance on contractual fees for directly accountable service provision. DCIL's experience also illustrates the existence of a powerful economic imperative to shift organisational goals and priorities in order to conform with contracting criteria.

The criteria for community care purchasing stipulate that contractual expenditure must be for a specific community care 'service' delivered to social services clients and provided on behalf of the social services department. In this sense it must relate to a service which the authority is empowered to provide (e.g. under Section 2 of the 1970 Chronically Sick and Disabled Persons Act). Grant payments towards other services cannot be included. Contracts can allow for the cost of preparing to provide services but this must relate solely to the specific community care service in question. Similarly, payments towards the provider's administrative costs would only be admissible if this was 'explicitly part and parcel of the cost of a community care service' (ADSS 1993).

By contrast, the integrated living approach of the disabled people's movement in Derbyshire stresses that no one 'service' (such as personal assistance) can be considered in isolation from the totality of the 'seven needs'. In this sense it differs from the approach of some other independent living projects. However, it is entirely consistent with guidance from the Department of Health which recommended that home support services should not be conceived as operating in isolation from other forms of community support (DoH/SSI 1993). Indeed the guidance suggested that such services should be 'part of an integrated and coordinated spectrum of comprehensive community service provision' (DoH/SSI 1993, p.iv).

The introduction of service contracting threatens to undermine holistic integrated living supports by separating out certain specific functions. The practice of awarding separate contracts for named services means that it is much harder for providers to spread the risk of a particular service across all their activities. Each contracted service must in some sense operate discretely. Thus, Kramer and Grossman (1987) argue that the implementation of service contracting creates pressures towards the fragmentation of service design and management structure within provider organisations. The perceived danger is that integrated organisational management structures like DCIL's may be threatened by the fragmentation inherent in moves from general grant-aid funding to discretely accountable contracts.

Restriction of service design

As mentioned earlier, community care legislation does not affect local authority powers to make grant aid for functions beyond the narrow remit of community care packages (DoH/DSS 1990, para.1.17). However, there has been increasing concern that this kind of funding is less and less available. Pressed by ideological, fiscal and legislative constraint from central government, local authorities have pared discretionary grant aid budgets to the bone. In response, independent providers have been forced to seek tightly defined contractual funding wherever they can. For Hoyes and Means (1993, p.116) 'the current emphasis on negotiating service provision agreements rather than the direct provision of grants must raise doubts about the capacity or the will of social services to finance the provision of anything other than highly specific services'.

Witnessing these developments, the National Council for Voluntary Organisations (NCVO 1993) argued that the wholesale shift of resources from grant aid to contract fees was directing activity towards direct service provision and threatening other important functions. Similar concerns were clearly recognised by the Association of Metropolitan Authorities in the run up to community care implementation:

> ...the use of a contract rather than a standard grant may affect the traditionally innovative role which voluntary organisations have been valued as fulfilling. If voluntary organisations are increasingly funded, via contract arrangement, to provide a 'mainstream service', their other tasks e.g. advocacy, involving local people in self-help and community projects are in danger of being squeezed out. (AMA 1990, p.7)

Hoyes and Means (1993) suggest that there is an obvious danger for service providers when financially pressured social services departments occupy a near monopoly purchaser position. It is likely, they argue, that core funding for non-contracted expenditure such as training, administration, technology and political advocacy may be curtailed (see Manser 1974, p.426). Smaller providers in the voluntary sector would be specifically disadvantaged by such a trend compared to those backed by large national organisations. In this context, poorly funded local organisations of disabled people are at a distinct market disadvantage when compared to wealthy, national charities and voluntary sector organisations 'for' disabled people. Consequently, their advocacy and campaigning roles are more likely to be constrained by reductions in grant aid.

Such pressures are particularly significant when one considers that they contradict important principles in community care policy making. For example, Department of Health guidance on care management (DoH *et al.* 1991b, para.2.49) placed great rhetorical emphasis on advocacy in empowering users to make appropriate choices and welcomed independent sector initiatives as a means of facilitating this. However, the absence of specific resourcing for independent advocacy schemes creates a situation in which 'Independent agencies wishing to offer a universal [advocacy] service will have to raise funding from other sources or by charging' (DoH *et al.* 1991b, para 2.51).

The funding position on community development work is similar. While recognising the importance of community development work, the funding arrangements for community care do not make provision for it to be resourced through individual care packages. Thus, as the Department of Health acknowledged that 'Care management for individuals can highlight community needs and community resources but is not by itself a mechanism for delivering community development work. This is a function which should be separately resourced by social services/social work authorities' (DoH *et al.* 1991b: para.4.102).

As with advocacy services, the emphasis is on the local authority to identify and resource useful community development work from sources other than community care budgets. Yet, the economic, bureaucratic and ideological imperatives of marketisation combine to exert a powerful disincentive to the provision of just such services. It is, then, no coincidence that the movement for independent/integrated living has been more successful in marketing individual packages of self-managed personal assistance than it has in selling the broader concept of integrated living.

As the preceding analysis shows, the contractual framework for community care purchasing (in a climate of fiscal restraint on local authorities) creates pressures towards the restriction of service design. In particular, reductions in grant aid funding and tightly defined purchasing criteria work against the development of advocacy, community development work and campaigning activities. Yet, without these functions there is little prospect of achieving integrated living outcomes for disabled people in the wider social world.

Mission distortion

Organisations within the disabled people's movement are grounded in values which go far beyond the boundaries of mainstream service provision. Independent/integrated living is not only about participatory service designs; it is also about promoting participatory citizenship, social integration and equal rights. DCIL's very existence is founded on an organisational mission which reflects social definitions of disability and the collective philosophy of integrated living. However, the constraints of community care policy making threaten to shift the emphasis back towards individualised 'services'. The following extract from a recent report into DCIL's management structure encapsulates this concern: 'Managers fear that imposition of performance measurement requirements will skew the focus of the organisation and render it impotent' (Crosby 1994, p.1).

There is evidence that the combined influence of organisational fragmentation, restricted service design and the curtailment of non-contracted activities is indeed forcing some providers to develop in directions which distort their own original mission (Gutch 1992). For example, Hudson (1994, p.69) suggests that the replacement of grant-aid by contractual relationships may force voluntary organisations to provide services which detract from, or even contradict, their own organisational values. Potentially, Hudson argues, there will be occasions when purchasers 'capture' a provider to such a degree that the latter loses its original identity altogether. Thus, for Lipsky and Smith (1989, p.646) 'It is...critical whether nonprofit organizations operate according to standards derived from the community of interest from which they arise, or whether they are operated according to standards imposed by law and the values of public agencies'.

The potential for 'mission distortion' (Gutch 1992) is a very real concern for disabled people's organisations which engage in service provision. On the one hand, they remain committed to the core political values of the wider disabled people's movement. On the other hand, as providers, they are increasingly bound by the economic imperatives of a quasi-market place to prioritise individualised 'services' defined within those same disabling constraints. In this context, disabled people's organisations in Derbyshire have long been aware that 'Once an organisation loses sight of the principles which give it stability, purpose and a sense of direction, they start to work to somebody else's agenda' (*INFO: the Voice of Disabled People in Derbyshire,* June 1992, p.1).

The disabled people's movement has sought to challenge the professional and administrative dominance of disability services through the articulation of a social model of disability and through the design and management of supports under the control of disabled people themselves (K. Davis 1993; De Yong 1983; Finkelstein 1991). The concern of organisations like DCIL is that the bureaucratic imperatives of marketisation impose a significant counter pressure to this historic quest. Far from fostering strategic innovation and enabling welfare alternatives, marketisation may actually be forcing providers back towards more traditional forms of service design.

Propper (1993, p.48) shows how the specification of production processes in service contracts (with associated penalties for non-compliance) discourages innovation and variety. This he argues, produces a more general tendency for service production to become more and more homogenised. This line of argument is reminiscent of Weber's (1952) contention that the competitive marketplace can create an 'iron cage' of bureaucratic rationalism. Drawing on Weber's work, DiMaggio and Powell (1983) identify a tendency towards 'institutional isomorphism' in the production of services (i.e. a tendency for service providers to become more and more like one another in the long term). Thus: 'highly structured organizational fields provide a context in which individual efforts to deal rationally with uncertainty and constraint often lead, in the aggregate, to homogeneity in structure, culture, and output' (1983, p.147).

In the context of community care, this kind of bureaucratic politics is shaped both by the bounded rationality of the purchasing criteria and by the hegemony of disabling values (Oliver 1990). The combined pull of these two factors generates an aggregate market pressure on service providers to move away from holistic, integrated living supports and towards fragmented, individual model services (see Figure 5.4).

This model also illustrates one reason why it has been easier to establish 'independent living' schemes within the existing legislative framework than to develop the more holistic goals of 'integrated living'. With the removal of legislative barriers to direct payments in 1996, the primary obstacle to self-managed personal assistance schemes is now the attitudes of purchasing authorities and individual care managers. Where this battle for 'hearts and

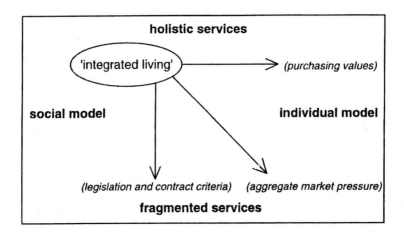

Figure 5.4 Market pressures on service design

minds' can be won, such schemes are pushing at an open door. By contrast, organisations committed to the holistic development of integrated living are fighting on two fronts simultaneously. On the one hand, they need to persuade the commissioning authorities of the added value of a social model approach; on the other hand, they need to find creative ways in which to resist policy pressures towards individualism.

Conclusions

The analysis presented in this chapter highlights a number of contradictions in the marketisation of community care services. First, the 'quasi-market' environment for community care purchasing presents barriers to contractual freedom and consumer choice. Second, local authority purchasing decisions are not based on economic considerations alone. Relationships of domination and subordination exist between contracting parties, between competing providers and between disabled people and the agencies of the welfare state. In this sense, community care markets are mediated by, or embedded within, the existing social relations of welfare production.

Marketisation impacts on the organisational structure and goals of providers in a number of ways. The experience of the case study organisations in Derbyshire shows how reductions in grant aid and the imposition of service contracting can lead to generalised financial impoverishment and a loss of autonomy. The combination of annual uncertainty, organisational fragmentation and a reduction in non-contracted activity can distort mission values and, on occasion, threaten the very survival of provider organisations. Such pressures are particularly strong for organisations which adopt a holistic approach to service design and for those whose mission values promote 'non-service' activities.

There is a need for effective systems of sustained advocacy, for community development work, for collective organisation and for political campaigning within the movement. However, as the evidence reviewed in this chapter shows, the marketisation of community care weights the system against such developments by focusing the allocation of resources on specific individualised 'services'. At the same time, the development of tighter service specifications and contract compliance conditions has resulted in more sophisticated mechanisms of surveillance, regulation and control over the form and content of these services.

It is, then, important to consider contractual decision making and the definition of purchasing criteria as more than purely technical processes. By highlighting individualised 'packages of care', such processes reinforce disabling discourses and obscure the potential for alternative approaches to barrier removal in the wider world. In this way, the implementation of service contracting has accentuated many of the core value conflicts in British disability policy making. The fact that these developments have also consolidated existing power relationships between disabled people and professional elites further emphasises their ideological significance. As LeGrand (1991, p.1266) notes, 'a common criticism of conventional markets (and a common justification for their replacement by bureaucracies) is that they foster and maintain inequalities and therefore social injustice'.

However, the outlook is not entirely bleak. There are still opportunities and resources to support independent/integrated living solutions. For example, money previously earmarked for the Independent Living Fund is now channelled through the social services revenue support grant as the ILF Transfer Fund (formerly the Independent Living Transfer). Although these funds are no longer ring-fenced, it is certainly the government's intention that they should be used for 'their original purpose' (see DoH circular LASSLA[95]13). As Simpson and Campbell (1996, p.25) note, some authorities have used the transfer to support independent living projects. In other places Joint Finance arrangements have provided resources, especially for new projects (e.g. in Hillingdon, Hampshire and Shropshire). There are also possibilities for Joint Commissioning and Joint Funding, although these can be difficult to put in place.

In December 1996, DCIL were awarded £300,000 from National Lottery funds to augment their Personal Support Service (so that all the elements of unfunded activity could be incorporated as originally envisaged). For the time being, there is a real possibility that DCIL will be able to implement integrated living support services to disabled people in Derbyshire free from the constraints of resource rationing. However, it is ironic that this development could only be achieved through the charitable culture of 'good causes' against which the disabled people's movement has consistently campaigned. Suffice to say that it is an ill wind that blows nobody any good.

The stakes are high for organisations like DCDP and DCIL. Their public commitment to challenge the form and content of mainstream service provision places them in a vulnerable position. They depend for financial income (and in some sense political legitimacy) on maintaining productive partnerships with the very authorities they seek to challenge. Such relationships are delicate, especially in a climate of financial retrenchment. Wrongly timed or poorly directed challenges can undermine relationships of trust. Taking the bull by the horns, representatives of DCDP met once more with Social Services in late 1996 to review their relationships. From this meeting a new working party has been established to work towards stronger partnerships in the interests of local disabled people.

Despite the legislative and economic constraints on local authorities there is still considerable scope for discretion and influence in purchasing decisions. As a result, the uneven regional development of independent/integrated living in Britain reflects both local political agendas and the strength of self-organisation amongst local disabled people. Where disabled people's organisations have engaged directly with the social services authorities they have often gained a stake in shaping the implementation of community care policies (for example, in Hampshire, Wiltshire, Avon or Derbyshire). In this situation, the challenge for such organisations is to demonstrate the quality of independent/integrated living solutions in ways which influence the purchasing strategies of statutory authorities. Consequently, the following two chapters are devoted to a more detailed analysis of strategies for achieving quality (in terms of service processes and outcomes respectively).

CHAPTER 6

Improving Services

Self-managed support services provide many elements of 'added value' for the disabled people who use them. They also create new spaces in which disabled people have been able to forge positive identities and explore enabling alternatives to 'care'. However, existing approaches to quality assurance do not always give credit to the value of these innovatory approaches. The development of more appropriate quality assurance procedures is therefore an important task. The discussion in this chapter draws on collaborative work with DCIL, and on other related studies, in order to develop these themes. Some of the general arguments were originally developed for a paper in *Critical Social Policy* (Priestley 1995c) and some of the initial data analysis was disseminated in report form by DCIL (Gibbs and Priestley 1996; Priestley 1996c).

In search of standards

The significance of quality issues has been emphasised during the 1990s by the implementation of the NHS and Community Care Act. Arrangements for service contracting require would-be providers to articulate the benefits of their services in measurable terms. For organisations committed to the principles of independent/integrated living, this raises important issues. Specifically, the benefits of services designed within a social model of disability need to be expressed in terms valued by purchasers, who have tended to operate within an individual model. As the research participants at DCIL pointed out: 'The determination of quality measures which will meet disabled people's perception of quality would be invaluable in the struggle to dispose of the medical (rehabilitative) model of disability' (DCIL Director's Report, December 1993).

The call for standards

The Griffiths Report contained nothing specific on quality, apart from the
need to register and inspect residential homes. However, *Caring for People*
established a clear link between service specification and quality. Indeed, the
White Paper suggested that, 'It will be essential that whenever they purchase
or provide services, Social Services Authorities should take steps to ensure
that the quality to be delivered is clearly specified and properly monitored'
(DoH *et al.* 1989, para.3.4.9). In the run-up to implementation of the 1990
Act, this preoccupation with quality standards was consistently reiterated in
policy guidance from the Department of Health (1992), the Audit Commission (1992a, 1992b, 1993a) and the Social Services Inspectorate (DoH/SSI
1993).

One of the main criticisms of previous arrangements was that services had
generally arisen *ad hoc,* from established custom and practice, rather than
from any reference to agreed quality standards. For example, the Audit
Commission (1992b) were concerned that few social services departments
had made progress in defining how their broad policy values might be
achieved in practice. Similarly, the Department of Health concluded that,
while there was a clear recognition of the need for quality assurance, few
authorities had developed adequate criteria for judging success against
targets (DoH 1993a). Moreover, emerging policy guidance envisaged that
the explicit statement of standards would *in itself* improve the quality of
services (DoH/Price Waterhouse 1991, para.10).

There has been some support for uniform national standards of service
quality. For example, the Social Services Inspectorate (DoH/SSI 1993)
argued that consistent standards for home support services would help to
ensure good practice (although they recognised that resources, eligibility
criteria and service details would continue to vary according to local
circumstances). The Commons Health Committee recommended that the
Department of Health should develop criteria for assessing community care
implementation as a priority (House of Commons 1993, para.7). In
particular, they expressed concern that there was no 'social care' equivalent
to *The Patients' Charter* (1993, para.8). Consequently, their report
recommended that the government should develop a 'Community Care
Charter', as part of its Citizens' Charter initiative, in order that service users
might have a better indication of the service quality they should expect as a
result of community care implementation.

Following the development of Citizens' Charters (Audit Commission 1992c, 1993b, 1994) the Department of Health set out a draft framework for developing local community care charters which would focus on the needs of users (DoH 1994b). The framework suggested that these documents should establish user entitlements to full, accurate and accessible information about community care services; offer high standards of assessment; specify standards about time scales for assessment (especially on discharge from hospital); promote individual care plans and include quantifiable performance standards. However, the efficacy of this approach has been treated with some scepticism both by policy analysts (Warburton 1993) and those within the disabled people's movement. Oliver (1992b, p.31) for example, questions the whole charter approach and concludes that it has done little to promote the citizenship of disabled people in any meaningful way.

In 1992, the Department of Health published research by the King's Fund into aspects of service quality (DoH 1992). The King's Fund team were concerned that existing definitions of quality reflected organisational preoccupations with efficiency and professional practice and that, in so doing, they often marginalised user definitions. They identified four functions of an organisation's concern for quality (demonstrating value for money, demonstrating achievement of policy objectives, improving the experience of the service user and assisting in the management of Departmental change). However:

> The most significant finding of this report is that of these four primary functions we found that in general the third, the experience of the service user, can be too easily overlooked. Again and again we found definitions of QA in use and evidence of standard setting which overwhelmingly represented the views of managers and professionals rather than those of service users. (DoH 1992, para.2.1.3)

The report concluded that effective quality assurance systems would require reliable systems for listening to users (and the front line staff who work with them). This listening process, it was hoped, would create an environment in which the primary definitions of quality were those of service users rather than service providers. Consequently, the report suggested that interventions to improve service quality should be focused at the point of service delivery (although responsibility for quality should remain with the provider organisation as a whole). Indeed, Department of Health guidance on the operation of markets in 'social care' indicated that, 'Local authorities should give more voice to users and utilise their perceptions of quality and outcomes alongside, or maybe even in lieu of, complex/expensive monitoring' (DoH 1994a, para 9.18).

There has also been a shared concern that this is not happening in practice. For example, the Department of Health was particularly critical of the lack of progress in developing user-led criteria for measuring satisfaction with, and control over, support services for 'younger physically disabled people' (DoH 1993a). Similarly, organisations of disabled people have often been frustrated in their attempts to secure adequate user representation and control. Indeed, staff at DCIL felt that 'little more than lip-service' was being paid to the principle of user participation in the implementation of community care purchasing (DCIL Director's report, December 1993). There is, then, a degree of rhetorical convergence in the competing agendas for change. In particular, all the stakeholders appear committed to the development of more effective systems for involving users in the development and monitoring of quality standards.

Local concerns

DCIL had become increasingly aware that the contractual framework of community care required them to clarify and articulate quality measurement criteria for supports which had previously been subsumed within a more general organisational philosophy. Within this context, services for which they contracted with the local authority would need to be measurable against specified quality standards:

> Some of these are quantifiable in simple terms – others require personal statements from our 'customers' which acknowledge the realisation of personal goals, self-confidence and satisfaction with supports provided... Without this, it is more than possible that the outputs of our different activities will be seen as the purpose of individual service elements instead of the means to achieving independent, integrated living for disabled people. (DCIL and Derbyshire County Council, Appendix to Proposed Partnership Service Agreement 1994–95, p.2)

The suggestion, then, was that the quality of DCIL's support services would have to be measured in comparable ways to traditional 'care' services in order for their 'added value' to be demonstrated. This in itself presents problems for a movement which was founded on critiques of those same mainstream services (K. Davis 1993; Davis and Mullender 1993; Oliver and Barnes 1991; Oliver 1992b). At the same time, such measures would need to recognise the radically different concepts of quality embodied within an integrated living approach. These concerns were also recognised by the Derbyshire Coalition, who were acutely aware of the importance of quality measurement issues in any service agreement with the purchasing authorities. Thus:

> Getting rid of discrimination is a hard task. Finding practical ways of doing it is what DCIL's Constitution is about. But our objectives of independence, participation and social integration are not easy things to define and measure. Yet this is what the Agreement is binding us to do. (DCDP, Proposed Amendments to Service Agreement, undated)

The fear was of a double jeopardy – a realisation that existing quality measures might undervalue integrated living outcomes and participatory services, but that alternative measures might fail to meet the established criteria of traditionally minded purchasers. Thus, it would be imperative that the statutory funding agencies appreciated 'the quality implications of this way of working' (DCIL briefing paper, May 1995). There were then significant barriers to overcome in defining quality measures. In particular, the successful implementation of DCIL's integrated living philosophy would require agreement with purchasers that such quality measures were valid.

Process-oriented approaches

Although the political agenda of the disabled people's movement centres on outcomes, there has also been much emphasis on the service delivery process. For example, user satisfaction, choice, respect, and reliability have featured prominently in disabled people's research (Begum 1990; Morris 1993a, 1993b; Zarb and Nadash 1994; Zarb, Nadash and Berthoud 1996). As one member of the Derbyshire Coalition summarised, quality for individual disabled people will often relate to a 'sense of responsiveness, understanding, acceptance, equivalence, supportiveness and appropriateness' in the services which they receive (field notes, March 1996). The discussion in this chapter deals mainly with issues of process (the following chapter then deals with debates around outcomes).

For Osborne the human services product must not only fit its purpose by meeting individual needs; it must also be provided in an appropriate and sensitive manner. Thus, evaluation of human services 'requires attention not just to the achievement of stated purposes, but also to the process of their achievement' (Osborne 1992, p.440). Ackoff (1976) suggests that traditional approaches to service quality measurement have failed to recognise the importance of aesthetic factors (such as the 'style' of delivery and the pursuit of ideals). For Ackoff, people ascribe value to means as well as ends. Similarly, Parmenter is concerned that 'we have tended to emphasise regular features or structures to the neglect of processes in our study of disability, possibly because it is easier to measure static structures more reliably' (1988, p.9).

Certainly, process measures have acquired significant currency in the rush to develop quality standards for community care. For example, the Commons Health Committee (House of Commons 1993) suggested that flexibility, continuity and reliability would be useful measures of service quality. Similarly, the government emphasised the need to establish the correct 'tone' for services provision (DoH et al. 1991c). Services, it was argued, should be welcoming, positive, proactive and open to challenge. The development of local Community Care Charters has followed this pattern by stressing the importance of the delivery process. Precedence is often given to general service values (such as courtesy, respect and fairness) and to detailed assurances (such as the conduct of assessments, arrangements for meeting staff, answering telephone calls, safeguarding personal information and so on).

Increasingly, process-oriented quality definitions have been imported into welfare services from industry, a trend which is consistent with a 'production of welfare' model (Davies and Challis 1986; Knapp 1984; Osborne 1992) and with the developing marketisation of welfare. However, the industrial analogy has its limitations. Nelson (1970) for example, notes that quality information about social care products is generally only available *after* consumption while industrial products can often be quality measured before purchase (see also Ritchie and Ash 1990). Moreover, there is an obvious danger in relying too heavily on process measures, since they provide no absolute guarantee of enabling outcomes. Knowing that the phone will be answered within a specified time period may build confidence amongst service users but it does little to ensure independent living or equal citizenship.

Some experiences of quality

The development of user-led standards begins with the experiences of disabled people themselves. In this context there have been a number of recent studies from within the disabled people's movement which demonstrate the benefits of self-managed personal support. For example, Oliver and Zarb's

(1992) analysis of personal assistance schemes in Greenwhich showed that, with appropriate back-up, direct payments could facilitate better quality support at no extra cost to purchasers. Subsequent research with wider samples of disabled people (Kestenbaum 1993a, 1993b; Lakey 1994; Morris 1993a, 1993b) has produced similar conclusions.

Zarb and Nadash's (1994) study for BCODP illustrated many of these quality issues in more detail and also showed that self-managed support could be substantially cheaper than other options (see also Zarb *et al.* 1996). In particular, disabled people involved with these studies valued the increased flexibility, choice, control and reliability which self-management offered them. The interviews with people using DCIL's Personal Support Service endorse these findings. The following review deals with five specific indicators of process quality which were important to the interviewees in Derbyshire. These were flexibility of response, choice and control, the number of staff involved, confidentiality, and relationships with the service provider.

Flexibility

Flexibility of service response is emphasised in the rhetorical agendas of both community care and the movement for independent/integrated living. In 1992, the Audit Commission (1992b, para.52) argued that community services should be as flexible as possible in responding to individual needs for support at different times. For example, they noted that staffing arrangements should allow for evening or weekend work and provide a quick response to changing circumstances. Thus:

> ...an elderly or physically disabled person relying on the local authority for social care should not have to be helped to bed at 7pm, because of inflexible staffing conditions. Nor should someone with mental health problems find social support impossible to find at weekends or on Christmas day.... (Audit Commission 1992b, para.3)

Similarly, the Social Services Inspectorate (DoH/SSI 1993, p.9) concluded that home support services should be flexible enough to accommodate user choices commensurate with a normal community lifestyle. In particular, they stressed the need for support services to take account of an individual's needs for employment, social activities, weekend support and help in emergencies (see also Thompson 1993).

All the interviewees felt that flexibility was important. However, their past experiences suggested that this kind of flexibility was often lacking in local authority domiciliary services and private agencies. More than one person reported being unable to make basic lifestyle choices (such as having a hot lunch or going to bed when they wanted) because of the timing of their support. The following two comments illustrate some of the restrictions imposed by the scheduling of mainstream support services:

> ...they wouldn't let me keep changing my times. I had to ring up the sub-office in [town] and tell them I wanted to change my times. And it was just getting too much...I felt as if I just couldn't organise my life in any way. I couldn't just say, have a lie in, because I'd got to ring social services just to have a lie in.... (Carol)

> I had to go home [to bed] every Friday night at half four...Saturday was always a problem. I got all the desperate ones on Saturday night or on Sunday. (Richard)

Such experiences suggest that mainstream community services were meeting the *prima facie* policy goal of maintaining people in their own homes. However, that was often all that such services did achieve (see Kestenbaum 1992; Morris 1993a). When the administrative requirements of a service provider dictate what time its clients will get up, go to bed, eat their meals or go out then it can hardly be said to facilitate 'independent' living. Such experiences illustrate graphically how inflexible domiciliary services can restrict lifestyle choices to a degree not out of place in the most draconian of residential establishments. Indeed, for Oliver (1992b) such inflexibility over ordinary life choices undermines disabled people's citizenship through the denial of 'social rights' (Marshall 1952).

Choice and control

A second key requirement for the service users in Derbyshire was that there should be maximum choice and control, not only in the timing of their support but also in the range of tasks covered. Thus, as Department of Health guidance acknowledges, many of the important aspects of quality reside in 'the attention to detail that matters to the individual' (DoH *et al.* 1991c, para.6.14). As Margaret put it:

> ...you cannot live your life with a list of things you can't do Mark. And if you're my arms and legs then there are a million and one things within a home set-up that need doing. How can you run your life when you're paying people to be your arms and legs but you can't do this that and the other, quite reasonable things. It's not going down a coal mine and

getting a sack of coal. You're talking about reasonable things in your own home. (Margaret)

Choice and control was sometimes restricted by family and friends who could not or would not assist with certain tasks. This was particularly evident when thinking about social situations, as the following comments illustrate:

> ...my parents was speaking for me and not letting me speak... All the support as I had was through my parents. My parents did everything for me...it was getting to the stage with my parents where they would only take me to certain places. (Joe)

> ...my father takes me out a lot but he gets a bit fed up sometimes. (Carol)

> ...it's so embarrassing if he takes me shopping and he doesn't like ladies' shopping anyway. I mean no man does do they?...I mean he doesn't want to sit there while two women are talking and what have you. (Liz)

Choice and control were more commonly restricted in the delivery of statutory support services. For example, Liz was particularly frustrated when she discovered that home help staff could no longer dust, clear out drawers or do ironing. Margaret reported that her local authority support workers would not clean the oven, wash the floor, clean the windows or walk the dog. Similarly, home helps were not able to assist with basic 'medical' tasks such as sorting tablets or helping with eye drops and inhalers. Local authority staff could not always use a person's preferred method of lifting or wheelchair transfer. These were all tasks which were considered as 'fundamental' by the participants.

The goal of self-determination in establishing a pattern of daily living was perhaps the single most important issue for the people involved in this study. Their subjective judgements, about the quality of support they had received from local authority staff, private agencies and unpaid helpers, suggested that choice and control over the content of personal assistance would always be an essential measure of good quality service provision. In this respect, their views reinforce the findings of similar studies (Kestenbaum 1992; Morris 1993a; Zarb and Nadash 1994). For the Coalition in Derbyshire, the goal is one of equal citizenship 'in which disabled people have the same choices as the general population' (minutes of meeting between DCIL, DCDP and DCC, March 1993). As one member of the Coalition put it, 'by full control over our lives we mean the opportunities to make the same choices, the opportunities to make the same decisions as would be taken for granted by other citizens' (Interview transcript).

However, it is important to remember, as Craig (undated, p.63) notes, that choice for service users can never be an absolute value. It will inevitably be shaped by other factors such as income, geography, age, gender or race, each of which may impact dramatically on the ability to exercise lifestyle choice or citizenship rights within specific social contexts or communities.

Staffing

A third factor identified by all the PSS users concerned the number of staff involved in a package of support. Everyone felt that there should not be more people involved than was absolutely necessary. Having a small number of regular helpers was seen as preferable for two reasons. It reduced the number of new people coming into the home and it ensured that staff became familiar with daily tasks and routines. Such views are consistent with work by the Social Services Inspectorate (DoH/SSI 1993, p.9) and with research carried out for disabled people's organisations (Oliver and Zarb 1992; Zarb and Nadash 1994).

All those who had used local authority domiciliary services or private agencies complained about the high turnover of staff. Richard, who had had 37 different staff from one private agency, described the situation as 'unbearable'. Carol reported having up to 16 different home helps during a single week. In addition to the stress and uncertainty of coping with different people every day, there was widespread frustration with the problem of training new staff in basic tasks, as the following two comments illustrate:

> When we had all these different home helps you had to keep telling them. Every time you had a new one you had to tell them again. And if they didn't come from one week to the next you'd have to tell them again. And it just got, well, it was ever so depressing...I was going to have it printed on the bathroom wall, instructions. (Carol)

> You're standing there saying do this, don't do that, put that in, put that there. You may as well do it. It is so exasperating...I'd got these people, knowing I wasn't going to keep them...knowing they were of no use to me whatsoever on a long-term basis, and I was going to have to start again. So, I could only see right into the future a long, load of aggro really. (Margaret)

There was a good deal of resentment about the level of emotional and practical effort invested in constantly retraining new staff in preferred methods of support with the wide range of daily activities. In addition, the unpredictability and sheer volume of staff turnover compounded personal feelings of vulnerability and perceptions of unwelcome 'gaze' (Foucault 1973) from outsiders, particularly when there was no control over the selection of staff.

Confidentiality

This aspect of the service delivery process caused much uncertainty and anxiety. Those who had used local authority domiciliary services were particularly worried that staff could get together to talk about them. In a more general sense there was concern about the basic level of confidentiality involved in using staff who also visited other people. For example, more than one person had overheard home help staff talking about the other people they visited. As Carol put it:

> ...they would sit and gossip about other folks and it just got too much...you hear them talking about other people and you think well they must talk about me. They're bound to. (Carol)

High staff turnover, and an absence of sustained personal relationships with staff, thus compounded feelings of insecurity and raised concerns about the privacy of the home, family life and the body:

> I felt as if I just couldn't organise my life in any way. I couldn't just say, have a lie in, because I'd got to ring social services just to have a lie in. And I felt as if the whole world knew every time I went to the toilet, what times, you know. The whole office knew because they had to know, to organise them to come, but I didn't want everybody knowing. (Carol)

> Another thing I get a little tired of, there's more people seen my body, you know all the different home helps...and you just get used to it you know.... (Liz)

By contrast, everyone felt much more comfortable in secure, long-term relationships with individual staff they had chosen themselves through the process of self-assessment and self-management. The values of trust, respect and confidentiality were generally reflected in personal relationships with personal support workers. Control over recruitment meant that most people got the staff they wanted and that their working relationships were based on partnership ('doing with' rather than being 'done to'). Indeed, the relationship often involved reciprocal support, with the 'service user' helping the personal assistant (see Ann Rae 1993, p.50). This kind of reciprocity and mutual respect represents an important challenge to the discourse of dependency by normalising the unequal relationships inherent in a culture of 'service provision'.

Additional support

The final area of process quality identified by the respondents concerned their relationships with the provider organisation. DCIL was perceived by service users as more 'understanding' than the local authority, the health trusts or private sector agencies. The fact that support was provided by an accountable and participative organisation working to a disability-led agenda was an important factor in this respect. A provider organisation which involves disabled people so prominently, and which emphasises aspirational values, clearly has many strengths. However, these strengths also create vulnerability, since service users may have higher expectations. For example, Hugh made the following point:

> I don't mind being let down by the professionals...they will fail you because it's a job at the end of the day. I do feel a greater depth of disappointment with DCIL, because I expect them to have the gut feeling that I have when I deal with disability issues. And if that doesn't come through then I am disappointed. (Hugh)

All the service users drew additional support from DCIL – from the service manager, from peer advocates and from community workers. The holistic nature of DCIL's management structure meant that people did not necessarily distinguish between these different roles. However, the additional back-up provided beyond the basic package of personal assistance was seen as an essential feature of the service by all the participants. These views reinforce the importance attached to Personal Assistance Support schemes in other studies (DIG 1996; Oliver and Zarb 1992; Simpson and Campbell 1996). They also help to emphasise that self-managed personal assistance cannot be considered as a 'service' in isolation from other modes of support.

Most people had found peer support workers to be particularly useful, especially in setting up their package of support and as positive role models. Everyone valued the opportunity for support from another disabled person, in particular, from someone who had used services themselves:

> I think the disabled [person] is more help than a social worker or whatever. They may know the theory but they don't know what it's like in practice. (Richard)

…somebody was there who'd been through it, who'd faced the system and got total independence despite the system. I'd been walked over by the social services certainly and knowing that somebody was there who'd been through it made it easier. (Terry)

The additional support provided by DCIL was valued for a number of reasons. First, people wanted to draw on support from another disabled person who had experience of using services. Second, they benefited from supported self-assessment and help with putting together a package of support. Third, all but one person wanted someone else to manage the finance and employment of their support workers. Finally, additional community development work was essential to some people in their attempts to achieve integrated living.

Re-inventing the wheel?

Viewed in the context of similar studies, the preceding review suggests that disabled people look for a number of specific quality indicators in community support services. These can be summarised as follows:

- choice and flexibility in the timing of personal assistance
- control over the range of tasks performed by personal support workers
- a small number of regular staff dedicated to a personal service
- privacy, respect and minimal intrusion from the provider organisation
- organisational values which foster trust, partnership and participation
- peer support from other disabled people who have experience of using services
- access to supportive back-up services.

Such conclusions are not new or particularly surprising. They are consistent with both the stated agenda of community care policy making and with the growing body of research emanating from the disabled people's movement. Indeed, there is a great deal of rhetorical agreement amongst the main stakeholders on most of these issues. In particular, there is considerable agreement in principle on the importance of user involvement and choice. Moreover, there are dangers in adding unnecessarily to the proliferation of service standards (DoH 1992, para.2.7.5). Ultimately, there is no point in 're-inventing the wheel' or simply paraphrasing existing work in this area.

For example, a sample study of early arrangements for care assessment by the Social Services Inspectorate suggested that useful quality measures might include user involvement, choice, normalisation, service responsiveness, non-discrimination, communication and outcomes for users (SSI 1991, p.16). Subsequently, the SSI argued that service delivery should also reflect core values of user control and respect (DoH/SSI 1993). In particular, they suggested that it might be helpful to look for the performance of tasks to user specifications (what to wear, how to prepare food, where to put things); the provision of support at times to suit the user (getting up, going to bed, etc.); the selection and employment of workers by users themselves; respect for choice; allowing users to do things for themselves; the right to refuse help; user satisfaction and so on (DoH/SSI 1993, p.10).

More specifically, the guidelines suggested eight core service values which would enhance the quality of home support services:

1. Autonomy and independence of decision-making, including the assumption of risks as well as responsibilities associated with citizenship.

2. Choice of lifestyle, occupation, and the best way to maintain independence, including the opportunity to select independently from a range of options.

3. Respect for the intrinsic worth, dignity and individuality of the person and his/her racial and ethnic identity and cultural heritage.

4. Participation and integration into society, and in the formation of policies, plans and decisions affecting the individual's life.

5. Knowledge about conditions and prospects, options and opportunities, and ways of improving individual circumstances.

6. Fulfilment of personal aspirations and abilities in all aspects of daily life, including the chance to develop new skills and knowledge.

7. Privacy from unnecessary intrusion, and the safeguarding of confidentiality.

8. Equality of opportunity and access to services irrespective of age, disability, gender, sexual orientation, race, religion or culture.

   (Quoted from DoH/SSI 1993, p.4)

Taken at face value, there can be little scope for major disagreement about such goals. All of these indicators are entirely consistent with the agenda of the movement for independent/integrated living. Yet problems remain and the reality of most service provision does not match the rhetoric. What is lacking is a clear indication of mechanisms for achieving such standards within purchaser and provider organisations. In order to address this problem it is necessary to think about standards which relate to the form of service production as well as its content.

Improving service quality

At the time of writing, the majority of disabled people in Britain continue to draw on service provision for elements of their personal support. Given that the new direct payments legislation is permissive rather than mandatory, that 'older' people are excluded (Barnes 1997) and that many 'younger' disabled people remain unsure about self-managed options, this situation is likely to continue for the foreseeable future. Moreover, as Zarb and Nadash (1994, p.80) note, 'payments schemes do not automatically ensure disabled people having greater choice or control over their support arrangements unless they are set-up and managed efficiently. On the other hand, it is quite possible to build a considerable degree of control into a genuinely user-led service.'

Consequently, the search for effective forms of quality assurance remains an important task. In a climate of intensive resource rationing, and with a proliferating array of potential providers, it will be increasingly important for potential service users to know how flexibility, choice, reliability and respect are to be assured. At the same time, organisations within the movement for independent/integrated living need to demonstrate clearly to purchasers and users how their approach differs from the other available options. The following discussion explores some strategies towards these ends.

Satisfaction ratings and complaints

It is tempting to suppose that the most direct way of increasing user involvement is simply to ask people what they think of service quality. For example, in its initial guidance to social services staff, the Department of Health (DoH *et al.* 1991b, para.5.31) argued that care managers should be encouraged to relate their own job satisfaction 'to high levels of satisfaction among users and carers'. Subsequent guidance on home support services went further, asserting that 'The most important gauge of the success of home support services is user satisfaction with results' (DoH/SSI 1993, p.27).

However, self-reported satisfaction ratings have been widely criticised as measures of service quality. For example, Moum (1988) illustrates their susceptibility to 'mood of the day effects' and 'yeah saying' (see also Huxley and Mohamad 1991). Brown, Bayer and MacFarlane (1988) suggest that many disabled people express high levels of satisfaction in the absence of informed knowledge about the options available. This effect, they suggest, is especially marked for people with learning difficulties who may have been denied major life experiences and life choices in the past. Similar limitations were recognised by the Social Services Inspectorate in their appraisal of early arrangements for community care assessment, concluding that 'the vast majority of users and carers were so grateful to receive anything at all that any notion of consumer rights was unrealistic at this stage' (SSI 1991, p.21).

The major legislative emphasis has been on the development of formal 'complaints' procedures (the provisions for establishing such procedures were introduced into Section 7B of the Local Authority Social Services Act 1970 by Section 50 of the 1990 Act). Herd and Stalker (1996) note that complaints procedures are easily overlooked as a means of involving disabled people in provider organisations. For example, disabled people who feel alienated from organisations which have disempowered them in the past may not believe that their views will be taken seriously. Additionally, complaints may be seen as 'options of last resort' rather than as a means of service development (Herd and Stalker 1996, p.32). While disabled people remain alienated from, and under-represented within, provider organisations there is a danger in substituting formal complaints procedures in place of developed arrangements for advocacy. Conversely, participative organisations, in which disabled people play a prominent and controlling role, are more likely to generate realistic and informed responses from service users.

In its response to the Commons Committee's *Third Report* (House of Commons 1992) the government also expressed concern about an over-reliance on user satisfaction (DHSS 1993). However, their emphasis was on lowering user expectations rather than raising them. In order to make sense of user satisfaction ratings, they argued, it would be necessary to establish clear and explicit statements about the limits on choice that users could expect. This point was reemphasised in a letter to social services departments from the SSI's chief inspector, who pointed out that practitioners would 'have to be sensitive to the need not to raise unrealistic expectations on the part of users and carers' (CI[92]34, para.25).

Presumably, the aim of this approach was to limit the expression of low levels of satisfaction with service options by dampening 'unrealistic expectations'. Conversely, the movement for independent/integrated living has sought to encourage aspirational statements from users about their personal goals and satisfaction with support services. Thus:

> It is axiomatic that if people are to enjoy personal autonomy, they must in the process of self-assessment be freed from the pressure to downgrade the attainment of their own programme to fit in with the timetable, style or content of the services provided. (DCIL Director's report, August 1993)

The danger with such an approach is that it may encourage the expression of user aspirations which cannot be met within existing service limitations or budgets. Its strength is in identifying barriers to independent/integrated living within the service delivery process itself.

Developing appropriate training

The values of front line staff and service managers are a critical factor in the implementation of permissive central government policies (Hogwood 1987, p.171; Hardy, Wistow and Rhodes 1990; Young 1981, p.45). If enabling organisational values are to be translated into the service delivery process then they must be shared by staff within provider organisations (DoH 1992; DoH/SSI 1993, p.25). Thus, policy guidance on community care has emphasised attitude change as a mechanism for reform. For example, the Department of Health suggested that community care would 'challenge all those in the caring services to re-think their approach to arranging and providing care' (DoH *et al.* 1991a, para.105). This, it was argued, would require a radical shift in practitioners' style of working.

For organisations like DCIL, the development of more enabling modes of support has been contingent upon effective recruitment and training. It is often hard to attract staff with an understanding of social model principles. Cultural representations and popular discourses can all too easily reinforce images of personal tragedy, impairment and otherness in the minds of prospective job applicants. Yet, service providers committed to independent/integrated living need to recruit workers with a completely different set of values if they are to improve quality at the point of service delivery. As one DCIL manager put it:

> You are talking about staff that have been retrained from day one. We are talking about people who are going to go into this work from a totally different viewpoint. You're talking about people who in some ways are going to have a totally different motivation for coming into the trade....
> (Interview transcript)

Specific guidance for practitioners noted that staff would have to 'rid themselves, as far as possible, of their own prejudices' (DoH *et al.* 1991c, para.3.30). This message was reiterated by the Audit Commission. They characterised the scale of change as a 'cultural revolution' in which 'winning the hearts and minds of social services members and staff...is key to the success of community care' (Audit Commission 1992b, para.42). From a disability perspective, Paul Abberley (1995) argues that staff within the 'caring' professions have been historically socialised, through professional training, to work within a framework of disabling values and ideologies. In this context, it is significant that disabled people using self-managed personal support schemes have often expressed a preference for staff who have not been previously trained (Morris 1993a; Zarb and Nadash 1994).

If training is to be effective then it needs to encompass the core values of independent/integrated living (participation, social integration and equality) – not only in its content but in the form of its delivery. Within the disabled people's movement, strategies for training have sought to move beyond 'disability awareness' training and towards 'disability equality' training (DET). This approach was originally conceived and pioneered by a small group of disabled women in London (particularly by Jane Campbell, Michelline Mason and Kath Gillespie-Sells). By the mid 1980s there was an expanding register of 'ET' trainers and established guidelines for good practice (Campbell and Gillespie-Sells 1988; French 1996).

Disabled people have been increasingly successful in promoting this approach. It is now an established (if small) part of social work training courses in Britain and has influenced the development of policy initiatives internationally. For example, the United Nations *Standard Rules on the Equalization of Opportunities for People with Disabilities* demand that all staff training should reflect 'the principle of full participation and equality' (UN 1993, Rule 19.2). Moreover, the rules stipulate that disabled people's organisations should be involved in training development and that 'persons with disabilities should be involved as teachers, instructors or advisers' (UN 1993, Rule 19.3). Similarly, Department of Health guidance on care management and assessment suggests that, 'The most effective way of demonstrating the centrality of users' needs and wishes will be by consulting users and carers over the training programme and inviting them to contribute to the training itself' (DoH *et al.* 1991a, para.106).

The experience of organisations like DCDP and DCIL shows that it is possible to challenge attitudes at a local level through recruitment and training procedures which convey the values of participation, integration and equality. Such procedures need to reflect these values not only in their content but also in their form, through the active participation and control of disabled people and their organisations. Disability Equality Training provides a useful framework for this kind of working (although it requires the development of well organised and well resourced organisations of disabled people for its implementation on a wider scale). However, it would be naive to suppose that training alone could guarantee improved service quality, even at a local level. In addition, purchaser and provider organisations need to establish effective mechanisms for assuring that training principles are translated into enabling service processes and outcomes.

Designing quality assurance systems

Designing a quality assurance system need not be complex or difficult provided that there is a basic level of agreement about the terms of reference (this may be the biggest barrier of all). In particular, it will be necessary to establish who is responsible for quality assurance, who should be involved in monitoring, and the kind of criteria to be used. The resolution of these issues is likely to vary according to local circumstances – including the kind of service under scrutiny; the terms of the service specification; the relationship between commissioner and provider; geography and the level of self-organisation amongst local disabled people. However, some general principles may help.

First, it is likely that service providers will bear the primary responsibility for quality assurance. Social services departments are responsible for ensuring that quality standards are incorporated into service specifications (DoH/DSS 1990, para.4.18). However, the emphasis is on providers to propose and demonstrate standards together with systems for their assurance (HMSO 1990). Common and Flynn (1992, p.26) argue that this is logical, since 'it is they who deal with the client and have to implement appropriate procedures' but Ritchie remains concerned about the tendency 'to shift responsibility for quality to a lower level without shifting control of resources; issuing specifications for brick quality without issuing straw' (1994b, p.153).

Second, the values and goals on which a service is based need to be made overt. Different provider organisations will generate different quality assurance systems which reflect their organisational values and goals. Bradley (1990) expresses concern that quality assurance systems often maintain a 'lowest common denominator', rather than providing 'benchmarks' to inspire performance. Similarly, O'Brien (1990) emphasises the importance of 'vision' in developing high quality disability services (Rhodes 1987; Ritchie and Ash 1990). O'Brien argues that QA systems should strive to be visionary, by incorporating the ongoing discussion, clarification and sharing of ideals relating to a better future for disabled people. Such a process should seek to identify tensions between the existing situation and the service ideal. It should seek out opportunities to act consistently with this vision wherever possible.

By contrast, Department of Health research (DoH 1992) warned that it may be 'counter productive' to attach notions of excellence to quality assurance. For example, where staff are aware of resource limitations they may become increasingly cynical about aspirational quality standards. Taken at face value, such an approach seems sensible given the current pressures on purchasers and providers. However, it is important not to lose sight of visionary and innovative service goals in the quest for pragmatic quality assurance. Quality assurance systems based on social models of disability require provider organisations with a visionary commitment to participative services, to social integration and to the removal of disabling barriers in the wider world. It is hard to envisage how provider organisations not committed to these values could demonstrate effective quality assurance systems within this model.

Finally, a successful quality assurance system would need to operate within a participative organisational structure. Bradley and Bersani (1990) suggest that as disabled people become more integrated ('invisible') in society, the need for effective monitoring becomes more pressing yet, 'real' homes should be free from the bureaucratic scrutiny often associated with quality assurance. The Department of Health have also been keen to note that 'the form of monitoring should be designed to cause as little disruption as possible to the users' daily pattern of living' (DoH 1991c, para.6.3). In this context, Bradley and Bersani (1990, p.347) suggest that, 'using other people with disabilities to serve as independent monitors can assist in maintaining the integrity of consumers and their living and working arrangements'.

Similarly, Herd and Stalker (1996, p.26) argue that:

> Users of specific services are an indispensable resource in gathering the information required to review or evaluate any service. Statistical analysis of the 'raw data' of services will always be necessary. The evaluation of the experiences of service users, by service users, will add a uniquely valuable dimension to the assessment of service quality.

For example, the practice of employing peer support workers (and a commitment to carrying out disabled people's research projects) would allow for such monitoring to be easily incorporated within the service design. Similarly, provider complaints procedures which give service users the right to appeal to an independent panel of other disabled people, including another person who uses personal assistants, are an important form of peer accountability. In addition, where a provider organisation is controlled by, and democratically accountable to, local disabled people there is the added value of intrinsic quality safeguards. Viewed in this context, disabled people's organisations and Centres for Independent/Integrated Living are particularly well placed to design and implement this kind of quality assurance system.

Towards a measure of participation

The preceding analysis suggests that it might be possible to formulate an approach to process quality measurement based on user participation within the service design (and within the provider organisation as a whole). Bornat *et al.* (1985) use the term 'participation standards' in this way in their work on services for older people. Similarly, the Social Services Inspectorate (SSI 1991, para.22) and Herd and Stalker (1996) list a range of 'participation' items for quality measurement. Within the movement for independent/integrated living, user participation has been a central to the philosophy of self-assessment and self-management.

Participation as a quality standard

Both the 1986 Disabled Persons Act and the 1990 NHS and Community Care Act highlight the need for service user involvement. Additionally, the prevailing climate of marketisation means that ever more emphasis has been placed on the role of the consumer (Flynn 1988). Evaluating the effectiveness of user involvement is then an important aspect of quality assurance for service providers and purchasers alike. However, it is important to be clear what we mean by involvement. On the one hand, there has been much talk of 'consultation'; on the other hand, there have been more radical calls for real participation and control in decision making (Beresford and Campbell 1994; Drake 1996; Morris and Lindow 1993; Priestley 1996b).

It is impossible to discuss user participation without reference to power. If providers are committed to increasing user power then they must contemplate a corresponding reduction of their own power (Means and Smith 1994, p.71). Thus, Jenny Morris and Vivien Lindow (1993, p.1) argue that, 'Community care organisations must treat service users as their equals and as experts with something unique and important to say about services and how they are delivered'.

The Department of Health's initial guidance on care management and assessment suggested that the power imbalance between professionals and users could be addressed by sharing information more openly and 'by encouraging users and carers, or their representatives, to take a full part in decision making' (DoH *et al.* 1991a, para 38). Connelly (1990) provides numerous examples of local initiatives which seek to involve disabled people both individually and collectively in this way. However, Means and Smith (1994) argue that local authorities' preoccupation with empowerment through 'exit' or 'voice' (Hirschman 1970) can never be a substitute for an approach based on rights and citizenship. Thus: 'Despite the obstacles to achieving a rights based approach, we have no doubt that such a perspective is essential for the empowerment of service users' (Means and Smith 1994, p.101).

Ritchie (1994b) identifies two strands of debate on user power. First, there has been much talk of power through consumer rights and choice in the market place. However, Ritchie argues that consumerism has not resulted in any real shift of power to service users. Similarly, Ramon (1991) points out that 'buying power' does not necessarily equal 'empowerment'. By contrast:

> The other strand of user power is genuine involvement in decision making at an individual and collective level – from choosing your own home help to lobbying for a better regional policy on adapted transport. It is this sort of power that has the potential for transforming the nature of care in the community. (Ritchie 1994b, p.10)

Both strands are evident within the movement for independent/integrated living. While the campaign for direct payments legislation has focused attention on buying power, disabled people's organisations in the wider movement have emphasised the need for greater voice and control in service planning and delivery. Strategies for involvement have been varied. Some disabled people's organisations have sought a 'seat at the table' within commissioning authorities. Others have used protest and campaigning to exercise 'voice' from outside. Centres for Independent/Integrated Living have engaged disabled people directly in the production of their own welfare and that of others. BCODP has promoted the establishment of a national representative council within the policy making community. However, policy makers within local and central government have remained sceptical about the potential for 'legitimating user views' and 'securing appropriate representation' (DoH 1992, para 2.1.7).

The idea that disabled people should be actively involved in provider organisations was reinforced in 1993 when the United Nations accepted the right of disabled people and their families to 'participate in the design and organization' of the services which concern them (UN 1993, Rule 3). At a national level, the British Government announced its intention to establish a 'national users and carers group' in 1993 (DHSS 1993, p.10). Although welcome in principle, these proposals were greeted with less than enthusiasm by disabled people's organisations. For the disabled people's movement, true participation means much more than simple consultation. Rather, it implies the development of real partnerships in the organisational management of change. DCIL for its part, has argued that user participation should itself be defined as a 'service' and accepted as such in the terms of contractual agreements with purchasing authorities.

In order to address issues around the quality of service user involvement in this study we carried out an action research project in collaboration with the Living Options Partnership Network. A series of focus groups were held in Derbyshire bringing together service users and disabled people's organisations with staff from the social services department and two local NHS trusts. The workshops focused on two existing examples of user involvement and two new services. The aim of the project was to assist the participants in developing their own approaches to user involvement, and also to come up with more general guidelines for purchasers and providers. The results of the project were presented in a short report and disseminated widely amongst disabled people's organisations, service commissioners and providers (see Gibbs and Priestley 1996; Priestley 1996b).

Getting people involved

It was clear from the initial discussions that many people may be unsure what user involvement is all about. For organisations committed to developing user participation this means being clear about the purpose of user involvement from the start. For example, what happens in a 'consultation' group and what power does it have to change things? On a more basic level, some of the participants felt very disempowered by not being listened to in the past. Consequently, they felt that disabled people would often need time and support before being expected to participate. To this end it was suggested that user representatives should be allowed to meet together in safe settings which are under their control prior to any formal involvement.

Real participation means involving as many users as possible at all points in the service. Thus, there is a place for involving people as individuals exercising power over the services they receive and for involving disabled people's organisations in strategic planning and service evaluation. As Jenny Morris and Vivien Lindow conclude, 'Community care organisations need to be clear when it is appropriate to encourage participation by an individual user and when it they need someone who represents users' (Morris and Lindow 1993, p.3).

It was clear from the workshop discussions in Derbyshire that people may be worried about the commitment required. Consequently, they needed to know what was expected of them. Everyone has other commitments in their lives and it is unrealistic, for example, to expect service users to attend every meeting of an ongoing group. It is worth remembering that disabled people have to give up other things to come to meetings. While professionals, consultants and speakers are paid to be there, service users are usually not and providers should always consider how people can be adequately remunerated for their input.

The workshop participants were able to identity several barriers to participation which could easily be overcome with forethought. For example, most people need time to think through the issues and plan what to say before a meeting so the topic(s) for discussion need to be set as far ahead as possible. Planning the dates of meetings well in advance, and deciding on the issues to be covered, helps increase both attendance and the effectiveness of contributions. On a practical level, inadequate access and transport make involvement difficult for many disabled people (especially in rural areas). For this reason, organisations committed to participation need to make sure that appropriate transport is arranged well in advance and that any venue to be used is fully accessible.

Access to information is a critical factor in this respect (particularly for visually impaired people, deaf people and those with learning difficulties). More generally, Herd and Stalker note that knowledge is power and that staff often have more information than people who use services. Thus, 'Meaningful consultation with disabled people and their organisations is not possible without accessible information. The absence of clear information and the resulting lack of knowledge may prevent the representatives of disabled people from playing an effective part in planning services' (1996, p.4).

Information was promoted as first among the 'seven needs' by the integrated living movement in Derbyshire. Without it, people cannot make informed choices or influence the pattern of service provision effectively. Organisations of disabled people (and CILs in particular) have a crucial role to play as peer providers of information services. For example, DCIL pioneered the development of comprehensive telephone advice, while Glasgow CIL have promoted World Wide Web access to information on independent living and self-managed personal assistance. Barnes (1996c) reviews his research for BCODP into 200 information providers and concludes that there is an urgent need for more resources to support specific locally-based providers (see also Simpkins 1993). The shortage of peer support and information for black disabled people and other marginalised groups is particularly important in this respect (Begum 1992; Priestley 1994b, 1995a).

Reducing intimidation

It was evident from the workshop sessions that some people will be more used to groups than others, and that this can have an adverse effect on those who are not comfortable in such situations. People are easily intimidated so it is important to make sure that 'professionals' and more experienced disabled people do not dominate group meetings. Indeed, some of the user participants voiced fears of elitism amongst experienced user representatives as well as amongst professionals. It takes time and experience to build the confidence necessary for effective user involvement, so it is important to make sure that people get more support when they first join a group. Proper training and support systems are required to achieve this and a period of 'apprenticeship' may be useful for new representatives.

Many people find formal meetings confusing at first. To make the process of meetings more accessible, participants need to avoid jargon and acronyms in agendas, discussions and minutes (for example, by using people's names rather than professional titles or initials). Similarly, it is important to avoid formal 'standing orders' and 'motions' unless everyone knows how they work. Rigid bureaucratic structures limit the scope of user involvement, especially when they are imposed by professionals in order to maintain closure and power. Ultimately, service users should be able to determine the form as well as the content of their involvement.

Involvement of service users as 'outsiders' rather than 'insiders' compounds intimidation and it is common for people to feel isolated between meetings. Professionals have a whole range of contacts and networks of support to draw on if they want to talk about how a meeting went or to discuss an issue that was raised. In a participative organisation there should be appropriate formal and informal support systems for user representatives too. In this context, people may be able to draw on collective resources and personal support by forming or joining organisations controlled by disabled people. However, as Herd and Stalker (1996, p.10) point out, such organisations need adequate resources to cover the costs of administration, training and peer support for involvement.

Getting results

It was clear from the Derbyshire workshops that people often wonder what happens to their ideas and whether anyone takes any notice. As one woman put it, 'I've been involved in lots of these meetings and we never get to hear what happens as a result of them'. Consequently, people may be unsure how much power they really have to change anything. As another user commented, 'There is a definite line beyond which we are not welcome'. For these reasons, the limits of user power and involvement should always be made clear (see Herd and Stalker 1996, p.39). For example, it is important to determine whether user representatives can make decisions about expenditure or organisational policy. Can they invite (and exclude) professionals from meetings? Do they have a power of veto?

Topics for consultation are often limited to what is possible rather than what is desirable. It is important that users should never be restricted in the issues they wish to raise. For example, people should be encouraged to express visionary ideas about equality and integration and not just about the location of notice boards or the colour of the wallpaper. Particular note should be made of goals which are not immediately attainable and efforts made to identify interim targets towards their achievement. Above all, it is important to recognise that 'services' are only one part of disabled people's lives. Users should be encouraged to express views about how (or whether?) a service impacts on disabling social relations and barriers in the wider world.

Even where consultation is limited to the achievable and the pragmatic implementation of user decisions can easily be blocked or ignored within large bureaucratic organisations. Effective user involvement requires a strong political commitment at the 'top' of the provider or purchaser organisation. This commitment needs to be a contractual requirement for staff at all levels. For example, Derbyshire County Council's *Code of Good Practice* on user involvement recognises that effective participation entails the transfer of power to users. Thus: 'Greater service user involvement will sooner or later necessitate changes in power and control, and thus may strike at the heart of the way many agencies are run' (Derbyshire County Council Social Services Department 1994, p.2).

This kind of user power is difficult to measure and we discussed a number of approaches in the workshops before focusing on one issue which seemed most relevant – has the purchaser or provider organisation ever made changes against its wishes because service users wanted them? Above all, it is important to make sure that there are real outcomes from user involvement and that everyone knows what has been done as a result of their input. People worry about being exploited and if users have no real power to change anything then the service provider or purchaser should question whether their involvement ought to be invited at all.

A user involvement checklist

The outcome of the Living Options project in Derbyshire was a *User Involvement Checklist* (Gibbs and Priestley 1995; Priestley 1996b). The approach which we adopted in developing this simple evaluation tool was to pose a series of closed questions about user involvement within organisations. By factoring out the data from the workshops and the steering group discussions we were able to arrive at a list of ten basic questions. These were then circulated back to all the workshop participants for comment, validation and amendment. Our final agreed list looked like this:

- Does your organisation want to increase user power?

- Are your staff required to demonstrate a commitment to user involvement?
- If you impose limits on user power, do you make these clear to everyone?
- Are your environments, processes and information accessible to disabled people?
- Do you involve disabled people's organisations as well as individual users?
- Do disabled people control your user involvement process?
- Do disabled people control your agenda for consultation issues?
- Do you provide user representatives with the same support systems as staff representatives?
- Do you communicate the outcomes of disabled people's involvement back to them?
- Has your organisation ever made changes against its will because disabled people wanted you to?

We envisaged that simple standards like these could be employed by disabled people as a quality measure for assessing an organisation's commitment to user involvement. We also hoped that such a list could be used by purchasers or providers as a kind of 'charter' for the participation of disabled people within their organisations. We wanted to challenge mainstream organisations by giving them aspirational targets for good practice and we recognised that few (if any) organisations could claim to meet all of the criteria we had set. However, we also wanted to frame our 'standards' in a practical way that made them seem achievable. The order of the questions was intended to reflect a hierarchy of empowerment similar to Hoyes *et al.*'s (1993) 'ladder of empowerment' (see also Nocon and Qureshi 1996, p.50).

The Checklist approach was initially validated by presenting it to the European Symposium of Disabled People's International (Gibbs and Priestley 1996). Delegates recommended its mass distribution and a copy was included in the conference report (see Walker 1996). It had already been adopted as policy by DCIL's management committee with recommendations for adoption by the purchasing authorities in Derbyshire. We were also able to present the checklist approach to a conference of purchasers and disabled people's organisations organised by the NHS Management Executive and to disseminate it via the conference report (Priestley 1996b). Although we did not pursue a formal pilot of the basic tool ourselves, it has now been adopted by a number of local authority social services departments, health authorities and disabled people's organisations as a basis for assuring effective user involvement in purchasing and providing community care services.

There are profound organisational implications for those adopting such an approach. Effective user participation means increasing user power. Yet the language of 'empowerment' which is so current within social services departments belies its own disabling assumptions. Those who believe they are in a position to 'empower' others must also accept that they have power over them – the power to commission, the power to purchase, the power to allocate resources, the power to withhold any of these things; the power to decide where someone lives and with whom, what time they will get up, eat and go to bed, who will see them naked, how far and how often they will travel. These are very great powers indeed.

The message from the disabled people's movement is that empowerment is not something which can be 'done to' disabled people by others. Rather, it is something that they must, and do, claim for themselves through self-organisation, collective self-advocacy, direct action and self-managed personal support. As one member of Derbyshire Coalition put it 'The only people that can really effectively remove the oppression are the oppressed, not the oppressors' (Interview transcript).

Conclusions

The discussion in this chapter highlights some goals for quality community support services, together with some strategies for their implementation. The analysis of evaluation research with DCIL's service users supports the findings of similar studies, by emphasising the importance of flexibility, choice, control and respect in personal support services. The analysis of strategies for change indicates that, while appropriate recruitment and training can challenge disabling attitudes amongst staff, it is also necessary for purchasers and providers to implement effective quality assurance mechanisms.

Effective QA systems will be led by provider organisations who can demonstrate a genuine, visionary commitment to the principles of participation, integration and equality. Such organisations need to articulate clearly and concisely specific standards for choice, self-determination and respect in terms of the service delivery process. These standards need to be monitored in an unobtrusive way which engages the full participation of disabled people. Above all, quality service provision is most likely to be assured within organisations that can demonstrate participative and accountable organisational structures. However, effective user involvement requires accessible information, venues and transport arrangements. It requires sustained peer support, training, administrative back-up and payments for user representatives. It requires effective mechanisms for feedback and dissemination. Community care organisations committed to user involvement then need to ensure that such supports are adequately resourced and that they are directly accountable to disabled people.

The recognition that organisational structures which empower users have intrinsic value is important when considering the significance of disabled people's organisations. Such organisations provide living models of the way in which disabled people can be effectively engaged in all aspects of welfare production – as individual consumers, exercising choice through self-assessment and self-management; as advocates, providing peer support and positive role modelling; as representatives, contributing to the strategic development and evaluation of service design; as participative citizens, seeking to identify and remove disabling barriers in their communities; as political actors, within a wider movement for social change. Participation is, then, a fundamental part of the enabling challenge to discourses of personal tragedy, dependency and 'care'. Kath Gillespie-Sells (1995, p.157) quotes Alinsky's (1971) *Rules for Radicals:*

> We learn when we respect the dignity of people, that they cannot be denied the elementary right to participate fully in the solutions to their own problems. Self respect arises only out of people who play an active role in solving their own crises and who are not helpless, passive puppet-like recipients of private or public services. To give people help, while denying them a significant part in the action, contributes nothing to the development of the individual. In the deepest sense, it is not giving but taking – taking their dignity. Denial of opportunity for participation is the denial of human dignity and democracy. It will not work.

The argument presented in this chapter suggests that organisations controlled by disabled people have a unique role to play in the pursuit of service quality. They are well placed to act as providers of participatory community support services to individuals. They are equipped to provide training expertise in the needs-led culture. They are also established as the accountable representatives of disabled people's collective needs for inclusive citizenship and social integration. The challenge for service planners and commissioners will be how far they are prepared to use their purchasing power to enable such organisations to fulfil these roles.

The participation of disabled people also poses many challenges to the established social relations of welfare production. Participative welfare blurs the traditional boundaries between 'providers' and 'users'. It challenges the hierarchical structures of powerful welfare bureaucracies and it threatens the ability of vested interest groups to maintain oppressive professional discourses. In this context, it is perhaps significant that our work on user involvement in Derbyshire was described by one senior public health consultant as 'neo-Leninist nonsense' simply because it suggested that the performance of health professionals might be judged by their patients (quoted in DCIL Director's Annual Report, September 1996).

In order to complete the analysis of quality issues it is necessary to go beyond the actual process of service delivery and to consider outcomes. While users may appear to value a particular 'service' it is the outcomes of that service that are the real issue. As Culyer (1990) points out, demand for a service may often be confused with demand for the characteristics of that service. For example, it is not 'personal assistance' or 'payments' that the disabled people's movement has struggled for, but the greater 'independence' or 'integration' which such supports might bring. In this sense, quality issues extend beyond the socially constructed boundaries of 'service provision'. Rather, they must also be concerned with aspects of citizenship and equality in the wider world. Thus, the following chapter is concerned with the relationships between quality of service, quality of outcomes and quality of life.

CHAPTER 7

Beyond Services

Services may be produced in a variety of ways, some of which are more appealing than others, but unless their inputs and processes enable people to make real changes in their lives they are of little value. For this reason, any consideration of service quality issues must necessarily include a focus on outcomes and on quality of life. Whilst there are some obvious links between quality of service and quality of life there is no obvious causal connection between the two. For example, a person may get a poor service but experience a better quality of life due to other contributory factors (and vice versa). Thus, a proper consideration of outcomes extends beyond the socially constructed boundaries of 'service provision' to include issues of citizenship, inclusion and equality in the wider world. The discussion in this chapter develops these themes in more detail. Some of this material was originally developed for a paper in *Critical Social Policy* (Priestley 1995c).

What kind of outcomes?

The kind of outcomes envisaged in the Griffiths Report were broadly speaking, those of normalisation – 'enabling the consumer to live as normal a life as possible' (para.1.3.2). Similarly, the government's initial policy guidance (DoH/DSS 1990, para.3.24) stressed that service provision should seek to 'preserve or restore normal living'. Clearly, there are many deficiencies in an approach based on 'normalisation' (see Brown and Smith 1992) not the least of which is to determine who's norms should be employed as the 'gold standard'. Disability itself has often been defined in terms of deviation from cultural and bodily norms. Conversely, attempts by the disabled people's movement to identify and remove disabling barriers have necessarily involved redefinitions of those same norms and values.

Some examples

Within local authorities, there has been a tendency to use destinational outcomes as a proxy for 'normal' or 'independent' living (Nocon and Qureshi
1996). Thus, particular emphasis is placed on the need to enable more people
to remain in their own homes or 'similar environments'. By 1993, the government were able to report 'anecdotal evidence' to suggest that fewer people
were being forced into residential care (DoH 1993a). In reality, many younger disabled people had in fact been transferred from hospitals directly into
residential institutions under the guise of 'community' care. As one DCIL
manager put it:

> Initially it would not occur to most people that in administrative terms
> 'community' was meant to mean 'not a hospital'. So in the record of
> implementation, a positive management outcome could conceal what
> measures of personal outcomes would have identified for at least some
> individuals as plain human rights abuse. (letter, September 1996)

Furthermore, in a climate of resource rationing, cost assessments of 'need'
continue to be made relative to the price of residential care. Although
Derbyshire have managed to avoid setting an arbitrary cost ceiling (above
which home support is unavailable) they have found it necessary to establish
procedures for reviewing the cost of home based services 'which are above
the relevant weekly nursing home rate' (Derbyshire County Council Social
Services Department 1996 Community Care Plan). In this way, the normative yardstick of incarceration continues to dominate local rationing
decisions and cost-benefit analysis.

Domicile is certainly an important outcome and it features high in the
'seven needs' promoted by the integrated living movement (after
'information' and 'counselling'). It was also an important factor for many of
the service user participants in this project. As Terry put it:

> I would say that they've kept me from going into care. They admitted it
> to me, and actually said at a meeting, social services said that they would
> have put me into care...without knowing I'd got this package coming,
> I'd have been in care certainly, without a doubt...I'd have
> stagnated...they might as well have put me in care. (Terry)

However, appropriate housing on its own does not provide an absolute guarantee of integrated living or improved life quality. Indeed, there is evidence
that community care implementation has consigned many disabled people to
'remain in their own homes' due to inadequate support for wider social

integration (see Morris 1993a, 1993b). As Cummings (1988) argues, it is much easier to create a 'normal' physical environment than to normalise social interactions and, for this reason, outcome measures need to be much more broadly based.

The agenda for change promoted by the movement for independent/integrated living sets much store by the notion of self-determination. Outcome quality within this context has much to do with maximising choice and control over the pattern of daily living. However, the notion of 'choice' promoted by organisations like DCDP is not an absolute. Rather, it is qualified relative to certain social norms. Thus: 'by full control over our lives we mean the opportunities to make the same choices, the opportunities to make the same decisions as would be taken for granted by other citizens. So, there's always reference to some norm of civilised or…acceptable qualities'. (Interview transcript)

In this sense, the kind of outcomes envisaged by the movement for independent/integrated living are really no different to the sort of life opportunities available to other members of the community. The early struggles of disabled people in Derbyshire to establish independent living solutions like the Grove Road project (K. Davis 1981) demonstrated real outcomes for the participants. However, the simple underlying social objective was 'just to establish ourselves like any bugger else'. Thus:

> …we weren't going beyond what was not normally or usually accepted as being the way human beings lived and behaved. And there was a very clear political element in that. We weren't arguing for improved or reorganised services in order that we would have a better life than anybody else… Everybody could probably do with a better quality of life, you know. And we weren't wanting to single ourselves out as a group of people who, having steered public money in a particular direction, providing different sorts of services, were going to end up as privileged members of the human race as a result of that. (Interview transcript)

The emphasis for DCDP was to facilitate opportunities for disabled people to take part in the ordinary life of the community in the same way as non-disabled people, through a restructuring of public welfare provision. The decision to relate political demands for choice and control to some social norm is a pragmatic rationale. It is also important in establishing claims to equal citizenship rights for disabled people, but it raises some difficult problems. In general terms, there is a broad agreement between all the stakeholders that outcome measures are a useful way of looking at quality and that quality of life should be an important feature of outcome measurement. However, there are significant difficulties in such an approach and it is not entirely clear who should take the lead role in defining quality of life measures.

User-defined outcomes

As the previous chapters show, there is much disagreement between disabled people and those who design and manage the services which they use. Specifically, outcomes defined by rehabilitation professionals are often framed within a medical rather than a social model of disability. For example, health service commissioners may judge the quality of a physiotherapy service by the degree of increased motility in a patient's leg joints and thereby recommend a programme of regular attendance at a hospital clinic. The patient, on the other hand, may feel happy using a wheelchair and be much more concerned about integrated living outcomes. Ironically, the requirement to attend regular daytime sessions at an out-patients clinic then becomes a barrier to full-time employment or education for that person.

Effective procedures for self-assessment are, in this sense, central to establishing a process through which people can articulate the kind of barriers they experience in their lives, and the kinds of supports that might be necessary to remove those barriers. For this reason, Conroy and Feinstein (1990) argue that service outcomes should be judged primarily from the disabled person's viewpoint as consumer. Following this line of argument, and building on the initial work we had done on user involvement, DCIL argued that the direct experience of service users (and their representative organisations) should form the primary data for determining the quality of service outcomes. Thus, 'people's preferred outcomes would lead on service objectives and by implication content; actual outcomes monitored by user/consumer organisations would provide commissioners with measures of provider performance' (DCIL Director's Annual Report 1996).

While it is easy to assert that user-defined outcomes should take precedence over purchaser-defined outcomes, it is more problematic to measure them in any standardised or transferable way. The resolution of this difficulty for DCIL has been to adopt user-defined outcome measures as the *prima facie* criteria for judging the success of service interventions. Such self-determined goals may be quite broad (for example, the degree to which a person considers the life choices available to them as 'normal') or they may be quite specific, in terms of a particular aspirational statement. As one DCIL manager put it:

> When somebody says to me, first day out of hospital, I want to go back to work, the only outcome measure I'm concerned about for the entire weight of health resources that are still to be put into that person, social services resources that are going to be put into that person in their continuing life, is to what extent does it advance that primary ambition to return to work. If it does not advance that primary aim, you're going to have to bloody well justify it as far as I'm concerned. (Interview transcript)

Having your choice and exercising it

A further difficulty in the use of norm-referenced outcome measures arises from the differential ability of certain groups to exercise choice. Reflexivity is not a universal privilege and lifestyle choices are limited for many people within a community. Dimensions of exclusion associated with income, social class, race, gender, sexuality or age are as just as important as disabling barriers in this respect. Differential incorporation and restricted access to employment, education, health, welfare and leisure facilities are established features in the structural exclusion of poor people, elders, black people, women, children, gay men and lesbians as well as disabled people. This makes it difficult to delimit the nature and extent of disabling barriers, although there have been some notable attempts to achieve this in Britain (see Barnes 1991; Zarb 1995a).

The use of choice to denote quality is also problematic when we consider that choice may not need to be exercised in order for it to have value. Indeed, it could be argued that the existence of accessible environments and services may impact positively on quality of life, even for those who do not use them. This makes little sense in the context of cost-effectiveness studies, which rely heavily on input and output measures. For example, it may seem very cost-ineffective to spend scarce resources on improving wheelchair access to a community facility if only a few wheelchair users exercise their new found choice to use it. As one of the research participants noted:

> ...if you're a landlord and you've been persuaded to spend a thousand quid on a ramp for the front door and you know you've got to sell X number of pints of beer to get that money back and you don't see anybody using a wheelchair for the next ten years you think what the bloody hell have I spent that bleedin' money on? (Interview transcript)

The important point is that increased quality in these terms may have as much to do with the *existence* of choice as the *exercise* of it. It is easy to imagine many scenarios in the field of public sector service provision where low take up of an enabling support system would be judged as indicative of its redundancy in quality terms. For example, a community transport service which allowed greater freedom of movement for people excluded from mainstream public transport could be said to increase quality of life in a community by providing the opportunity to travel.

The fact that large numbers of people do not immediately take up such an opportunity may have nothing to do with the value of the service itself. It is likely that disabled people within that community may be restricted in their use of such a service by other factors. A lack of money, an absence of social contacts outside the home or a shortage of accessible destinations would all impact dramatically on the outcome of transport services although such restrictions have nothing to do with the 'service' itself. As one member of DCDP put it:

> ...it's very hard to evaluate the quality of dial-a-ride if the place that you would get the bus to, like the pub, you can't get into when you get there. So you don't bother getting the bus there in the first place. Taking these things in isolation is quite difficult in a way. (Interview transcript)

However, in an economic climate of resource rationing, it is likely that low usage figures might lead to the withdrawal of a service like this. The idea that outcome quality can be latent as well as actual is a difficult, and somewhat abstract, concept but it has very real implications. It also illustrates the impossibility of measuring service outcomes in isolation from the wider social context in which 'services' play only a small part.

The brief examples reviewed in the first part of this chapter highlight the significance of outcome measures, together with a number of problems in their use. In particular, they illustrate some of the analytical tensions between 'choice' and 'normalisation'. Moreover, it is important to remember that the achievement of integrated living outcomes for disabled people requires more than just better 'services' or better 'care'. Rather, it is contingent upon the removal of disabling barriers in the wider world. This makes it difficult to think about outcome measures within the culturally and bureaucratically constructed boundaries of 'service provision'.

Some examples of service outcomes

The need for work on outcome measures in this study was highlighted in early 1996 when a social services report on DCIL's Personal Support Service was withheld on the grounds that it lacked personal information about outcomes for users. For the authority, tangible information about user outcomes would be a determining factor in any decision to continue funding the service manager's salary. DCIL, for its part, remained convinced that user perceptions 'could only lend support to continued funding for the programme' (DCIL Director's Annual Report, September 1996). For this reason, user outcomes, as well as service processes, featured prominently in our collaborative evaluation of the service.

Outcomes for users

All the Personal Support Service users were able to identify tangible outcomes resulting from their experience of self-assessment and self-management. Most of these were associated with being able to accomplish specific daily activities and routines which they had previously been unable to do due to lack of support. For example:

> I can go shopping when I want to. I can go out for a day if I want to, under the restraints that there are. I can go for lunch, We can go for morning coffee somewhere…there are lots of appointments, I've been to meetings…and I could only do that sort of thing because I've got people to rely on. (Terry)

> …it was getting to the stage with my parents where they would only take me to certain places. Now, with the support services, the people what I've got don't hesitate to take me in there. (Joe)

> It's given me more independence from me dad, and it's given him a bit more. He won't admit it but it has…it's nice to be able to say, if somebody says why don't we go so and so, it's nice to say yeah, OK, without having to ask my dad. (Carol)

In some ways, it is easier to identify and record these kind of practical outcomes than the more intangible benefits associated with cognitive 'well-being'. However, it quickly becomes clear that the task is not as simple as it might first appear. Any kind of generalised 'checklist' which sought to encompass the range and diversity of practical benefits derived from self-managed personal support would be so wide ranging as to render it useless as a measurement tool (this problem is closely akin to the difficulty of defining a 'job description' for personal support workers). For this reason it would be impractical, not to say undesirable, to draw up any definitive list of daily living activities that might constitute an integrated living outcome measure.

Quality guarantees about getting up or eating when you want to can easily be accommodated within standards for service flexibility. By contrast, quality guarantees about choice in employment, education, personal relationships, social contact or community participation depend on factors beyond the administrative remit of 'community care' or 'services'. Yet these are the very things that often matter most to people. Service providers can and do make aspirational statements about integrated living outcomes but service provision alone is not a sufficient condition for their achievement (although for some people it may be a necessary one). The provision of 'services' is then only one amongst a number of factors which contribute to integrated living (see Figure 7.1).

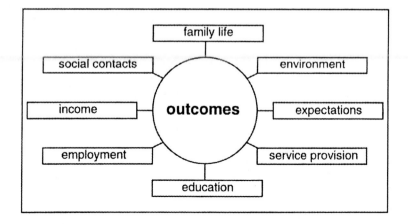

Figure 7.1 Factors contributing to life quality outcomes

Some of the most clearly articulated outcomes for DCIL's service users were highly subjective. These cognitive outcome statements generally related to feelings of increased self-confidence, self-efficacy or self-esteem as the following comments illustrate:

> [The] assistance afforded to me…is enabling me to form a solid base and give me confidence to actually look to the future, a thing which I was unable to do before moving. I had previously spent many long hours sitting on my own with a blanket over my head, too frightened to move because I was alone and sometimes afraid to even pick up the phone to ask for help. This is a situation that I dread returning to. (Terry, in a letter to his care manager, March 1994)

> …it's made me completely different. My frame of mind has altered completely because now I am in control whenever I want to be. (Richard)

> They've allowed me to get back to something approaching what I was before, albeit for short periods…I've actually seen it. I've done something for an hour. I've just reached it. I've reached what I used to do…afterwards, absolutely shattered, but I've done it, and it's because I've got people there. (Terry)

Such responses support an approach to quality of life based on self-reported 'well being' (rather than objective measures of 'welfare'). However, there are considerable methodological difficulties involved in the development of quality measurement tools which emphasise the cognitive or affective nature of service outcomes for users. In particular, life satisfaction is a critical factor for individual service users but it is very difficult to measure reliably.

The problem is partially resolved by trying to gauge satisfaction in terms of change over time (either by comparing user responses 'before and after' or simply by asking people how things have changed) but this approach is also fraught with difficulty. First, changes in perceived well-being over time can be due to any number of uncontrolled variables (such as unemployment, childbirth, winning the lottery, having a 'bad day', etc.). Second, there are all sorts of dangers involved in any evaluative research with disabled people which ventures into an interpretative psychology (Hunt 1981). Nonetheless, it is important to accept that experiential factors remain a key determinant of quality for service users and that any approach to outcome measurement would need to give due privilege to that experience.

Outcomes for other disabled people

Self-assessment and self-management blur many of the traditional boundaries between 'providers' and 'users'. In addition, supports which facilitate integrated living and active citizenship bring disabled people out of isolation and make their contribution available to the wider community. Consequently, it is important to recognise that the outcomes of support services may extend beyond the individual who receives a 'package of care'. For example, self-managed personal support enabled Richard to work as a volunteer at DCIL. Thus, the package supported not only his own social integration but also that of numerous other disabled people in the locality. The knock-on benefits to others were undoubtedly a positive 'outcome' yet they might easily be overlooked in a more individualistic approach to service quality measurement. The following extract illustrates similar contributions to disabled people in the community made by another of the interviewees:

> This package has allowed me to take part in community activities. I'm a chairman of an access group, I'm a secretary for, um, transport, I'm treasurer for community action network...I support another access group in [town]...and it's purely because I've got the support with me...I support a lot of other people in the community with the work I'm doing. It has a knock-on effect. And I do an awful lot of work that I couldn't do without the package. And I would think I possibly save a lot more for the services than is spent on me.... (Terry)

These two brief examples indicate the difficulty in adopting an individualistic approach to outcome measurement. Integrated living benefits not only the direct recipients of 'services' but also their families and communities. Today's service users become tomorrow's peer advocates and positive role models. As active citizens, disabled people bring many more economic and social benefits to their communities than would be possible within the confines of residential or 'day care' establishments. Integration itself brings social benefits to non-disabled communities impoverished by their exclusion of difference. Thus, an adequate approach to outcome measurement needs to recognise not only the quality of life for individual service users, but the added quality of life which integration brings to the communities in which they live.

Outcomes for the community

The logic of an approach to quality measurement based on social integration and equality suggests that services should impact not only on the individual service user but also on the community in which she or he lives. Indeed, the Department of Health went so far as to argue that 'helping people to belong to and feel part of their local community is the best form of community care in terms of both cost and likely therapeutic impact' (DoH *et al.* 1991b, para.4.106). Their guidance stressed that although care management for individual service users might highlight community needs and resources it could not in itself be considered as a mechanism for delivering the necessary development work (1991b, para 4.102). Moreover, community development work was seen as an essential counter balance to the individualism of 'needs' assessment. Thus:

> It is particularly important to preserve the community dimension at a time when services are becoming increasingly specialist in nature, with the attendant danger of narrowing, or fragmented, focus on individual needs. The emphasis on targeting those in most need may also be seen to pose a threat to preventative/promotional community work. (DoH *et al.* 1991b, para.4.100)

Self-managed personal assistance schemes cannot, on their own, bring about changes in the wider world and organisations like DCIL have long viewed community development as an essential service component. Community development workers have been involved in a variety of interventions to facilitate integrated living outcomes. Some of these have been prompted by work with individual services users. Other interventions are more general in their scope and impact. In Derbyshire, community development workers help to disseminate information, provide peer counselling, train volunteers and support self-help groups. They have also been active in initiating and supporting a range of autonomous local groups which focus on locally defined access issues, promote local participation and provide a base for awareness-raising in their communities.

Clearly, integrated living supports have a considerable impact in terms of outcomes for local disabled people. However, the removal of social and physical barriers can have many positive outcomes for other members of the community, not only those with specific impairments. Integrated living strategies are then entirely consistent with an approach based on 'service to the whole community' (Local Government Management Board 1991). Indeed, as DCIL has argued:

The outcomes of community development directly benefit thousands of Derbyshire people; the growth of accessible transport, awareness of communication impairment such as acquired deafness, learning difficulties, Access on the high street, accessible premises for meetings, involvement of disabled people in public affairs. It may be a local access group which demands a ramp into the local post office, or a pedestrian crossing which can be used safely by blind or partially sighted people – but behind every local pressure group has been a DCIL Community Development Worker, and in every planning victory can be seen DCIL Information and Training. These are changes which benefit everyone – people with young children, older people, people who live in isolated parts of the county. (Presentation by DCIL's director to the social services department, December 1994)

As the preceding discussion shows, the achievement of integrated living outcomes for disabled people requires interventions which go far beyond the administrative boundaries of 'individual packages of care'. True participation, integration and equality in the wider world are likely to be advanced not only by good quality personal support services but also by a range of more collective action. In particular, the removal of social and physical barriers is unlikely to be achieved without effective community development work, collective self-organisation and political campaigning.

Quality of life

The degree of increased choice offered by self-managed personal support amounted to a major change in quality of life for the service users involved in this study. Indeed, 'quality of life' has become something of a buzz-word in talking about outcomes for service users (see Bradley and Bersani 1990; Nocon and Qureshi 1996). For this reason, process measures of service quality need to be complemented by an approach which can accommodate outcomes in terms of life quality. Unfortunately, many of the existing approaches to quality assurance in purchasing authorities still focus on process at the expense of life quality (House of Commons 1993). However, quality of life is hard to measure and extends far beyond the narrow confines of 'care' or 'service provision'.

Definition and measurement issues

The literature on quality of life is diverse and wide ranging (e.g. George and Bearon 1980; Megone 1990; Rescher 1972; Robertson 1985). Osborne

(1992) reviews some of the existing approaches and attempts to group them under the headings of 'welfare' and 'well being'. However, it would be unwise to reduce the complexity of life quality definitions to a simple dichotomy. Quality of life may be defined in terms of physical, cognitive, material or social well-being (Blunden 1988) or equated solely with health status and physical functioning (Kaplan 1985; Williams 1987). It may be related to the experience of material consumption (Ackoff 1976; Gillingham and Reece 1979) or considered in more existential terms – such as the ability to engage in rational or virtuous activity (Megone 1990). It may be measured across whole communities or as an idiosyncratic property of the individual (Brown 1988).

These differing approaches give rise to differing conceptual frameworks which, in turn, influence the selection of evaluation criteria and quality measurement tools. Ultimately, the value base used to define 'quality' shapes the form and content of disability services (Ritchie 1994a, 1994b). Indeed, the cultural values used to judge both disabled people's quality of life and the quality of the services available to them are derived from, and determined by, a variety of dominant discourses about the role of disabled people in society as a whole. Thus, Hirst (1990, p.72) asserts that the way in which disability is depicted has implications for social policy, because the value judgements used in decision making are not only technical but also political. For this reason, the social construction of 'quality' is inextricably bound up with the social construction of 'disability'. As Knoll (1990, p.235) notes, 'the definition of program standards and quality is a process that transcends empiricism. This process ultimately appeals to the fundamental values of a society'.

Consequently, such standards are not immutable but dynamic, arising from an ongoing dialectic in which public opinion, political ideology, bureaucratic imperatives, theory, practice, research activity and social movements all make a contribution. Within the current state of this dialectic, the pursuit of greater quality of life for disabled people often runs against the general drift of dominant cultural values and professional discourses.

Bradley and Bersani (1990) argue that widely held values about quality of life for non-disabled people often run counter to the values and life expectations imposed on disabled people as 'service users'. For example, quality of life might be said to include the ability to exercise preferences for interdependence over independence (French 1993), choice over productivity or privacy over integration. Similarly, Ritchie and Ash (1990, p.21) argue from their work on quality that, 'Services which seek to promote valued lives for people with learning disabilities are working against the grain of major economic and social trends. They are working, within resource constraints against long-established patterns of service designed to achieve the exact opposite.'

The way in which quality of life is defined is inherently value-led. The values which underlie its definition are rarely made explicit yet they have a profound influence on the way in which policy is formed, implemented and evaluated. This raises questions about the potential efficacy of any attempt to measure quality of life. In particular there are many measurement difficulties in assessing the loose qualitative concepts which contribute to quality of life (Conroy and Feinstein 1990, p.276). Thus Hall (1976) argues that there may be insuperable problems in seeking to measure the 'intangible' aspects of life quality. Hall suggests that measurement difficulties are apparent even where there is some consensus of definition. Where there is little or no consensus (for example in the case of 'tolerance' or 'equality') such difficulties are further compounded.

Numerous approaches to these problems are evident in the literature. Some are generic approaches to quality of life measurement while others are specifically targeted at disabled people. As the following analysis shows, the former have masked the oppression of disadvantaged groups (including disabled people) by employing aggregate measures to whole populations, while the latter have contributed to the continued oppression of disabled people by reinforcing the medicalisation and individualisation of disability.

Generic approaches

During the past 30 years, social indicators research has dominated the quality of life literature. Such research is characterised by the search for aggregate measures of welfare within whole communities or populations. However, the choice of indicators is as varied as the number of studies with each author seemingly arriving at a new list (Bloom 1978; Flax 1972; Liu 1976; Schmalz 1972). In this context it is important to recognise that the selection of social indicators is fundamentally a political choice. Thus, Bauer (1966) argues that social indicators enable researchers and policy makers to assess where they stand with respect to certain values and goals. Similarly, Carr-Hill (1984) notes that social indicators research has not adequately recognised that different sets of social indicators are suited to different political ideologies.

Thus, Carr-Hill uses the term social indicator as 'a measure of the condition or state *with respect to a given social objective'* (1984, p.174).

The major limitation of social indicators, as employed in the established literature, is that they are essentially aggregate measures of life quality for whole communities. Thus, they present difficulties for the researcher who is interested in quality of life for specific groups which are alienated and excluded from many of the benefits which that community has to offer. For example, Knox (1980) argues that measures of access to employment, public services and amenities provide important social indicators of life quality within a community. However, disabled people (along with women, black people, children and elders) are frequently excluded from access to just those facilities which benefit the non-disabled members of a community, such as housing, education, transport, employment or leisure.

The second major approach to generic quality of life measurement has concentrated on psychological rather than material factors. For example, writers such as Marans and Rogers (1975) argue that social indicators, like income or participation levels, are inadequate because human meaning is only attached to objective measures when they are related to subjective indicators. To use Osborne's (1992) taxonomy (outlined earlier), these psychological indicators tend to deal with 'well-being' rather than 'welfare'. Within such an approach the most commonly employed measure of subjective well-being has been 'life satisfaction' (Andrews and McKennel 1980; Knapp 1976; Neugarten, Havighurst and Tobin 1961).

Most life satisfaction studies employ large-scale surveys to elicit responses from statistically significant population samples (Flanagan 1978). However, such studies have produced widely varying views on the criteria which should be used. Hall (1976) reviews the largest British study, noting that the most frequently mentioned factors included satisfaction with family and home life, being 'contented' and having a good 'standard of living'. Hall notes, with some concern, that perceptions of social justice, equality and altruism were among the least mentioned influences on life satisfaction.

Another major difficulty is that correlations between social and psychological indicators are notoriously low. Individuals experiencing apparently high levels of welfare often report low levels of well-being and vice versa. (Perry and Felce 1995; Schneider 1976). Indeed, as Zautra and Goodhart (1979) note, increased levels of personal welfare may lead to increased levels of expectation and, thereby, produce decreased subjective judgements of life quality.

Conversely, Zautra and Goodhart (1979) identify a tendency for life satisfaction responses to be revised upwards by respondents (see also Mastekaasa and Kaasa 1987). Thus, Brown *et al.* (1988) argue that very many disabled people express high levels of life satisfaction in the absence of informed knowledge about the options available. This effect, they suggest, will be especially marked for people with learning difficulties, who may have been denied major life experiences and life choices in the past. As one member of the Derbyshire Coalition put it, 'how do you know what good quality is if you've never experienced it?' (interview transcript).

A third general approach has been the application of ecological theory to quality of life measurement (Milbrath 1982). The emphasis here is on measuring the relationship between the individual and their environment. From such a perspective life quality is characterised as the degree of 'fit' between people and their physical, economic or social environments. Zautra and Goodhart make use of this model in their work on mental health, suggesting that particular problems arise for people who find themselves part of a disabled social minority, 'This produces a condition in which there is a poor 'fit' between the person and the environment, since the values, standards, and lifestyles of the dominant culture make it more difficult for minority persons to meet their needs' (Zautra and Goodhart 1979, p.4).

Baker and Intagliata are concerned that quality studies have tended to concentrate exclusively on either the environment or the individual's perception of it, rather than on the purposeful interaction between the two. The important point for them is that people not only perceive environments, they also act to change them (1982, p.74). Thus, Brown *et al.* (1988) argue that the degree of control which disabled people are able to exercise over their environment is an important quality of life indicator. Similarly, Schalock *et al.* (1989) develop an ecological approach which values the degree of control that a person has over their immediate environment, the level of their community involvement and their social integration.

Parmenter (1988) sees the state of being disabled as relative to others within a community and also suggests that we should be primarily concerned with the processes of interaction between person and environment. In the context of this study, it is important to remember that social models of disability are fundamentally concerned with the disabling nature of environments. For this reason ecological theory offers a useful framework for thinking about quality of life, since it emphasises the degree of match (or mismatch) between the needs of individuals/groups and the socio-material environment within which they operate. Specifically, quality measures which seek to identify and remove social or physical barriers to integration and participation are entirely consistent with the ecological 'goodness of fit' concept.

Specific approaches

In addition to generic strategies it is important to consider approaches to life quality measurement that focus specifically on the lives of disabled people. As the following analysis shows, this literature reveals a tendency towards medico-functional rather than socio-political definitions of disability. Moreover, many such approaches consider functional impairment *de facto* and *a priori* as a reduction in life quality. In general, this inadequacy arises out of confusions between 'illness' and 'disability' (cf. Barnes and Mercer 1996).

Kaplan notes that health is the most consistently valued quality of life indicator (to the extent that it is regarded as universal and may even be omitted from some survey forms). Kaplan then makes the conceptual leap of assuming that the terms 'health status' and 'quality of life' are equivalent, defining the latter as 'the impact of disease and disability upon daily functioning' (1985, p.116). Thus he narrows his definition of life quality to exclude many issues of great importance to disabled people (such as appropriate housing, access to employment and recreation, the physical environment and so on). Similarly, Williams uses the term quality of life as synonymous with 'good health' measured by physical mobility, pain and distress, capacity for self-care and ability to pursue 'normal social roles' in relation to family, work and leisure (1987, p.203).

Measures of quality which focus specifically on the lives of disabled people have thus been dominated by functionalist approaches that are fundamentally at odds with a social model of disability (Nocon and Qureshi 1996, p.74). Consequently, the notion of functional 'dependency' has often been regarded as a determinant factor in attributing reduced quality of life (Brisenden 1989, p.9). Katz, for example, regards the use of assistance with *any* function (such as making one's own breakfast) as a measure of dependency and therefore reduced life quality, 'Independence means without supervision, direction, or active personal assistance… This is based on actual status and not on ability. A patient who refuses to perform a function is considered as not performing the function, even though he is deemed able' (Katz 1963, p.94).

Within this kind of medical model approach, the increased choice and self-determination afforded by self-assessment and self-management would not be acknowledged as an increase in life quality. Although such an approach makes little sense in the context of the movement for independent/integrated living it forms the basis for many of the quality measurement systems currently employed within commissioning health authorities.

The increasing attention on quality of life issues within commissioning authorities has been driven not so much by concern for the citizenship of disabled people as by the bureaucratic imperatives to ration scarce resources. Consequently, the marketisation of welfare has been mirrored by an increasing use of econometric approaches to policy evaluation. In particular there has been a marked trend towards approaches based on cost-benefit analysis (Klarman 1965; Warner and Hutton 1980; Weisbrod 1961). Some of these approaches employ classical cost-benefit analyses, which judge outcomes solely in terms of their monetary benefits (Jones-Lee 1976), others involve a cost-utility analysis, which may take a slightly broader view (Culyer 1990).

There are a number of methodological weaknesses in cost-benefit analysis. Drummond (1986) expresses concern at the lack of accurate measurement of true costs and consequences. On a more conceptual level, Shiell *et al.* suggest that all economic measures fail where they do not allow for human meaning in the experience of life quality. Thus, they argue that there can be no welfare equivalent of the 'gold standard' for judging service interventions (1990, p.112). In the context of disability policy, the major shortcoming of cost-benefit approaches has been their reliance on medical and functional definitions of life quality in terms of 'health' (at the expense of social or political indicators). An example helps to illustrate the point.

Quality Adjusted Life Years (QALYs) have become increasingly popular as a measurement tool in health policy analysis (Bush, Chen and Patrick 1973; Weinstein and Stason 1977). The QALY, or 'well year', is an arithmetic measure derived by considering the life expectancy of an individual adjusted downwards for the supposed reduction in quality of life arising from ill health or impairment. For example, a person with an estimated 20 years of life expectancy whose quality of life is judged to be reduced by 50 per cent would attain a QALY life expectancy score of ten years. If a service intervention could raise that person's quality of life to, say, 75 per cent then the measure would judge this service as a gain of five (QALY) years life expectancy.

There are clearly many technical difficulties in using this kind of measure (Kind, Gudex and Godfrey 1990; Loomes and McKenzie 1990; Shiell *et al.* 1990). However, on a more fundamental level, such approaches implicitly devalue the worth of disabled lives through the equation of impairment with negative life quality. Thus, they are clearly incompatible with a social model approach to outcome evaluation. The assumption that disabled people's 'well' life expectancy is reduced by lack of bodily function is in fact more compatible with a 'social death' model of disability. The implication of this kind of measure is that disabled people who outlive their QALY life expectancy become a kind of 'living dead'. Indeed, there is increasing concern that the use of such measures in genetic screening and treatment rationing promotes the practice of eugenic abortion and euthanasia (Shakespeare 1995).

The preceding review illustrates the variety of current approaches to life quality measurement and highlights many difficulties in their application to disability policy evaluation. Aggregate measurements of life quality for whole communities (such as social indicators research and large-scale psychological studies) have tended to contribute to the oppression of disabled people by obscuring both their community presence and their needs. At the same time, life quality measures targeted specifically at disabled people have sustained that oppression by medicalising the state of disability, and by valuing functional outcomes over barrier removal in the wider world. In general terms, such approaches have much more to do with surveillance, governance and the maintenance of a normalising gaze than with improving quality of life for disabled people.

Quality and equality

The concern for many among the disabled people's movement is that the definition of outcome measures should not be constrained within the framework of 'community care'. This restrictive definitional focus limits the consideration of disability issues to administrative and distributive notions of welfare production and precludes their consideration within an alternative discourse of social justice (Silvers 1995; Young 1990). In view of this argument it is important to reconsider some of the points made at the beginning of this chapter.

Beyond quality of life

Assuring service quality alone can never be a sufficient condition for improving disabled people's quality of life (although it may sometimes be a
necessary one). There is a danger in becoming preoccupied with the techni-
calities of quality assurance systems at the expense of life quality issues which
are beyond the reach or scope of 'services' (Oliver 1991). Specifically, there is
a danger of employing 'quality' as an inadequate conceptual substitute for
the more important goal of 'e-quality' (Priestley 1995c). Quality of life is
hard to define and any attempt to do so is inherently value-led. The selection
of measurement indicators is not only a technical process but also a political
one. For this reason the ability of particular groups to define 'quality', and the
value base which they use to do it, will also determine the kinds of services
which are thought to have 'value'.

This argument is particularly significant when we consider that the power
to define quality measures resides largely with professional interest groups
(rather than with those disabled people who use services). The tendency of
such groups to define quality within the traditional discourses of tragedy,
individualism and otherness creates an evaluative framework in which the
functional 'benefits' of care, treatment or rehabilitation are valued above
integrated living outcomes and barrier removal. Within the market
framework of community care, such evaluations are inevitably linked to
purchasing decisions which in turn shape the form and content of the
support services available to disabled people.

For Ackoff there is a fundamental flaw in the preoccupation of service
planners with the measurement and improvement of life quality. Ackoff
argues that the problem is not how to improve other people's quality of life
but '*how to enable them to improve their own quality of life*' (1976, p.299, original
emphasis). Importantly, this problem does not require measures of quality of
life for its solution. Thus, Ackoff concludes that 'the key to improved quality
of life is not planning for or measurement of others, but enabling them to
plan and measure for themselves' (1976, p.303). This would seem to reach to
the core of the argument presented by organisations within the disabled
people's movement. By creating a framework of participative support
structures, integrated living services provide new opportunities for the
self-definition of life quality and outcome measurement. Thus, as O'Brien
points out, 'human services organisations cannot manufacture better lives.
People weave better lives from the resources afforded by individual effort,

personal relationships, available opportunities, and help from services'
(1990, p.20).

Services and civil rights

As a service user, Kennedy (1990, p.40) argues: 'I am not asking for a *better*
service because I have a disability; I am asking for *equal* service because I am
equally a citizen. Quality assurance to me means that I will be treated like
anybody else. I need no special treatment' [original emphasis]. In a similar
way, the Local Government Management Board make an explicit link
between the notions of quality and equality, linking recent work on quality
assurance by local authorities with recent advances in equal opportunities
(LGMB 1991). They argue that the two themes are related through the over-
arching concept of 'service to the whole community'. Thus, 'The phrase
service to the whole community describes an approach which integrates
quality and equality, a way of working which sees these two themes as inter-
related and interdependent rather than separate' (LGMB 1991, p.1).

It is inherent within this approach that the service provider (and the
purchasing authority) is required to recognise each person not only as an
individual customer but also as a member of a particular group within that
community. If applied to the present context, such an approach would require
authorities to recognise, and respond to, disabled people both as customers,
with *individual needs* for services, and also as members of an oppressed group
in the community, with *collective needs* for equal citizenship and civil rights.

The goals and practices of the movement for independent/integrated
living are particularly well suited to this kind of approach. For organisations
like DCDP and DCIL, the provision of personal support to individual
disabled people is inextricably bound up with collective action for
integration and participation in the wider world. As Bracking (1993, p.12)
argues, the campaign for self-operated personal assistance schemes must be
viewed within the political struggle for civil rights rather than within the
narrow quest for better 'services'. Thus, he is concerned that, 'Local
authorities, health authorities and charities tend not to see independent
living as a basic human right as we do. For them independent living is still a
"welfare" issue' (1993).

Consequently, the movement for independent/integrated living has
sought to define its objectives within the broader panoply of disabled
people's participation and equality within society. From this perspective, the
measure of success for policy implementation is determined by the degree to

which it promotes and advances these broader political aims. Ultimately, enabling outcomes relate not just to better services but to a better society.

The following extract was supplied by a member of the Derbyshire Coalition in response to questions raised during the fieldwork for this study. It was an attempt to differentiate between quality, as perceived by individual service users, and as it relates to the broader aims of the disabled people's movement:

> A 'quality' society would provide the means of independence and full social participation. Such quality would be measured by reference to facts which demonstrate that disabled people as a distinct social group had both the rights to, and the means of equal social participation, e.g., it would count up bits of legislation; the content of legislation which could take rights away; the absence of disabled people needing to resort to law; the effect of legislation measured in anything from the numbers of accessible buses or buildings to the number of books in a library accessible to people with visual impairments to the availability of supports like technical aids or personal assistance; and by numbers of disabled people in jobs; the amount of their income; and the ways in which the choices and preferences they exercised matched those of the population at large. (Field notes, March 1996)

Reaching any level of social consensus about the validity of such an approach is problematic, since it poses a direct challenge to traditional ways of thinking about disability and welfare. As an approach to quality, it extends far beyond the administrative confines of 'community care' to issues of inclusion, citizenship, equality and participation in the wider world. If outcome measures are considered in this context then there are enormous implications for the design of services aimed at achieving them.

Desegregating services

Disabled people's organisations have consistently contrasted segregated forms of service provision with supports towards the goal of an inclusive society (Barnes 1990, 1991; Finkelstein and Stuart 1996). Such an approach is important because it challenges the administrative segregation of disability 'services', within a distinct (and culturally devalued) system of welfare distribution. It is certainly consistent with the Audit Commission's conclusion that 'support for individuals should help sustain as normal and independent a life as possible, *using ordinary services whenever feasible*' (1992b, para.3, my emphasis). More specifically, it is entirely consistent with the United Nations'

Standard Rules which state that, 'Persons with disabilities are members of society and have the right to remain within their local communities. They should receive the support they need *within the ordinary structures* of education, health, employment and social services' (UN 1993, para.26, my emphasis).

The achievement of such aspirational goals is no small task and requires a wholesale reevaluation of traditional ways of thinking about disability and welfare. Although the community care agenda has sometimes coincided with disabled people's demands for decarceration from *physical* segregation in residential institutions, it has consistently failed to challenge the *administrative* segregation from which those same institutions arose (Priestley 1997a; Stone 1984). Thus, as Finkelstein and Stuart (1996) argue, it has also failed to challenge the central values of a 'disabling culture' which distances disabled people from non-disabled people (see Chapter 2, or Barnes 1996a).

Sutherland (1981) and Morris (1993a, p.45) argue that little progress can be made until impairment and old age are seen as part of our common life experience. Similarly, Finkelstein and Stuart (1996) argue that the dominance of individual model thinking has, until recently, masked the possibility of an integrated approach to service development. Consequently, the priority for the disabled people's movement in Britain (and for disability theorists) has been to promote social model arguments. Only now, they conclude, is it possible to expand our horizons on the 'untravelled road from fantasy to reality'. Thus, they begin to envisage a future redefinition of service provision in which, 'it would no longer make sense to identify disabled people's needs as special any more than, for example, to regard a stand-up urinal as a provision for the special needs of able-bodied men!' (Finkelstein and Stuart 1996, p.172).

To reshape the form and content of welfare production towards this end would require a wholesale redistribution of resources and responsibilities. It would challenge the power, and even the existence, of whole professions, organisations and government departments. It would require, for example, the abolition of segregated 'special' education (Barton 1996b); universal access to the built environment (Walker 1996); fully accessible public transport systems (Heiser 1996); an end to discrimination in employment (Gooding 1996b) and a complete restructuring of the social security system (Berthoud 1996). In fact, it is hard to think of any substantive area of social policy making which would not be affected by such a far-reaching agenda. Yet this is the implicit, often explicit, goal of the disabled people's movement.

Conclusions

The disabled people's movement has been primarily concerned with acting to remove disabling barriers towards social integration and equal citizenship. In this sense, it is more concerned with outcomes than with processes, with ends rather than with means. However, in the realpolitik of policy debate there has been a necessary focus on more specific campaigns – closing residential institutions, raising benefit levels, creating more participatory services, accessing direct payments and promoting anti-discriminatory legislation. The potential danger in this climate of pragmatism is that we may sometimes lose sight of the movement's visionary focus on outcomes – participation, social integration and equal citizenship.

Both central government and the disabled people's movement have placed a rhetorical emphasis on independence, choice and integration as outcomes for community support services. Both have used normative definitions in attempting to define appropriate outcomes for service users (although there have been disagreements in deciding whose norms should be applied to the task). There is some convergence in the assertion that service users themselves should lead in determining the kind of outcomes to which services ought to be directed. For their part, the service users who participated in this study valued both cognitive and practical outcomes. Their experiences suggested that good quality services were those which facilitated greater self-esteem, self-determination, social integration and quality of life.

Although there are a wide variety of approaches to life quality measurement, it is useful to distinguish between those which deal with whole communities and those which focus specifically on the lives of disabled people. The former have obscured the marginalisation of disabled people from their communities (along with other oppressed groups). The latter have consolidated oppressive social relations by confusing disability with illness. On a more positive note, there seems to be some mileage in thinking about life quality in ecological terms – as a function of the relationship between person and environment. Ultimately, the real challenge for support services is not how to measure quality of life but how to enable people to measure and improve their own life quality (Ackoff 1976).

Outcomes cannot be considered without taking into account issues of equality in the wider world. Indeed, the current preoccupation with quality measurement in service provision has been increasingly employed as an inadequate substitute for equality in the wider world (Priestley 1995c). In order to facilitate integrated living outcomes, it is necessary to engage directly with social and physical barriers which extend far beyond the administrative boundaries of 'services'. For this reason, the achievement of real and positive outcomes for service users will depend not only upon participative delivery structures but also upon effective community development work, collective self-advocacy, campaigning and political struggle. As Jenny Morris concludes:

> The ideology of caring which is at the heart of current community care policies can only result in institutionalisation within the community unless politicians and professionals understand and identify with the philosophy and the aims of the independent living movement. (Morris 1993a, p.45)

As this analysis indicates, there are enormous difficulties in approaching outcome measurement within the framework of 'community care'. The preoccupation with 'care', individualism and administrative segregation makes it difficult to talk in the same breath about participation, citizenship or equality issues. Support services framed within this latter value system do not sit comfortably within a policy evaluation framework arising from the former. This is particularly evident when one considers the relationship between quality measurement and the rationing of scarce resources by purchasing and commissioning authorities.

The added value of integrated living supports, which engage directly with disabling barriers beyond the 'individual package', may easily be ignored within individualistic approaches to quality measurement. In particular, a purchasing framework which cannot accommodate integrated living outcomes, in terms of participatory citizenship and civil rights, will fail to provide the supports necessary for their achievement. The final chapter in this study considers this problem by reexamining the central conflict of values in terms of disabling barriers and strategies for change.

CHAPTER 8

Barriers and Strategies

The preceding chapters illustrate in some detail how value conflicts over the definition of disability and welfare are played out in the implementation of community care policies. Although the analysis has drawn extensively on data from one unique case study, it also highlights some more general issues. In particular, the experience of the movement for independent/integrated living shows how definitions of 'need', 'quality' and 'outcomes' can function ideologically, by legitimising disabling relationships of domination and sub-ordination in the production of welfare. Moreover, disabling discourses of 'care', individualism and administrative segregation have obscured disabled people's claims to participation, social integration and equality in the wider world.

The analysis presented in the preceding chapters highlights a number of significant barriers to change – the attitudes of individual care managers and front line staff; the bureaucratic politics of commissioning authorities; the administrative and legislative constraints of the contractual framework; the cultural imperialism of disabling values; the economic imperatives of a welfare state in crisis. The analysis in this final chapter summarises the range and extent of such barriers and considers some strategies for change. The discussion draws on three levels of analysis – organisational change at a local level, policy change at a national level, and socio-economic change in a global context.

Bridging the implementing gap

Although there are many fundamental differences between the policy agenda for community care and the philosophy of integrated living there are also many areas of rhetorical convergence. For example, there is much common ground in the promotion of user involvement, choice, self-determination and independent living outcomes; although, as Pilgrim, Todhunter and Pearson (1997) argue, shared 'interest' is not the same as shared 'interests'. In practice, the framework for community care implementation often works against the achievement of these same policy goals.

There is, then, much evidence for the existence of a substantial 'implementation gap' between the rhetoric and the reality of community care. Although many of the barriers to the liberation of disabled people operate at a structural level (Abberley 1987; Oliver 1990; Ryan and Thomas 1980) there are some opportunities for bridging this gap at a local level. Specifically, the existence of discretion and relative autonomy in policy implementation creates opportunities for disabled people, and their organisations, to challenge organisational cultures and established ways of working.

Street level bureaucracy

Wherever policy implementers have discretion there is scope for policy making – even where those actors are individuals and where the degree of discretion is limited. For example, Smith (1981) observes how receptionists, filing clerks and typists can influence social work policy at the point of service delivery (see also Winkler 1981). However, as Burch and Wood (1989, p.177) note, such discretion is generally more 'rule bound' than that exercised by professionals. In addition, lay people may be able to exercise considerable discretion, especially as elected local councillors. Far from being the passive recipients of central government policy, it is clear that many front-line actors have the opportunity to prioritise, negotiate, arbitrate and obstruct policy implementation in a very real way.

Consequently, the implementation framework for community care provides a great deal of scope for 'street level bureaucracy' (Lipsky 1978). The decisions of local planners and assessors can have dramatic consequences for individual disabled people and for the pattern of services available within a community. For example, Hardy et al. (1990) describe the case of a hospital consultant who would not allow people with learning difficulties 'into the community' unless he thought that it would improve their quality of life (which he did not). Similarly, one of the participants in this study described his previous experience of institutionalised residential 'care':

It [the residential home] was a barrier to us living in a decent home, but it was there because a handful of people had made a decision that it would be there. They were individuals who collectively were expressing certain attitudes towards people like [us] and giving effect to how they felt and saw problems through making that decision. (Interview transcript)

It would be naive to reduce the consideration of disabling barriers to a discussion about individual attitudes amongst planners, purchasers and providers. However, where discretion and relative autonomy in policy implementation are combined with disabling value assumptions, individuals and professional groups do have the power to shape local service provision in highly oppressive ways. Such processes are particularly evident in relation to 'care' assessment and management (Priestley 1998b). At a very basic level, individual attitudes can and do create real barriers to integrated living for disabled people.

Much has been written about the power of the professions (cf. Friedson 1970; Wilding 1982) and disabled people have been particularly subjectified by them. For example, McKnight (1981) and Abberley (1995) illustrate how professionalised services have both created and maintained disabling social relations within the welfare production process. Professional closure, and the growth of institutional welfare bureaucracies, have further reinforced the boundaries between professionals and their 'clients' (Hugman 1991). However, there is also evidence of an emerging counter-tendency in the growth of 'consumerism', self-help and the movement for independent/ integrated living (Zola 1987).

Connelly (1990) argues that the traditional relationship between social services departments and disabled people is beginning to change, as service boundaries and ideas about disability are increasingly challenged. This analysis is supported by evidence of change at a local level within some social services departments. For example, Jones (1996) and Evans (1996) review developments in Wiltshire from the perspectives of management and user organisations respectively. Such experiences suggest that it has been possible to move towards models of choice and control within the bounded rationality of community care. Supports for integrated living, which promote self-management, are an important catalyst in this process. By engaging disabled people directly in the design, management and delivery of services, they promote user-led solutions and challenge the cultural imagery of disabled people as impotent or dependent.

More specifically, the movement for independent/integrated living has enabled disabled people to demonstrate that they can be effectively engaged, not only as consumers but also as the producers of welfare. The increasing presence of disabled people in the management and delivery of services is therefore a significant factor in effecting change at a local level. Herd and Stalker (1996) point out that the current under-representation of disabled people as employees within provider organisations is a particularly poor use of potential resources and expertise. While accepting that the absence of disabled people in such organisations is not the sole reason for service failures and deficiencies, they suggest that:

> Service providing agencies can be strengthened and their role enhanced within the communities which they serve if members of those communities – in all their diversity – can contribute as employees to the work of such agencies. This is as true for disabled people as it is for members of any marginalised and under-represented group of people. (1996, p.21)

Similarly, Chinnery (1991) stresses the need for more disabled people to be employed within the 'caring' professions (particularly at a managerial level). However, Sally French (1988, 1994) invites caution in this analysis, providing numerous examples of the barriers which disabled people face in pursuing such a career within mainstream organisations.

By contrast, those working within organisations controlled by, or accountable to, disabled people have often been able to make real advances in an enabling workplace environment. For example, Etienne d'Abboville (1991) describes how the Spinal Injuries Association was able to develop approaches to social work within a social model of disability. From this example, he argues that disabled people's organisations, and specifically centres like DCIL, are better equipped to engage in participatory forms of service provision than more traditional organisations (compare Phelan and Cole 1991). Thus: 'Unless disabled people are themselves involved in the design and, some would say, the delivery of services, the fundamental structure of service provision will remain flawed' (d'Abboville 1991, p.84).

On an individual level, hundreds of local disabled people have become involved in the production of welfare for others through involvement with local planning groups, access campaigns, information provision, home visiting, community education and the arts. This process is illustrated in the following extract from Derbyshire:

Once awareness is raised and access improved, disabled people can and do involve themselves in community activity. People whose only outing was previously to the Day Centre find themselves booking transport through DCIL and staffing an information desk. People who came to DCIL in despair, for counselling, for vital information, benefits advice etc., train as peer counsellors and use their own experience to support others. (DCIL, presentation to Derbyshire Social Services Department, December 1994)

This approach suggests a blurring of the established hierarchy between 'providers' and 'users'. In so doing, it illustrates how user participation can create opportunities for resistance to the discourse of 'carers' and 'cared for'. Moreover, self-empowerment in an enabling environment of peer support builds community and collective identity. Thus, John Evans draws attention to the way in which:

...disabled people have directly become empowered by living independently e.g. taking control of their lives, creating choices, being decisive and assertive, articulating their needs, being an employer, and being an advocate just to mention a few. As well as these more individual qualities, there is also empowerment in terms of raising one's awareness and becoming committed to a cause and the politicisation that goes with this process. (Presentation to the Association of Metropolitan Authorities, 16 February 1992)

As Bracking (1993, p.11) points out, it is important to remember that the concept of independent/integrated living evolved from within the disabled people's movement, rather than from within non-disabled society. Bracking argues that Centres for Independent/Integrated living were particularly important in this process. They have demonstrated that disabled people can run their own support services and they have located those support services within a broader political movement for citizenship and equality.

Discretion and the 'enabling' authority

As the preceding chapters illustrate, policy continues to be 'made' during the so-called implementation phase (Hupe 1990). Implementation is not a passive process and the simplistic differentiation between 'policy makers' and 'administrators' is largely misplaced. Thus, Barrett and Fudge (1981) dispute the way in which 'top-down' analyses treat implementers as mere agents, while marginalising the study of power, conflict and value systems within, and between, organisations (see also O'Toole 1986). For similar reasons,

Hjern (1982, p.307) concludes that, 'To understand how politics and administration are linked now requires an understanding of more than just how
clause is related to clause. It also takes an understanding of how organisation
is linked to organisation'.

In Britain, central government administers little of its 'own' policy and an
increasing amount of social policy formed at the centre is implemented by
local authorities, arms-length government agencies and QuaNGOs.
Although there is much evidence that local government has become
increasingly subordinate to centralised constraint (Cochrane 1991; Crouch
and Marquand 1989; Widdicombe Report 1986) it is also clear that relative
autonomy in policy implementation has led to a great deal of 'uneven
development' between different localities (Duncan and Goodwin 1988).

The ability of local authorities to shape policy depends upon the
existence of discretion and relative autonomy. As Hogwood (1987) points
out, 'flexible' or 'permissive' policies are more susceptible to discretion
during implementation than 'mandatory' or 'proscriptive' ones. Hill (1981)
amongst others, notes that social policy in general creates more opportunity
for discretion than that in other areas (such as economic policy). Thus, Hill
uses the example of the 'meals on wheels' service to show how permissive
legislation (together with a lack of directive guidance) can often account for
local variations in service provision.

Community care policy has been highly permissive and policy making at
the centre has consistently sought to divest responsibility to 'enabling' local
authorities. For example, in response to a Commons Health Committee
report on community care (House of Commons 1993) the government were
keen to point out that it would be local authorities, rather than central
government, who would be held accountable for the implementation of
community care policies. Thus, 'Local authorities have "eagerly sought" the
responsibilities of community care and...it is they who will be held
accountable by users and carers and their local community...the Secretaries
of State for Health and Social Security have no direct management function'
(DHSS 1993, p.2).

It is local authorities who must establish local needs and develop strategic
objectives for service development. Within those authorities, the framework
for care assessment and management divests further discretion to
professional groups and individual staff at the front line. It is worth noting
that this discretion is tempered by the proliferation of directive guidance and
regulation from central government, and that the proscriptive nature of

purchasing criteria creates a significant counter-weight towards centralised control and surveillance. However, local authorities do retain a significant degree of autonomy in assessing local needs and in shaping the pattern of supports which are available to local disabled people. The existence of local discretion and relative autonomy provides scope for both pessimism and optimism. On the one hand, local councillors, chief executives, service commissioners and care managers may impede the enabling potential of community care policy where it conflicts with organisational values and interests. On the other hand, permissive policies open up spaces for the creation of innovative support structures (within the 'bounded rationality' of financial and legislative constraint).

The analysis presented in the first part of this chapter suggests that there is scope to challenge the ideology of community care at a local level. It also suggests that disabled people's organisations are uniquely well placed to take a leading role in this struggle. At an individual level, self-assessment and self-management provide care managers with tangible evidence that the discourse of welfare dependency has become outmoded. At a collective level, the self-organisation of disabled people provides local politicians and planners with coherent voices for change. Where disabled people's organisations have made in-roads into local authorities they have been able to influence the implementation of community care policies in very real ways (particularly through Disability Equality Training and representation on planning groups).

As the experience of the movement for independent/integrated living shows, there *are* opportunities for effective local action in awareness raising, attitude change and political dialogue. Such activities can, and do, challenge established values and ways of working. However, the opportunities for influence remain contingent upon a number of factors, including the level of local commitment to user involvement, the political agenda of the local authority and the level of self-organisation amongst local disabled people. In this context, it is important to remember that advances towards integrated living have generally occurred where the demands of disabled people and their organisations have coincided with local political agendas.

For example, initial demands for self-managed personal assistance schemes by disabled people in Hampshire clearly struck a chord with the Conservative authority's interest in consumerism and market choice. In Derbyshire, the Coalition's agenda for participation and equality fitted well with the Labour authority's interest in equal opportunities. Conversely, where the promotion of integrated living solutions has conflicted with local political agendas there has been much resistance. Thus, DCDP's attempts to *replace* existing service provision in Derbyshire (with user-led alternatives) were perceived as unwelcome privatisation, and as an attack on public sector accountability. The existence of local discretion means that 'enabling' authorities can still choose to be disabling when it suits them.

As these examples show, the existence of local discretion and autonomy in community care policy making remains a double-edged sword for the disabled people's movement. On the one hand, it offers the possibility that local campaigning can lead to positive influence in the implementation process. On the other hand, it places the burden of persuasion on disabled people themselves. Local autonomy has been an important factor in the historical development of independent/integrated living. However, in the absence of a mandatory legislative framework, community care continues to operate within a needs-based, rather than a rights-based, system of welfare production (Oliver and Barnes 1991, 1993). This, in turn, leaves the definition of local 'needs' vulnerable to relationships of power between local disabled people and the commissioning authorities.

Although there may be some scope for challenging disabling attitudes and practices amongst discretionary actors at a local level, organisations like DCDP and DCIL have more far-reaching goals. As one DCIL manager put it, 'what this organisation seeks to do is somehow change the basis on which all services are provided...and it is a revolutionary thing to try and do'. (Interview transcript)

To restructure such a system is no small task. It would require an end to the physical segregation of institutional care; the removal of administratively segregated 'special' services into the mainstream; and a redefinition of the relationship between 'providers' and 'users'. In this sense, the agenda promoted within the movement calls for a more fundamental redefinition of the social relations of welfare production. In particular, the goals of integrated living and equal citizenship are undermined by the continued administrative segregation of service provision for disabled people (Finkelstein 1991; Stone 1984). It is important to remember that those same services have increasingly been named by disabled people amongst the primary barriers to participation, integration and equality in the wider world (Abberley 1995; Finkelstein 1991; Oliver 1992b; Oliver and Barnes 1993).

The scope of legislative change

The research for this book was carried out between October 1994 and May 1997 and much water has passed under the bridge during that time. When I began this study, direct payments were not an option for most service users and there seemed little immediate prospect for anti-discriminatory legislation. Yet, both these provisions have reached the statute book (in one form or another). In addition, the election of a Labour government in May 1997 raises questions about the future direction of disability policy making. In the light of these developments, it is important to review the potential for policy change at a national level. The following discussion examines the prospects for change offered by implementation of the 1996 Community Care (Direct Payments) Act and 1995 Disability Discrimination Act. More generally, this analysis suggests that legislative change cannot be a sufficient condition for ensuring the sort of broader social change promoted by the disabled people's movement (although it may sometimes be a necessary one).

Direct payments

Griffiths (1988) had specifically ruled out the prospect of extending local authority powers to make direct cash payments to individual service users (at that time Section 29 of the 1948 Act, Schedule 8 of the 1977 Act and Section 45 of the 1968 Act specifically prohibited English authorities from making payments in lieu of 'services'). Thus, until recently, the only examples of direct payments were administered by central, rather than local, government. For example, Maggie Davis (1993, p.17) draws attention to the fact that patients at St Thomas Hospital had been granted special DHSS payments (the Domestic Assistance Addition) to employ personal assistants at home during the 1960s and 1970s. The success of this scheme she suggests posed a threat to existing institutions and thus led to its withdrawal in the 1988 social security reforms.

Probably the most significant development was the establishment of the Independent Living Fund (ILF) in 1988. The ILF was launched jointly by the Disablement Income Group and the Department of Social Security, with the intention of assisting disabled people of working age to remain in their own homes through cash payments (up to a weekly maximum). In its first year of operation (1988–89) the Fund paid out £1 million of the £5 million available. By 1992–93 more than £100 million was being paid out to 21,000 people (see Kestenbaum 1993b, for a history of the ILF).

The ILF was closed to new applicants from November 1992 and replaced by two new funds. The Independent Living (Extension) Fund was set up to deal with the ILF's existing caseload while the Independent Living (1993) Fund was intended to take on new applications. Moving the second reading of the Disablement (Grants) Bill in February 1993, Nicholas Scott pointed out that the ILF had been intended as an 'interim' measure pending community care legislation. However, he also remarked on its success, confirming government support for the 'main concepts behind it, which are giving cash to disabled people and recognising that by doing so we give them independence and the power to determine how best to meet their own care needs' (*House of Commons Official Record,* 15 February 1993, c36).

The principle had already been endorsed by the Association of Directors of Social Services at their Annual General Meeting in 1992 and promoted in their evidence to the Commons Committee the following year (House of Commons 1993, Q448). The Committee recommended that central government should review existing research in this area with a view to making changes (House of Commons 1993, para.41). To this end, the Department of Health appointed a Technical Advisory Group and the Community Care (Direct Payments) Bill was published in November 1995. The legislation came into force the following year, permitting local authorities to make direct payments to people assessed as needing community care services (taking into account their financial circumstances in calculating the amount). It is too early to reliably predict the impact of policy implementation in this area, and much research is needed to establish the impact of direct payments policy amongst a wide range of service users in different local authorities. However, it is important to note some initial concerns about the limitations of direct payments legislation as a means towards integrated living for disabled people.

First, direct payments legislation does not circumvent existing arrangements for needs assessment. It affects the management of allocated resources but it does not impact on the criteria used to make that allocation. Thus, while more easily available direct payments may facilitate opportunities for increased self-management, they will contribute rather less towards a culture of self-assessment. The administrative and professional dominance over assessments of 'need' remains largely unchallenged. In a similar way, applications to the remaining ILF funds are still mediated by local authority assessors, reinforcing the principles of administrative dominance and professional power in determining disabled people's 'care' needs.

Second, it is becoming clear that many service users may be wary about the prospect of direct payments. Although disabled people's organisations campaigned strongly for the legislation, there have been differing opinions about the most appropriate arrangements for administering them. DCIL in particular has remained concerned that direct payments legislation may obscure important management issues, by focusing attention on the individual as purchaser. Indeed, there is a danger that, without effective organisational back-up, many individual disabled people may become even more vulnerable to abuse, exploitation or inadequate support arrangements in the market place. Furthermore, there is a perceived danger that direct payments schemes present an opportunity for, 'removing a problem outside mainstream services. They intend to give you your own money, that's fine. You get on with it but don't bloody complain to us. That's part of that process'. (Interview transcript)

In this context, it is perhaps significant that, of the Personal Support Service users involved with this study, only one person wanted to manage all the financial aspects of her package. Everyone else felt that they would continue to need the sort of back-up support that organisations like DCIL provide. The following comments illustrate the kind of arguments which they put forward:

> You've got like another person, another organisation that you can sort of put the responsibility on, it's not only me, which it would be if I was paying. I mean at the moment I'm just directing them in the hours. I've got nothing to do at all with the money apart from how many hours they do. I wouldn't want to. (Carol)

> I think it's dangerous, I think it's really dangerous to give a lot of money to people who need community care. You give anybody a few hundred quid and they'll blow it. You give people housing benefit in arrears and they spend it. With a lot, you'd get a lot of trouble. And I think it would be open to abuse, not by people who are dishonest but because people wouldn't cope. (Terry)

> ...I'd have to have somebody to put the adverts up for me and like help to do the interviewing...I'd have to have somebody to organise it. Handling money: they do good things like that, like interviewing and seeing that people are all right in the background. You see I couldn't do

> all that…I don't think I'd be able to manage… No, it wouldn't be for me I tell you. (Liz)

> What I would like is to be able to be plugged into DCIL for…an advocate, I certainly wouldn't change that. And I think they should be there to support me still, in a crisis. (Margaret)

> If you sever all links with DCIL, you're back to a situation where you're confronting the County Council without support. I don't think that's tenable because I've been through that… (Hugh)

Similarly, accumulated experience within the movement for independent/integrated living shows that additional support is a necessary prerequisite for self-assessment and self-management (Barnes 1997; DIG 1996; Oliver and Zarb 1992; Simpson and Campbell 1996). Managing one's own package of financial support can be a liberating experience. However, without adequate arrangements for information, advocacy, peer support, administrative back-up and payroll services it can also be a daunting prospect. This will be especially so for those disabled people who have been denied major life choices and experiences in the past.

As the examples from Derbyshire show, many people do not have the time, the confidence or the experience to manage the administrative and financial side of their support package. Some people need organisational support in dealing directly with their personal support staff. Others may often feel threatened when dealing with the purchasing authorities on their own. At this stage, such observations are necessarily based on anecdotal evidence but they do suggest that there remains an important role for disabled people's organisations, especially in the areas of advocacy, peer support, campaigning and community development work.

Direct payments legislation is an important policy development for the disabled people's movement. It challenges disabling discourses of 'care' and undermines cultural associations between disability and dependence. However, there are also dangers. First, the new direct payments legislation is discretionary and there will be no obligation on local authorities to make the option available more widely. Consequently, it is likely that the development of direct payments schemes in England will mirror the uneven regional development of past initiatives in independent/integrated living. Second, direct payments (taken as an isolated policy) reinforce the idea that disability is an individual problem which requires an individual response.

Taken on their own, direct payments cannot provide the means to participation, integration and equality in the wider world (although they are a considerable help towards those ends). Direct payments do not, in themselves, do anything to influence the causes of disability. They do not for example restructure the physical environment, the economic imperatives of the labour market, the education system or the cultural imperialism of disabling values. However, they do provide opportunities for more disabled people to gain the independence necessary to further those tasks. Finally, it is important to reiterate that the implementation of direct payments legislation is being played out within a needs-based system of distributive welfare rather than within a rights-based framework for inclusive citizenship.

Anti-discriminatory legislation

The community care White Paper recognised that support towards integrated living should be extended beyond the traditional responsibilities of social services departments, to include accessible employment, education and housing (see paras 2.4 and 3.5.1). Consequently, local authorities need to recognise that 'independence' for disabled people demands more than just 'care' services. It also demands access to 'ordinary community activities' (Leat 1998, p.30). Similarly, the Audit Commission advised that achievement of community care implementation goals would require action beyond the narrow scope of social services departments (Audit Commission 1992b, para.62). In particular, they argued that access to the wider environment would be an essential feature of successful implementation. Thus, 'If community care is to be a reality for physically disabled people wider initiatives are also required on such aspects as access to indoor shopping centres, other buildings, public toilets, transport and the suitability of pavements and crossings for disabled people' (1992b, para.22).

With this in mind, they concluded that the implementation of community care should not be regarded simply as a social services matter. Instead, community care should be seen, within local authorities, as a 'corporate approach' to local need (1992b, para.63). Such an approach is consistent with the broader agenda of the disabled people's movement. Taken in the bigger picture, it suggests an approach which transcends the socially and bureaucratically constructed boundaries of 'service' provision altogether, in favour of one based on a social model of disability and barrier removal in the wider world (Finkelstein and Stuart 1996).

Within this framework, disabled people's organisations have persistently campaigned for effective anti-discriminatory legislation. It is not necessary to review this campaign in detail here, and it has been well documented by various authors (Barnes 1991; Barnes and Oliver 1995; K. Davis 1994). Suffice to say that numerous attempts to introduce legislative measures between 1981 and 1995 met with considerable resistance from central government and were unsuccessful. However, under sustained pressure the government introduced its own Bill in 1994 and, after a stormy passage, the Disability Discrimination Act received Royal Assent on 8 November 1995 (although implementation of its major provisions has been staggered).

Ostensibly, the Act creates three basic 'rights' for people defined as 'disabled' – the right not to be discriminated against in employment; the right not to be discriminated against in the provision of goods, facilities and services; the right not to be discriminated against in the provision of premises. However, these are by no means universal rights and there are numerous exemption clauses (Northern Officers Group 1996). Consequently, the new legislation has been widely criticised by disability activists for failing to challenge systematic oppression in any real or meaningful way (Barnes and Oliver 1995; *Disability Now,* January 1997, p.1).

First, the Act defines disabled people in terms of particular impairments and functional limitations, rather than with reference to categories of exclusion or discrimination. In this sense it differs from the Race Relations Act or the Sex Discrimination Act, which do not require black people or women to be defined in biological terms. Consequently, the new legislation has been criticised for perpetuating the ideological association between impairment and disability (Chadwick 1996; Northern Officers Group 1996). Although the Act deals in 'rights' these are individualised rights based on a medical model of disability, rather than collective rights based on a social model.

Chadwick (1996, p.29) argues that the adoption of individual model definitions in the Disability Discrimination Act draws a line under the state's acceptance of financial responsibility. The limits on this responsibility, Chadwick argues, are to curb discrimination at the level of individual prejudice, and minor environmental barriers, while failing to address the structural features of disabled people's exclusion from full participation and citizenship. Thus, the ability to define disability in terms of 'natural' causes prevents any meaningful political discussion of large areas of disabled people's lives (Chadwick 1996, p.30).

Second, the rights to access and inclusion conveyed by the Act are in no sense absolute. In particular, the provisions for allowing 'justified discrimination' in the Disability Discrimination Act are far more extensive than those found in anti-discriminatory legislation relating to racism or sexism. Where the reason for discrimination is proven to be substantial and material it can be regarded as justifiable. Where an employer or service provider can show that 'adjustments' to normal practice are not 'reasonable' then there are grounds for justifiable discrimination. Consequently, there has been much concern about the burden of proof in establishing legal criteria for the terms 'substantial', 'justifiable reason' and 'reasonable adjustment' (Gooding 1994, 1996a; *Guardian*, 25 November 1994, p.8; Northern Officers Group 1996). At the time of writing it remains unclear how far legal precedent and government Codes of Practice will resolve such ambiguities.

Third, the provisions of the Act are not universal. Many organisations are exempt even from a basic duty to accommodate disabled people. For example, the police, prison, fire and armed services are excluded from all provisions of the Act. Similarly, the duty not to discriminate in employment does not apply to companies with less than 20 employees (i.e. 96 per cent of all employers in the UK!). In addition, educational institutions are required only to publish anti-discriminatory policies on pupil admissions, teaching and facilities. There is no mechanism for the enforcement of such policies (although further and higher education colleges need to report on their progress in implementing these policies). Consequently, the Act presents few challenges to the disabling social relations of segregated and 'special' education (Barton 1996b; Barnes 1991; Rieser and Mason 1992).

Fourth, there is no effective agency of enforcement for disability rights under the Act. Again, this presents a significant contrast with the legislation on race and gender discrimination, where the Commission for Racial Equality and the Equal Opportunities Commission have a role in pressing cases and enforcing legislative provisions. Instead, the Act establishes a National Disability Council (NDC) with advisory powers and a monitoring role. As the Northern Officers Group (1996) point out, what this means is that individual disabled people and their representative organisations carry the responsibility for identifying and bringing cases of discrimination to tribunals and the courts. It is too early to predict how the new Council will carry out its responsibilities (the NDC met for the first time in February 1997). However, without adequate representation from the disabled people's movement, and without enforcing powers, it is likely to remain open to the charge that it is an ineffectual mechanism for advancing citizenship rights.

As this brief review shows, there are many deficiencies in the Act as a piece of civil rights legislation. It reinforces causal associations between impairment and disability; it conveys 'rights' which are neither collective, absolute nor universal; it lacks the teeth of a proper enforcement agency. It is certainly a very pale imitation of the Civil Rights (Disabled Persons) Bill sponsored by Harry Barnes in the same session of Parliament and forcibly talked out by Conservative MPs. As Barnes (1991) and Oliver (1990) argue, effective legislation would have required not only a comprehensive anti-discrimination Act but also an accompanying freedom of information Act and well funded organisations of disabled people to ensure pressure for enforcement.

However, despite these limitations, it would be wrong to become too cynical. Given the sustained and often vociferous government opposition to demands for anti-discriminatory legislation, the passage of the Act must also be seen as an important advance for the disabled people's movement. The Act is a partial achievement from a hard-fought battle but it would not have happened at all without the effective self-organisation of disabled people within a politicised movement for change (Campbell and Oliver 1996).

While not devaluing the importance of the 1995 Act, Finkelstein and Stuart (1996) remain sceptical about the ability of anti-discriminatory legislation to effect significant change. Using the analogy of British race relations and the Commission for Racial Equality they argue that:

> The importance of British anti-discriminatory legislation should not be underestimated. Yet, this legislation has obviously not removed discrimination from the day-to-day experience of the ethnic minority population. This conclusion highlights limits to the gains that are possible through civil rights legislation. (1996, p.174)

Colin Barnes and Mike Oliver (1995, p.114) make similar associations with other anti-discriminatory legislation. The institutionalised nature of disability in Britain is, they argue, akin to racism, sexism and heterosexism. As such, it permeates 'the very fabric of British society' and is rooted in 'the very foundation of western culture'. Thus, they conclude, 'Our analysis suggests that the achievement of civil rights for disabled people will involve political struggles which go beyond campaigns for legislation. These will include consciousness raising, direct action, the strengthening of democratic and accountable organisations, and the promotion and control of research' (1996, p.115).

Similarly, Oliver (1996a) is concerned that the campaign for anti-discriminatory legislation should be seen as a 'step on the road' towards inclusion, rather than as a solution in itself. While welcoming recent developments with optimism, Oliver urges realism about the scale of the barriers still to be overcome. For example, he expresses concern about the relevance of legislative change at a time when there is evidence of increasing segregation in education (Norwich 1994) and where the abuse of disabled children remains widespread (Cross 1994). Consequently:

> as disabled people we need to recognise that the law will not do it for us. Even once we have got legislation we will still have to do it for ourselves. We will still have to force the politicians and the lawyers to take our concerns seriously. We will still have to go out on the streets. The road to liberation is one which we can only take for ourselves. (Oliver 1996a, p.25)

Steve Jones (1994) takes a more radical Marxist stance, arguing that all demands for legislative 'civil-rights' should be seen as a liberal bourgeois approach to 'equality'. The legislative loop-holes, and the liberal incorpora- tion of disabled people's 'representatives' in an ineffectual consultative council, lead Jones to argue that the campaign for anti-discriminatory legisla- tion can only legitimise existing alienation and exploitation under capitalist class rule. For Jones then, 'Real practical emancipation cannot evolve from the idealist political sphere or legal reforms – it can only come from a united working-class expropriating the owners of capital and forcing a change in the social relations of production' (1994, p.35).

To summarise, there have been some important policy developments in recent years which will undoubtedly impact on the further implementation of community care policy and integrated living projects. The advent of direct payments and anti-discriminatory legislation show that advances can be made. In particular, they provide some optimism for those who believe that targeted political campaigns by social movements can influence the pattern of social policy making in Britain. However, they provide rather less optimism about the impact of legislative reform as a mechanism for achieving participation, integration and equality in the wider world. It is important to be realistic about the scope of the gains which have been made and to remember just how difficult they were to achieve. In particular, it is important to recognise that even these limited developments would not have come about without the effective and sustained self-organisation of disabled people within a cohesive social movement for change.

Social change

So far I have considered the prospects for change at the micro-level of service provision and at the level of national policy. The final part of this chapter extends this analysis to the consideration of disabling barriers and social change in more general terms. This argument is necessarily speculative and cuts across some of the really 'big issues' in contemporary social science. For example, in order to envisage a society in which disabled people might be truly integrated with full equality it is necessary to rethink concepts like citizenship, culture, political economy and social movements.

Citizenship, commodification and welfare

In developing its *Standard Rules* the United Nations (1993) made a clear link between the equalisation of opportunities for disabled people and their participatory citizenship within member states. For example, the Preamble emphasises the need for disabled people to become 'active partners with States in the planning and implementation of all measures affecting their civil, political, economic, social and cultural rights'. Thus:

> The purpose of the Rules is to ensure that girls, boys, women and men with disabilities, as members of their societies, may exercise the same rights and obligations as others. In all societies of the world there are still obstacles preventing persons with disabilities from exercising their rights and freedoms and making it difficult for them to participate fully in the activities of their societies. (UN 1993)

Yet there is considerable evidence that disabled people have been systematically denied such citizenship rights in Britain (Barnes 1991; Oliver 1992b). Political rights have been denied through unequal access to the political process, to suffrage and to the ballot box. Social rights have been denied through differential levels of poverty (Berthoud 1996; Disability Alliance 1987; Martin and White 1988; Thompson *et al.* 1990), inadequate environmental access (Finkelstein 1975; Heiser 1996; Walker 1996) and basic lifestyle choice (Barnes 1990; Hunt 1981; Morris 1991a). Moreover, Oliver and Barnes (1993) argue that this kind of institutional discrimination has been specifically compounded by the development of social policy within the British welfare state. As Oliver puts it: 'not only has state welfare not ensured the citizenship rights of disabled people, through some of its provisions and practices it has infringed and even taken away some of these rights' (Oliver 1992, p.30).

In particular, the tentative citizenship rights incorporated in post-war legislation, such as the 1944 Disabled Persons (Employment) Act, have been progressively undermined by moves towards a needs-based system of welfare. This process, according to Oliver and Barnes (1993, p.269), has been masked by the rhetoric of recent community care policy making. As shown in this study, community care has consistently reinforced ideological associations between impairment, 'needs' and 'care' rather than between disability, exclusion and rights. Adèle Jones concludes that:

> ...the focus on 'needs' rather than 'human rights' is in direct conflict with the concept of empowerment. The concept of need is an approach that runs through all the legislation and is one which promotes pathology, inadequacy and inability as the basis for determining who has what services. (Jones 1992, p.38)

Against this background, the movement for independent/integrated living has made an important contribution. In particular, it has fostered the development of a participative disability culture which challenges discourses of dependency and passivity. However, within the prevailing climate of commodification and marketisation, the participation of disabled people has been constructed by policy makers simply as 'consumerism' (rather than as liberation or citizenship).

This argument could be equally applied to the relationship between other differentially incorporated citizens and the welfare state (e.g. black people, women, elders, children, lesbians and gay men). In Derbyshire, the equation between participatory services and participatory citizenship is clearly articulated in the Coalition's commitment to, 'promote a form of service that would underpin active, participatory citizenship rather than passive containment or custodianship and elevate the former as being the preferred policy objective of central/local government' (Field notes, DCDP, March 1996).

In this context, it is important to remember that government has a relationship with service users not only as 'customers' or 'consumers' but also as citizens (Priestley 1995c) and that consumerism cannot therefore be a sufficient guarantee of the public interest. As Stewart and Ranson (1988, p.15) argue:

> The public are not merely clients or customers of the public sector organisation. They are themselves a part of that organisation as citizens. Citizenship can be a basic value in the public domain. In building

citizenship management has to encompass a set of relationships for which the private sector model allows no place.

Thomson (1992) sees individual client contracts as a way to bolster active citizenship. However, Lipsky and Smith (1989) suggest that, because service contracting alters the politics of welfare delivery, it raises concerns about equity and citizenship. As the analysis presented in this study shows, there is reason to believe that the marketisation of community care services may actually be undermining the citizenship of its disabled 'consumers'. Indeed, there has been growing concern in the United States that the contracting out of public services is impacting negatively on citizens' rights, and that privatisation and civil liberties 'may prove to be mutually exclusive goals' (Sullivan 1987, p.466). For the Coalition in Derbyshire: 'The future for disabled people under a "mixed economy of care" amounts to little more than a reversion to the old idea of disabled people as being tragic cases rather than equal citizens, backwards into dependency in the interests of private profit' (*INFO: the Voice of Disabled People in Derbyshire,* June 1992, p.1).

More generally, Plant (1992) argues that the very notion of 'welfare rights' is based on an assumption that the *laissez-faire* market needs to be controlled and moderated by the broader obligations and rights associated with citizenship (for example, the obligation to pay tax and the right to receive a minimum level of economic and social status). For Plant this,

> ...implies some limit to commodification and commercialisation, in the sense that the basic welfare goods to which individuals have rights are not ultimately to be subject to the market mechanism, since the market cannot guarantee the provision of these goods, as of right, on a fair basis to all citizens. (1992, p.16)

Iris Young (1990) develops this line of argument in order to illustrate how the discourse of oppression, in which new social movements engage, often runs counter to many of the core assumptions of western capitalist societies. In this way, she argues that the discourse of collective social justice and citizenship conflicts with the distributive paradigm of welfare capitalism. For Young, 'Entering the political discourse in which oppression is a central category involves adopting a general mode of analyzing and evaluating social structures and practices which is incommensurate with the language of liberal individualism' (1990, p.39).

The marketisation of community care policy making has centred on the extension of negative civil and political rights (such as individual choice), while opposing many of the positive social and economic rights necessary to exercise them. It is no coincidence that the initial marketisation of community care occurred alongside strident political resistance to both anti-discriminatory legislation and the provision of direct payments with which disabled people might have been able to exercise 'choice' in the market. While the disabled people's movement has been partially successful in securing negative rights, it has, as yet, made rather less progress in obtaining the positive rights necessary to exercise active and inclusive citizenship.

From costs to causes

One of the most commonly identified barriers to integrated living is the presumed cost of implementation. For example, Ann Kestenbaum (1996) welcomes the need-led rhetoric of community care policy making but argues that economic constraints present barriers to the implementation of independent living solutions. Thus:

> In principle, a social policy that aims to keep people out of institutions should mean that their individual needs for Independent Living are addressed more appropriately. However, if the overriding considerations in implementing the policy are the reduction of welfare spending and the shifting of financial and moral responsibilities to families...then the possibilities opened up by community care for Independent Living in its full sense are likely to be very limited. (Kestenbaum 1996, p.4)

Jenny Morris (1993b) questions whether overall levels of resourcing are the real issue, and asks whether we should instead focus on the way in which existing resources are tied up in particular modes of service provision. Morris maintains an agnostic approach to this question but argues that significant change could be effected without raising overall welfare spending (by rechannelling the weight of investment from traditional modes of 'care' and 'rehabilitation' towards independent living schemes). For Morris then:

> ...it is not certain that the redistribution of resources which would be necessary would also need to be accompanied by an increase in the total amount of resources. Instead it may be that a fundamental shift in the use of existing resources would go a long way to achieving independent living for disabled people. (1993b, p.178)

Morris' analysis draws on other studies of independent living which suggest that the self-management of personal assistance may often be a cheaper option than traditional models of service provision (Zarb and Nadash 1994;

Zarb *et al.* 1996). However, there is an important distinction between the proven cost-effectiveness of self-managed personal assistance schemes, on the one hand, and the broader socio-economic agenda posed by the disabled people's movement on the other.

It would be wrong to over-emphasise differences of approach within the movement for independent/integrated living. To do so would be counter-productive and largely misplaced. The point is simply this: the development of effective self-managed personal assistance schemes *has* been possible within existing policy frameworks and within available 'service' budgets (albeit as a result of hard-won local battles by individual disabled people). However, the goals of integrated living (participation, integration and true equality) require more than just participative services. They also require barrier removal in the wider social world – in the built environment, in employment, in education.

Cost-benefit analysis is not an easy (or an appropriate) model to apply to agendas for radical social change, and it is hard to estimate the likely costs of such wide-ranging proposals. There would be gains as well as losses. As one DCIL manager pointed out, 'people who currently are eking out their existence in nursing homes could, in a different model of care, a different model of support, be employed. They could actually be earning and paying taxes and actually cost people, the exchequer and themselves [less]…' (Interview transcript).

In addition, the creation of universally accessible environments would bring benefits to many non-disabled people (Walker 1996). However, on balance it is probably fair to say that the long-term goals of the disabled people's movement could not be met simply by redistributing existing 'service' budgets. Rather, they would require a more wholesale redistribution of resources. Such a redistribution would directly challenge the economic imperatives of production and reproduction within a capitalist economy. In order to understand the implications of this broader agenda for social change, it is necessary to reconsider the relationship between disabling values, social policy and political economy.

George and Wilding (1976, p.129) argue that welfare polices are necessarily weakened when they are 'grafted on to an economic system intrinsically hostile to the welfare ethic'. Consequently, they see 'the conflict between the values of capitalism and the ethic of welfare as the underlying reason for the failure of social policies to achieve agreed aims' (1976). George and Wilding's emphasis on conflicting 'values' and 'ethics' provides a graphic image of the kind of ideological tensions illustrated throughout this study. It also accords with the way in which the disabled people's movement challenges the cultural imperialism of disabling values. As Finkelstein and Stuart (1996) point out:

> Lasting change requires more than merely winning the battle for civil rights for disabled people. It requires more than just the support of a benign government. It requires more than a disability commission with a key 'police' role over the delivery of services and responsibility for the representation of impairment in popular culture and the media. The engine of change requires the sum of these things but more. It requires all these things within a context of a fundamental transformation of the restricted cultural view of disability in the United Kingdom. (Finkelstein and Stuart 1996, p.175)

However, the causes of disability cannot be reduced simply to debates about 'values' or 'culture', although these are important (Barnes 1996a; Ingstad and Reynolds-Whyte 1995). Analyses which are conducted within an idealist discourse of 'culture' often fail to provide a sufficient level of explanation for the disadvantage experienced by disabled people. It is important to remember that disabling cultural values also reflect material relations of power. This is not a new debate and the implications have been explored at some length by social model writers such as Vic Finkelstein (1980), Paul Abberley (1987), Mike Oliver (1990), Tom Shakespeare (1994) and Colin Barnes (1996a).

Cultural values play a central role in legitimising disabling social relations, but we have to ask where such values come from, why certain values remain dominant over others and whose interests are threatened when dominant values are challenged (Abrams 1982). The answers to these questions are more likely to be found by talking about 'ideology' than by talking about 'culture' (1987). For these reasons, an adequate theory of disability needs to accommodate not only the relationship between individual and society, it also needs to accommodate both idealist and materialist levels of explanation (Priestley 1988a).

The recognition that policy values can function ideologically, by legitimising disabling social relations, reinforces the view that welfare policies can often be considered as examples of social control (Higgins 1980; Janowitz 1976). For example, Marxist and neo-Marxist commentators have often portrayed social policy implementation as providing the minimum sufficient conditions for reproducing the labour force while maintaining order and state legitimation (Mishra 1977, 1984; O'Connor 1973). The implication for Hugman (1991, p.21) is that 'The growth of the welfare state has exacerbated the contradictions between the economic and ideological aspects of society, so that to resolve the ensuing crisis the long-term interests of capital are placed before those of welfare'.

It is clearly beyond the scope of this study to examine theories of crisis in the capitalist state in any real detail. Suffice to say that numerous authors have analysed the inherent contradictions between capital accumulation and the expansion of state welfare spending (Gough 1979; Habermas 1976; Offe 1984). Within this dialectic, the demands of the disabled people's movement are doubly significant. Including disabled people on equal terms challenges the social relations of both production and reproduction. The prospect of full inclusion in employment challenges the economic imperatives of capital accumulation (particularly within Fordist modes of production). The removal of barriers to inclusion in mainstream education, leisure and welfare demands additional resources and undermines the legitimacy of the welfare state.

In this sense, some of the analogies between disability, race and gender begin to break down. As with disability, the cultural imperialism of racist and sexist values has served to legitimise historic relationships of domination and subordination (Fraser 1987; Lugones and Spelman 1983; Young 1990). The representation of black people and women, as biologically inferior or 'other', has been an important factor in maintaining the cultural legitimacy of Britain's patriarchal and imperialist legacy. The social relations of power arising from this legacy have, in turn, enabled the labour of black people and women to be additionally exploited in the British labour market (including unpaid 'caring' labour).

By contrast, the cultural construction of disabled people (in terms of tragedy, the impaired body and otherness) has been exploited ideologically to *exclude* them from the processes of production and reproduction altogether. Indeed, there is considerable evidence that the historic segregation of disabled people through 'service provision' has been premised upon the maintenance of an administrative disability category which defines those 'unable to work' in order to control labour force participation (Finkelstein 1991; Stone 1984; Priestley 1997a).

If such arguments are correctly premised then there are important implications for the movement. In order to dismantle the administrative segregation of disabled people, and the disabling cultural values which underpin it, it would be necessary to dismantle some of the most fundamental mechanisms of structural state control. Consequently, any attempt by the disabled people's movement to reclaim and redefine popular discourses of disability and welfare also challenges the social relations of production and reproduction within a capitalist economy. All this takes us a very long way away from 'community care'. However, if we are to accept the agenda of the disabled people's movement, that is probably where we ought to be.

CHAPTER 9

Summary and Conclusions

The content of this study arose from some very specific concerns expressed by disabled people involved with the Derbyshire Coalition of Disabled People and the Derbyshire Centre for Integrated Living in late 1993 and early 1994. At that time they were becoming increasingly concerned that implementation of the 1990 NHS and Community Care Act might undermine their ability to provide support to disabled people within an integrated living approach. In particular, they were aware of a significant conflict of values over the definition of quality standards for the contracted services which they sought to provide under the new purchasing arrangements. This conflict was all the more significant because, taken at face value, the philosophy of integrated living seemed to exemplify all the key rhetorical goals of community care. The evidence which I have presented in this study suggests that supports towards integrated living are indeed threatened by the implementation of community care policy. More generally, community care policy making in the 1990s has continued to reproduce disabling cultural values and social relations in the wider world. Despite the rhetoric of 'choice' and 'independence', the reality has all too often undermined those ends.

First, the preoccupation with 'care' has reinforced the association between disability and personal tragedy (rather than structural exclusion). The analysis of policy documentation showed in some detail how the discourse of care has been primarily concerned with defining those who should be cared for, those who should do the caring and the way in which this relationship should be organised. Thus, there has been a consistent failure to challenge the structured dependency of disabled people which gives rise to this 'need' for care in the first place. The emergence of the disabled people's movement has offered much resistance to such perceptions by generating a culture of participation. In particular, centres for independent/integrated living have demonstrated how disabled people can be actively engaged in the management and delivery of new forms of participative welfare. However, the experience of disabled people who use self-managed support schemes suggests that resource allocation through care assessment and management continues to constrain the options for 'choice' and 'independence' within narrow definitions of personal care and limited domestic assistance.

Second, the preoccupation with individual 'packages of care' has reinforced the currency of individual models of disability which locate the problem within the body (rather than within the systems and structures of a disabling society). The rhetoric of community care policy making, as evidenced in the primary legislation and subsequent guidance, is restricted to the assessment of individual needs, the purchasing of individualised packages and the provision of individualised services. Conversely, the development of the disabled people's movement has promoted social models of disability which emphasise the commonality of disabled people's oppression and which call for policy responses based on their collective needs. As this study shows, the movement for independent/integrated living has developed a variety of responses within this philosophy. However, the analysis of marketisation suggests that current purchasing arrangements favour individualised forms of 'independent living' over those which seek to address collective needs through 'integrated living'. As the case study illustrates, marketisation (within a climate of resource rationing) creates pressure towards discrete, individualised, personal support services and away from collective advocacy, community development and campaigning.

Third, the maintenance of disabled people within a separate administrative category of welfare production reinforces the cultural construction of disability as otherness. Historically, the segregation of disabled people from the 'community' has been produced by structural changes in the labour market and by the specific development of the British welfare state. The disabled people's movement has challenged this tradition of segregative welfare production on many fronts – especially through critiques of residential institutions and the promotion of integrated living alternatives. Similarly, the rhetorical agenda for community care policy making has promoted the production of welfare within non-institutional settings. However, the experience of service users in Derbyshire suggests that the purchasing framework for resource allocation still fails to provide the resources for effective community participation. Until social needs are accorded the same resource priority as physical and domestic needs, many disabled people will remain confined within their homes and denied the opportunity to contribute to the lives of their communities. Even with such resources, the goal of community integration can never become a reality unless we also pay attention to the removal of disabling barriers in the wider world.

For the primary research participants, these contradictions were exemplified in the definition of quality standards for community care purchasing and evaluation. As this study shows, the standards generated by government departments and local authorities have been dominated by a concern with the process of individualised care production. They are framed within an individual model of disability and are restricted to the consideration of discrete services. This agenda for policy evaluation assumes that disabled people are dependent upon 'care', that disabled people's needs are individual and predominantly physical, and that disabled people are 'users' rather than equal citizens. By contrast, the agenda of integrated living suggests that welfare interventions should be evaluated against measures of social participation, social integration and true equality. A social model approach to quality measurement suggests that the focus should be on outcomes and that the emphasis should be on removing disabling barriers. Moreover, it requires that we shift our gaze beyond the restricted horizons of 'service provision' and search instead for tangible measures of inclusion in society. From this perspective, it is impossible to separate issues of quality from issues of e-quality in the wider social world (Priestley 1995c).

Definitions of 'quality' derived from individual models of disability will always be at variance with those derived from social models and it is therefore no surprise that disabled people's organisations have found themselves at odds with the kind of values embodied in community care implementation. However, as this study shows, the individual model definitions used by policy makers are not simply the intellectual product of civil servants or politicians within government departments. They are inextricably bound up with cultural values about the role of disabled people in society and with the social relations of welfare production in a capitalist economy. They may be bureaucratically defined but they are also culturally embedded and structurally produced. Seen in this broader context, it is no coincidence that British disability policy has tended to favour charity over civil rights, administrative hegemony over user power, familism over community and individualised services over equal citizenship.

I have used this study to explore these conflicts and to assist DCIL in developing their own strategies for negotiating a changing policy environment. Using a grounded theory approach and coparticipatory methods, I have analysed in some detail the competing welfare ideologies of community care and integrated living. By placing my research skills 'at the disposal' of the primary research participants, it was possible for them to define the research agenda and to shape the specific research questions. In retrospect I would not lay any great claim to having produced a piece of truly 'emancipatory' research. However, the fact that it was possible to generate so much data and analysis from such open-ended beginnings is in itself a testament to the potential for working in this way. It does at least prove that a committed researcher (working within an accountable institution) can produce academically credible work in partnership with disabled people's organisations.

Those organisations face an unenviable task – how to fit the 'square peg' of inclusive citizenship into the 'round hole' of community care 'services'. These kind of tensions were central to the experiences of the research participants in Derbyshire. They also tell us something about strategies for change. At a local level, disabled people will need effective forms of self-organisation and self-empowerment. They will need to engage directly with established political bureaucracies and to challenge powerful professional interest groups. They will need to build strong collaborative partnerships and present a united voice. In a climate of intense resource rationing new funds are unlikely to be won. The campaign for local change will need to focus on demands for a transfer of existing resources from traditional dependency-creating services (in both the public and voluntary sector) towards the removal of disabling barriers and the creation of innovative support structures in which disabled people exercise participation and control.

This focus on participation, social integration and equality requires change in many contexts and at many levels. As the case study shows, it is possible to change services at a local level (although there may be many battles in 'winning the hearts and minds' of discretionary local actors). However, the goals of integrated living also require more far reaching changes. Recent developments on civil rights and direct payments suggest that, while some change is possible at a national level, legislation is unlikely to provide a long-term solution. Rather, the integrated living agenda suggests that a more fundamental redefinition of the social relations of production and reproduction is required. Ultimately, the liberation of disabled people requires us to question both the economic imperatives of capital accumulation and the legitimacy of a welfare state in crisis.

In order to understand the dynamics of this debate, and to develop strategies for change, we need to understand the relationship between disabling values and disabling structures. Welfare policies do not emerge or compete in a simple pluralistic way and the relative influence of competing values is contingent upon the distribution of power within a given society at a given time. It would therefore be naive to consider contemporary policy debates about disability as a simple conflict of 'values'. We have to ask where such values come from and why some values acquire dominance over others. Indeed, where there are underlying structural causes at work in the creation of disabling barriers these can only be explained with reference to material relations of power. Yet this kind of analysis leaves the disabled people's movement with a paradox.

On the one hand, the identity of the disabled people's movement is grounded in a sense of commonality derived from social models of disability, which demonstrate how socio-economic forces structure the experience of people with impairments within a capitalist society. On the other hand, the very existence of the movement is premised upon experiences of self-empowerment and a belief in the potency of collective action as a catalyst for change within that same structure. Clearly then, the story of independent living has much to convey about the relative significance of structure and agency in a changing welfare state.

If we believe that policy is shaped by the values of politicians and street level bureaucrats within welfare institutions, then our strategies for change will be directed towards winning the 'hearts and minds' of those institutions. Conversely, if we believe that both the values and the institutions themselves have been produced by material relations of production and reproduction, then there may seem little point in engaging directly with either. There is, of course, a reductionist tendency in both these positions. It would be more accurate to suggest, as Juckes and Barresi (1993, p.211) do, that it is the combination of subjective interpretation and objective social positioning which provides a basis for conscious political action (this action and the interpretation are then fed back into society through culture). As the self-organisation of disabled people shows, people with grievances have a great capacity to think and act subjectively, although the stance from which they do so is inevitably 'positioned' by their objective location within the social relations of production and reproduction.

The self-organisation of disabled people has continued to open up spaces in which new narratives of disability have been forged and in which collective identities have been strengthened. As Giddins (1991, p.54) accepts, this kind of identity, or reflexivity, is contingent upon 'the capacity to keep a particular narrative going'. That the disabled people's movement has not only been able to keep enabling narratives 'going' under such adverse circumstances but also to widen their political currency is testament to its counter-hegemonic potential (Campbell and Oliver 1996; Morrison and Finkelstein 1993; Oliver 1990).

Disabled people's organisations in Britain have made many advances: the birth of integrated living projects; the acceptance of a 'needs-led' agenda for community care; the partial implementation of direct payments and anti-discriminatory legislation; the incorporation of social model thinking into the mainstream of European Union and United Nations policy making. These are no small achievements and they have all been contingent upon the effective self-organisation of disabled people locally, nationally and globally. As Oliver (1990, p.112) concludes:

> disabled people cannot look to either the welfare state or traditional political activities to effect considerable material and social improvements in the quality of their lives. The only hope, therefore, is that the disability movement will continue to grow in strength and consequently have a substantial impact on the politics of welfare provision.

Yet there are many barriers to these processes. Street level bureaucracy, bureaucratic politics and marketisation all impact to the detriment of disabled people's self-organisation. In more general terms, British disability policy making is not played out on a level field and the policy community is weighted against the disabled people's movement. Moreover, there is much evidence that the structured dependency inherent in British disability policy making has been socially produced by the developmental processes of a capitalist economy operating within a patriarchal and imperialist legacy (Finkelstein 1981; Oliver 1990; Townsend 1981; Williams 1989).

However, it is important to avoid too deterministic an analysis. Widespread commodification and consumerism have exerted a significant counter force to the hierarchical constraints inherent in Fordist modes of production and welfare. The breakdown of rationalist bureaucracies, traditional forms of social stratification and national boundaries opens up possibilities for new forms of social organisation and political alignment. In particular, the emergence of new social movements indicates the existence of significant counter-cultures which challenge disabling social relations throughout the world. There is a sense then in which the postmodern (or late modern) condition requires a new response. As old forms of commonality and collective action have crumbled in the face of 'identity politics', so new boundaries of stratification and division have been drawn. Yet, increasingly we are also beginning to recognise the poverty of a politics based solely on difference.

The search is on for new forms of solidarity and communalism, for new forms of collective welfare production and for a new politics which celebrates difference while rejecting the differential incorporation which that difference so often reflects. Thus, Leonard (1997) sees the major social movements of our time as characterised by a convergence of interests, in that they share both a 'respect for diversity and a commitment to fight poverty and exploitation'. Within this 'confederation of diversities', the disabled people's movement is an indispensable ally. More than any other contemporary movement, it embodies both the celebration of difference and the common goal of social and economic inclusion.

To envisage a society which includes disabled people on equal terms with full participation is to envisage a society which has redefined its relationship to welfare, work and citizenship in ways which would benefit all other marginalised and oppressed groups. The achievement of this enabling society requires not only enhanced 'services', but also enhanced civil rights and citizenship. Such a restructuring would require major changes in the social relations of welfare production. It would threaten powerful interest groups and it would challenge the legitimacy of a welfare state in crisis. Ultimately, the achievement of participation and equality for disabled people would challenge the economic imperatives of capital accumulation. In this sense, the political agenda of integrated living reaches to the root causes of disability itself.

In the campaign for change we would rather not be starting from here. Yet, there is some guarded optimism that now may be a good time to act. Current debates about the future of welfare production and citizenship provide opportunities for the disabled people's movement to seek new alliances. Policy making communities in the 1990s are avidly engaged in wide-ranging debates about the whole future of welfare production, about citizenship and about constitutional change. There has been much talk about communitarian politics, about a Bill of Rights and about electoral reform. The involvement of disabled people's organisations with Charter 88 and the emerging links between BCODP and Liberty bring such debates directly into the movement.

The election of a Labour government in May 1997 heightened the significance of these debates. It is perhaps still too early to predict the scope for detailed policy change. Fortunes have been mixed. It is perhaps significant that government accountability to disabled people has been transferred from 'social security' to 'employment' and that there are promises to bolster anti-discriminatory legislation (although no specific plans emerged in the first Queen's speech). Speaking to the Labour Party conference on 1 October 1997 the Equal Opportunities Minister, Andrew Smith, announced that the government would move to implement its manifesto commitment to 'comprehensive and enforceable rights for disabled people' (DfEE press release 304/7). A Ministerial Task Force, including disabled people's organisations, is to undertake consultation. The provisions of the Disability Discrimination Act relating to 'goods and services' will be implemented and there will be moves towards the establishment of a Disability Rights Commission. October 1997, also saw the publication of the government's first Green Paper on special educational needs, promising further moves towards social inclusion.

As early as July 1997, the new government were promising £200 million from the windfall levy to 'help disabled people back into work' (Department of Social Security press release, 29 July 1997). However, by the end of the same year, possible benefit cuts were revealed (including the scrapping of Disability Living Allowance). In addition, government representatives were talking openly about new limits on 'community care'. By Christmas, the honeymoon was over, and the papers were once more carrying photographs of disability activists protesting at the gates of Downing Street.

The barriers to integrated living are many and varied. They range from the individual attitudes of front-line staff to the bureaucratic politics of purchasing authorities; from the detail of legislative constraint to the macro socio-economic environment of welfare capitalism in a globalising economy. However, there is some scope for change, although we should be pragmatic about the prospects for improvement in the short to medium term. There are many battles to be won and the sheer scale of those which remain requires the maintenance of a visionary agenda for the liberation of disabled people. As the example of disabled people's organisations in Derbyshire shows, acting locally and thinking globally has proved to be good maxim for action.

Glossary

(Abbreviated forms are cited in full the first time they appear in the text)

ABA	Association of Blind Asians
BCODP	British Council Of Disabled People
CIL	Centre for Independent/Integrated Living
CILG	Coventry Independent Living Group
CC	Derbyshire County Council
DCDP	Derbyshire Coalition of Disabled People
DCIL	Derbyshire Centre for Integrated Living
DHSS	Department of Health and Social Security
DIAL	Derbyshire/Disability Information Advice Line
DIG	Disablement Income Group
DoH	Department of Health
DPI	Disabled Peoples' International
DPOs	Disabled People's Organisations
GLAD	Greater London Association of Disabled People
HCIL	Hampshire Centre for Independent Living
ILF	Independent Living Fund
IYDP	International Year of Disabled People
LOP	Living Options Partnership
NFB	National Federation of the Blind
NHS	National Health Service
NLDB	National League of the Blind and Disabled
OPCS	Office of Population Census and Surveys
PAS	Personal Assistance Support

References

Abberley, P. (1987) 'The Concept of Oppression and the Development of a Social Theory of Disability', *Disability, Handicap and Society 2, 1, 5–19.*

Abberley, P. (1992) 'Counting Us Out: a discussion of the OPCS disability surveys', *Disability, Handicap and Society 7, 139–155.*

Abberley, P. (1995) 'Disabling Ideology in Health and Welfare – the case of occupational therapy', *Disability and Society 10, 221–232.*

Abrams, P. (1982) *Historical Sociology.* Shepton Mallet: Open Books.

Ackoff, R. (1976) 'Does quality of life have to be quantified?' *Operational Research Quarterly 27,* 289–303.

Adorno, T. (1973) *Negative Dialectics.* New York: Continuum.

Albrecht, G. (1992) *The Disability Business: Rehabilitation in America.* Newbury Park, CA: Sage.

Alinsky, S. (1971) *Rules for Radicals.* New York: Random House.

Allport, G. (1954) The Nature of Prejudice. Cambridge, MA: Addison-Wesley Publishing Company.

Andrews, F. and McKennel, A. (1980) 'Measures of self-reported well-being', *Social Indicators Research 8, 127–155.*

Association of Directors of Social Services (1993) *Advice on Interpreting the Conditions for spending 85% of the Special Transitional Grant for Community Care for 1993/94 in the Independent Sector.* London: ADSS circular.

Association of Metropolitan Authorities (1990) *Contracts for Social Care: the local authority view.* London: AMA.

Audit Commission (1992a) *Community Care: managing the cascade of change.* London: HMSO.

Audit Commission (1992b) *The Community Revolution: personal social services and community care.* London: HMSO.

Audit Commission (1992c) *Chartering a Course.* London: HMSO.

Audit Commission (1993a) *Taking Care: Progress with Care in the Community.* London: Audit Commission.

Audit Commission (1993b) *Staying on Course: The Second Year of the Citizen's Charter Indicators.* London: HMSO.

Audit Commission (1994) *Watching their Figures: a guide to the Citizen's Charter indicators.* London: HMSO.

Baker, F. and Intagliata, J. (1982) 'Quality of life in the evaluation of community support systems', *Evaluation and Program Planning 5, 69–79.*

Baldwin, S. and Lunt, N. (1996) *Charging Ahead: the development of local authority charging policies for community care.* Bristol, The Policy Press.

Ballard, R. (1979) 'Ethnic Minorities and the Social Services'. In V. Khan (ed) (1979) *Minority Families in Britain: support and stress.* London: Macmillan.

Barnes, C. (1990) *Cabbage Syndrome: the social construction of dependence.* Lewes: Falmer.

Barnes, C. (1991) *Disabled People in Britain and Discrimination: a case for anti-discrimination legislation.* London: Hurst/BCODP.

Barnes, C. (1992a) 'Qualitative Research: valuable or irrelevant?', Disability, Handicap and Society 7, 2, 139–155.

Barnes, C. (1992b) *Disabling Imagery: An Exploration of Media Portrayals of Disabled People.* Derby: BCODP.

Barnes, C. (1996a) 'Theories of Disability and the Origins of the Oppression of Disabled People in Western Society'. In L. Barton (ed) (1996a) *Disability and Society.* London: Longman.

Barnes, C. (1996b) Deaf and Disabled People Together – a disability perspective on the historical development of divisions. London: paper presented at the conference on 'Deaf and Disabled People – Towards a New Understanding' on 7–8 December 1996, Policy Studies Institute/Association of Deaf Service Users and Providers.

Barnes, C. (1996c) 'From National to Local: BCODP Research on the Information Needs of Local Disability Organisations'. In B. Walker (ed) (1996) Disability Rights: A Symposium of the European Regions. Headley, Hampshire: Hampshire Coalition of Disabled People.

Barnes, C. (1997) *Older People's Perceptions of Direct Payments and Self-Operated Support Systems.* Leeds: Disability Research Unit, University of Leeds.

Barnes, C. and Mercer, G. (eds) (1996) *Exploring the Divide: illness and disability.* Leeds: Disability Press.

Barnes, C., McCarthy, M. and Comerford, S. (1995) *Assessment, Accountability and Independent Living: confirmation and clarification of a disability led perspective.* Coventry, report of a conference organised by Coventry Independent Living Group (CLIG) and Coventry Social Services Department, Coombe Abbey, Coventry, 23/24 May 1995.

Barnes, C. and Oliver, M. (1995) 'Disability Rights: rhetoric and reality in the UK', *Disability and Society 10,* 1, 111–117.

Barnes, M. and Shardlow, P. (1996) 'Identity Crisis: Mental Health user groups and the "problem of identity".' In C. Barnes and G. Mercer (eds) (1996) *Exploring the Divide: illness and disability.* Leeds: Disability Press.

Barrett, S. and Fudge, C. (eds) (1981) *Policy and Action.* London: Methuen.

Barton, L. (ed) (1996a) *Disability and Society: emerging issues and insights.* Harlow: Longman.

Barton, L. (1996b) 'Segregated special education: some critical observations'. In G. Zarb (1996) *Removing Disabling Barrriers.* London: Policy Studies Institute.

Bauer, M. and Cohen, E. (1983) 'The Invisibility of Power in Economics: beyond markets and hierachies'. In A. Francis, J. Turk and P. Williams (eds) (1983) *Power, Efficiency and Institutions.* London: Heinemann Educational Books.

Bauer, R. (1966) 'Detection and Anticipation of Impact: the nature of the task'. In R. Bauer (ed) (1966) *Social Indicators.* Cambridge, Mass.: MIT Press.

Becker, H. (1963) *Outsiders.* New York: Free Press.

Begum, N. (1990) *Burden of Gratitude: Women with disabilities receiving personal care.* Coventry: University of Warwick.

Begum, N. (1992) *...Something To Be Proud Of...: the lives of Asian disabled people and carers in Waltham Forest.* Waltham Forest: Waltham Forest Race Relations Unit.

Beier, A. (1985) *Masterless Men: The vagrancy problem in England 1560–1640.* London: Methuen.

Beresford, P. and Campbell, J. (1994) 'Disabled people, service users, user involvement and representation', *Disability and Society 9,* 3, 315–325.

Berger, J. (1972) *Ways of Seeing.* Harmondsworth: Penguin/BBC.

Berthoud, R. (1996) 'Social security, poverty and disabled people'. In G. Zarb (1996) *Removing Disabling Barrriers*. London: Policy Studies Institute.

Berthoud, R., Lakey, J. and McKay, S. (1993) *The Economic Problems of Disabled People*. London: Policy Studies Institute.

Bloom, B. (1978) *Social Indicators and Health Care policy*. Louisville, Kentucky, paper presented at the second National Needs Assessment Conference, March 1978.

Blumer, H. (1946) 'Collective Behaviour'. In A. Lee (ed) (1946) *New Outlines of the Principles of Sociology*. New York: Barnes and Noble.

Blunden, R. (1988) 'Quality of life in persons with disabilities: issues in the development of services'. In R. Brown (ed) (1988) *Quality of Life for Handicapped People*. London: Croom Helm.

Boal, A., McBride, C. and McBride, M. (1989) *Theatre of the Oppressed*. London: Pluto.

Boggs, C. (1986) *Social Movements and Political Power*. Philadelphia: Temple University Press.

Bond, J. (1991) *The politics of care-giving: the professionalization of informal care*. Manchester, paper presented to the British Sociological Association Conference.

Bornat, J., Phillipson, C. and Ward, S. (1985) *A Manifesto for Old Age*. London: Pluto.

Bourne, J. (1980) 'Cheerleaders and Ombudsmen: the sociology of race relations in Britian', *Race and Class XXI*, 331–352.

Boyne, R. and Rattansi (eds) (1990) *Postmodernism and Society*. Basingstoke: Macmillan.

Bracking, S. (1993) 'An Introduction to the Idea of Independent Integrated Living'. In C. Barnes (ed) (1993) *Making Our Own Choices: independent living, personal assistance and disabled people*. Clay Cross: British Council of Organisations of Disabled People.

Bradley, V. (1990) 'Conceptual Issues in Quality Assurance'. In V. Bradley and H. Bersani (eds) (1990) *Quality Assurance for Individuals with Developmental Disabilities*. Baltimore: Paul H. Brookes.

Bradley, V. and Bersani, H. (eds) (1990) *Quality Assurance for Individuals with Developmental Disabilities*. Baltimore: Paul H. Brookes.

Brattgard, S. (1972) 'Sweden: Fokus: a way of life for living'. In D. Lancaster-Gaye (ed) (1972) *Personal Relationships, the Handicapped and the Community*. London: Routledge and Kegan Paul.

Brisenden, S. (1989) 'A Charter for Personal Care', *Progress 16* (published by the Disablement Income Group).

Brown, H. and Smith, H. (1992) *Normalisation: a reader for the nineties*. London: Tavistock.

Brown, R. (ed) (1988) *Quality of Life for Handicapped People*. London: Croom Helm.

Brown, R., Bayer, M. and MacFarlane, C. (1988) 'Quality of life amongst handicapped adults'. In R. Brown (ed) (1988) *Quality of Life for Handicapped People*. London: Croom Helm.

Burch, M. and Wood, B. (1989, 2nd edition) *Public Policy in Britain*. Oxford: Basil Blackwell.

Busfield, J. (1989) 'Sexism and Patriarchy', *Sociology 23*, 343–364.

Bush, J., Chen, M. and Patrick, D. (1973) 'Health Status Index in Cost-effectiveness: analysis of PKU Program'. In R. Berg (ed) (1973) *Health Status Indexes*. Chicago: Hospital Research and Educational Trust.

Campbell, D. and Harris, D. (1993) 'Flexibility in long-term contractual relationships: the role of cooperation', *Journal of Law and Society 20*, 166–191.

Campbell, J. and Gillespie-Sells, K. (1988) *Good Guide to Equality Training*. London: CCETSW Disability Resource Team.

Campbell, J. and Oliver, M. (1996) *Disability Politics: understanding our past, changing our future*. London: Routledge.

Campling, J. (1981) *Images of Ourselves: women with disabilities talking.* London: Routledge.

Carr-Hill, R. (1984) 'The Political Choice of Social Indicators', *Quality and Quantity 18,* 173–191.

Chadwick, A. (1996) 'Knowledge, Power and the Disability Discrimination Bill', *Disability and Society 11,* 1, 25–40.

Chetwynd, M. and Ritchie, J. (1996) *The Cost of Care: The impact of charging on the lives of disabled people.* Bristol: The Policy Press.

Chinnery, B. (1991) 'Equal Opportunities for disabled people in the caring professions: window dressing or commitment?', *Disability, Handicap and Society 6,* 3, 253–258.

Cixous, H. (1986) 'Sorties'. In H. Cixous and C. Clement (eds) (1986) *The Newly Born Woman.* Manchester: Manchester University Press.

Clay, R. (1909) *The mediaeval hospitals of England.* London: Methuen and Co.

Coats, A. (1976) 'The relief of poverty, attitudes to labour, and economic change in England, 1660–1782', *International Review of Social History 21,* 98–115.

Cochrane, A. (1991) 'The Changing Face of Local Government: restructuring for the 1990s', *Public Administration 69,* 3, 281–302.

Cohen, J. (1985) 'Strategy or Identity: new theoretical paradigms and contemporary social movements', *Social Research 52,* 663–716.

Common, R. and Flynn, N. (1992) *Contracting for Care.* York: Joseph Rowntree Foundation.

Connelly, N. (1990) *Raising Voices: social services departments and people with disabilities.* London: Policy Studies Institute.

Conroy, J. and Feinstein, C. (1990) 'A new way of thinking about quality'. In V. Bradley and H. Bersani (eds) (1990) *Quality Assurance for Individuals with Developmental Disabilities.* Baltimore: Paul H. Brookes.

Coward, R. (1984) *Female Desire.* London: Paladin.

Craig, G. (undated) *Cash or Care: A Question of Choice?* York: Social Policy Research Unit.

Craig, G. and Manthorpe, J. (1996) *Wiped off the map? – local government reorganisation and community care.* Kingston upon Hull: University of Lincolnshire and Humberside.

Crawford, T. and Naditch, M. (1970) 'Relative Deprivation, Powerlessness, and Militancy: the psychology of social protest', *Psychiatry 33,* 208–233.

Crosby, N. (1994) *Derbyshire Centre for Integrated Living: measuring capacity for strategic development.* Ripley: DCIL.

Cross, M. (1982) 'The manufacture of marginality'. In E. Cashmore and B. Tyroyna (eds) (1982) *Black Youth in Crisis.* London: Sage/Open University Press.

Cross, M. (1994) 'Abuse'. In L. Kieth (1994) *Mustn't Grumble.* London: Women's Press.

Crouch, C. and Marquand, D. (eds) (1989) *The New Centralism: Britain Out of Step with Europe?* Oxford: Basil Blackwell.

Culyer, A. (1990) 'Commodities, characteristics of commodities, characteristics of people, utilities, and the quality of life'. In S. Baldwin, C. Godfrey and C. Propper (eds) (1990) *Quality of Life: perspectives and policies.* London: Routledge.

Cumberbatch, G. and Negrine, R. (1992) *Images of Disability on Television.* London: Routledge.

Cummings, J. (1988) 'Options in Day Service Provision'. In A. Leighton (ed) (1988) *Mental Handicap in the Community.* Cambridge: Woodhead-Falkner.

d'Abboville, E. (1991) 'Social Work in an Organisation of Disabled People'. In M. Oliver (ed) (1991) *Social work: disabled people and disabling environments.* London: Jessica Kingsley.

Dalley, G. (1988) *Ideologies of Caring: Rethinking Community and Collectivism.* London: Macmillan.

Dalley, G. (1991) *Disability and Social Policy.* London: Policy Studies Institute.

Darke, P. (1994) 'The Elephant Man: an analysis from a disabled perspective', *Disability, Handicap and Society 9,* 327–342.

Daunt, S. (1996) *Home is the Hero?: Disability and Masculinity in Post-1918 Literature.* Dublin: Trinity College Dublin, M.Litt. thesis (unpublished).

Davidson, I., Woodill, G. and Bredberg, E. (1994) 'Images of Disability in 19th Century British Children's Literature', *Disability and Society 9,* 1, 33–46.

Davies, B. and Challis, D. (1986) *Matching Resources to Needs in Community Care.* Aldershot: Gower.

Davies, K., Dickey, J. and Stratford, T. (1987) *Out of Focus.* London: Women's Press.

Davis, K. (1981) '28–38 Grove Road: accommodation and care in a community setting'. In A. Brechin, P. Liddiard and J. Swain (eds) (1981) *Handicap in a Social World.* London: Hodder and Stoughton.

Davis, K. (1993) 'On the Movement'. In J. Swain, V. Finkelstein, S. French and M. Oliver (eds) (1993) *Disabling Barriers: Enabling Environments.* Milton Keynes: Open University Press/SAGE.

Davis, K. (1994) 'Disability and legislation'. In S. French (ed) (1994) *On Equal Terms: working with disabled people.* Oxford: Butterworth/Heinemann.

Davis, K. (1995) 'A Family Affair', *Coalition,* June 1995, 5–9.

Davis, K. and Mullender, A. (1993) *Ten Turbulent Years: a review of the work of the Derbyshire Coalition of Disabled People.* Nottingham: Centre for Social Action, School of Social Studies, University of Nottingham.

Davis, M. (1993) 'Personal Assistance – notes on the historical context'. In C. Barnes (ed) (1993) *Making Our Own Choices: independent living, personal assistance and disabled people.* Clay Cross: British Council of Organisations of Disabled People.

De Beauvoir, S. (1976) *The Second Sex.* Harmondsworth: Penguin.

Deegan, M. and Brooks, N. (eds) (1995) *Women and Disability: The Double Handicap.* New Brunswick, NJ: Transition Books.

De Hoog, R. (1985) 'Human services contracting, environmental, behavioural, and organizational conditions', *Administration and Society 16,* 427–454.

De Jasay, A. (1992) *Choice, Contract, Consent: a restatement of liberalism.* London: Institute of Economic Affairs.

De Yong, G. (1981) 'The Movement for Independent Living: origins, ideology, and implications for disability research'. In A. Brechin, P. Liddiard and J. Swain (eds) (1981) *Handicap in a Social World.* London: Hodder and Stoughton.

De Yong, G. (1983) 'Defining and Implementing the Independent Living Concept'. In N. Crewe and I. Zola (eds) (1983) *Independent Living for Physically Disabled People.* London: Jossey-Bass.

Department of Health (1992) *Committed to Quality: Quality Assurance in Social Services Departments.* London: HMSO.

Department of Health (1993) *Implementing Community Care for Younger People with Physical and Sensory Disabilities.* London: Department of Health.

Department of Health (1994) *Social Care Markets: Progress and Prospects.* London: HMSO.

Department of Health, Department of Social Security, Welsh Office, Scottish Office (1989) *Caring for People: Community Care in the Next Decade and Beyond.* London: HMSO.

Department of Health and Social Security (1993) *Community Care: Funding from April 1993: Government Response to the Third Report from the Health Committee Session 1992–93.* London: HMSO, Cm 2188.

Department of Health, Department of Social Security (1990) *Community Care in the Next Decade and Beyond: policy guidance.* London: HMSO.

Department of Health, Price Waterhouse (1991) *Implementing Community Care: purchaser, commissioner and provider roles.* London: HMSO.

Department of Health, Social Services Inspectorate (1993) *Inspecting for Quality: developing quality standards for home support services: a handbook for social services managers, inspectors and users of services and their relatives and friends.* London: HMSO.

Department of Health, Social Services Inspectorate, Scottish Office, Social Work Services Group (1991a) *Care Management and Assessment: summary of practice guidance.* London: HMSO/Scottish Office, Social Work Services Group.

Department of Health, Social Services Inspectorate, Scottish Office, Social Work Services Group (1991b) *Care Management and Assessment: managers' guide.* London: HMSO/Scottish Office, Social Work Services Group.

Department of Health, Social Services Inspectorate, Scottish Office, Social Work Services Group (1991c) *Care Management and Assessment: practitioners' guide.* London: HMSO/Scottish Office, Social Work Services Group.

DiMaggio, P. and Powell, W. (1983) 'The iron cage revisited: institutional isomorphism and collective rationality in organisational fields', *American Sociological Review 48,* 147–160.

Disability Alliance (1987) *Poverty and Disability, Breaking the Link: The Case for a Comprehensive Disability Income.* London: Disability Alliance.

Disablement Income Group (DIG) (1996) *Personal Assistance Support Schemes and the Introduction of Direct Payments: A report and recommendations.* London: DIG.

Dols, M. (1987) 'Insanity and its Treatment in Islamic Society', *Medical History 31,* 1–14.

Drake, R. (1996) 'Charities, Authority and Disabled People: a qualitative study', *Disability and Society 11,* 1, 5–23.

Driedger, D. (1989) *The Last Civil Rights Movement.* London: Hurst and Co.

Driedger, D. and Gray, S. (1992) *Imprinting Our Image: an international anthology by women with disabilities.* Charlottetown, P.E.I.: Gynergy.

Drummond, M. (1986) *Studies in Economic Appraisal in Health Care, vol. 2.* Oxford: Oxford University Press.

Du Bois, W. (1969 [1903]) *The Souls of Black Folk.* New York: New American Library.

Duncan, S. and Goodwin, M. (1988) *The Local State and Uneven Development.* London: Polity Press.

Dutton, K. (1996) *The Perfectable Body.* London: Cassell.

Etzioni, A. (1995) *The Spirit of Community.* London: Fontana.

Evan, W. (1963) Comment [on Macaulay (1963) op cit.], *American Sociological Review 28,* 67–69.

Evans, C (1996) 'Disability, discrimination and local authority social services 2: users' perspectives'. In G. Zarb (1996) *Removing Disabling Barrriers.* London: Policy Studies Institute.

Evans, J. (1993) 'The Role of Centres of Independent/Integrated Living'. In C. Barnes (ed) (1993) *Making Our Own Choices: independent living, personal assistance and disabled people.* Clay Cross: BCODP.

Eyerman, R. and Jamison, A. (1991) *Social Movements: a cognitive approach*. Cambridge: Polity Press.

Fanon, F. (1967) *Black Skins: White Masks*. New York: Grove.

Featherstone, M., Hepworth, M., Turner, B. (1991) *The body: social process and cultural theory*. London: Sage.

Finch, J. (1990) 'The politics of community care in Britain'. In C. Ungerson (ed) (1990) *Gender and Caring*. Hemel Hempstead: Harvester Wheatsheaf.

Finkelstein, V. (1975) 'To Deny or Not to Deny Disability?', *Magic carpet XXVII*, 1, 31–38.

Finkelstein, V. (1980) *Attitudes and Disabled People: issues for discussion*. New York: World Rehabilitation Fund – monograph 5.

Finkelstein, V. (1981) 'Disability and the Helper/Helped Relationship. An Historical View'. In A. Brechin, P. Liddiard and J. Swain (eds) (1981) *Handicap in a Social World*. London: Hodder and Stoughton.

Finkelstein, V. (1991) 'Disability: an Administrative Challenge? (the health and welfare heritage)'. In M. Oliver (ed) (1991) *Social Work: disabled people and disabling environments*. London: Jessica Kingsley.

Finkelstein, V. (1993) 'The Commonality of Disability'. In J. Swain, V. Finkelstein, S. French and M. Oliver (eds) (1993) *Disabling Barriers: Enabling Environments*. Milton Keynes, Open University Press/SAGE.

Finkelstein, V. and Stuart, O. (1996) 'Developing New Services'. In G. Hales (ed) (1996) *Beyond Disability: Towards an Enabling Society*. London: Sage/Open University.

Flanagan, J. (1978) 'A research approach to improving our quality of life', *American Psychologist 33*, 138–147.

Flax, M. (1972) *A Study in Comparative Urban Indicators: conditions in 18 large metropolitan areas*. Washington, DC: The Urban Institute.

Flynn, N. (1988) 'A consumer-oriented culture', *Public Money and Management 8*, 27–31.

Ford, C. and Shaw, R. (1993) 'Managing a Personal Assistant'. In C. Barnes (ed) (1993) *Making Our Own Choices: independent living, personal assistance and disabled people*. Clay Cross: British Council of Organisations of Disabled People.

Foucault, M. (1970) *The Order of Things*. New York: Random House.

Foucault, M. (1973) *Birth of the Clinic*. London: Tavistock.

Foucault, M. (1977) *Discipline and Punish*. New York: Pantheon.

Fox, N. (1995) 'Postmodern perspectives on care: the vigil and the gift', *Critical Social Policy 44/45*, 107–125.

Fraser, N. (1987) 'Women, Welfare, and the Politics of Need Interpretation', *Hypatia: a Journal of Feminist Philosophy 2*, 103–122.

Freeman, J. (1973) 'The origins of the Women's Liberation Movement', *American Journal of Sociology 78*, 792–811.

Freidson, E. (1970) *Profession of Medicine: a study of the sociology of applied knowledge*. London: Harper and Row.

Freidson, E. (1975) 'Dilemmas in the doctor patient relationship'. In C. Cox and A. Mead (eds) (1975) *A Sociology of Medical Practice*. London: Collier-Macmillan.

French, S. (1988) 'Experiences of disabled health and caring professionals', *Sociology of Health and Illness 10*, 2, 170–188.

French, S. (1993) 'Disability, impairment or something in between'. In J. Swain, V. Finkelstein, S. French and M. Oliver (eds) (1993) *Disabling Barriers: Enabling Environments*. Milton Keynes, Open University Press/Sage.

French, S. (1994) 'Disabled Health and Welfare Professionals'. In S. French (ed) (1994) *On Equal Terms: working with disabled people.* Oxford: Butterworth/Heinemann.

French, S. (1996) 'Simulation exercises in disability awareness training: a critique'. In G. Hales (ed) (1996) *Beyond Disability: towards an enabling society.* London: Sage/Open University.

Friedman, M. and Friedman, R. (1980) *Free to Choose.* Harmondsworth: Penguin.

Garland, R. (1995) *The Eye of the Beholder: deformity and disability in the Graeco-Roman World.* London: Gerald Duckworth and Co. Ltd.

George, L. and Bearon, L. (1980) *Quality of Life in Older Persons.* New York: Human Sciences Press.

George, V. and Wilding, P. (1976) *Ideology and Social Welfare.* London: RKP.

Gerber, D. (1990) Listening to Disabled People: the problem of voice and authority in Robert B. Edgerton's the 'Cloak of Competence', *Disability, Handicap and Society 5,* 3–24.

Gibbs, D. (1994) *The Impact of Trends in the Independent Sector on Disabled and Elderly Service Users,* paper prepared for the Rowntree Foundation Community Care and Disability Committee, Ripley: Derbyshire Centre for Integrated Living.

Gibbs, D. (1995) 'Killing the concept of integrated living', *Equalities News,* December 1995, 6.

Gibbs, D. and Priestley, M. (1996) 'The Social Model and User Involvement'. In B. Walker (ed) (1996) *Disability Rights: A Symposium of the European Regions.* Headley, Hampshire, Hampshire Coalition of Disabled People.

Giddins, A. (1991) *Modernity and Self Identity.* Cambridge: Polity Press.

Gillespie-Sells, K. (1995) 'What do users think about quality: the perspective of people with physical disabilities'. In D. Pilling and G. Watson (eds) (1995) *Evaluating Quality in Services for Disabled and Older People.* London: Jessica Kingsley.

Gillingham, R. and Reece, W. (1979) 'A New Approach to Quality of Life Measurement', *Urban Studies 16,* 329–332.

Gilroy, P. (1987) *There Ain't No Black in the Union Jack.* London: Hutchinson.

Glaser, B. and Strauss, A. (1967) *The discovery of grounded theory: strategies for qualitative research.* New York: Aldine de Gruyter.

Glendinning, C. (1992) '"Community Care": the financial consequences for women'. In C. Glendinning and J. Millar (eds) (1992) *Women and Poverty in Britain: the 1990s.* London: Harvester Wheatsheaf.

Glennerster, H., Power, A. and Travers, T. (1991) 'A New Era for Social Policy: a New Enlightenment or a New Leviathan?', *Journal of Social Policy 20,* 3, 389–414.

Goffman, E. (1961) *Asylums: essays on the social situation of mental patients and other inmates.* Harmondsworth: Penguin.

Gooding, C. (1994) *Disabling Laws, Enabling Acts: disability rights in Britain and America.* London: Pluto Press.

Gooding, C. (1996a) *Blackstone's Guide to the Disability Discrimination Act 1995.* London: Blackstone Press Limited.

Gooding, C. (1996b) 'Employment and disabled people: equal rights or positive action'. In G. Zarb (1996b) *Removing Disabling Barrriers.* London: Policy Studies Institute.

Gough, I. (1979) The Political Economy of Welfare. London: Macmillan.

Gramsci, A. (1971 [1948–51]) *Selections from the Prison Notebooks.* London: Lawrence and Wishart.

Granovetter, M. (1985) 'Economic Action and Social Structure: the problem of embeddedness', *American Journal of Sociology 91,* 481–510.

Grant, B. (1990) *The Deaf Advance: A History of the British Deaf Association.* London: Portland.

Green, H. (1988) *Informal Carers: general household survey 1985*. London: HMSO.

Griffiths, R. (1988) *Community Care: Agenda for Action: a report to the Secretary of State for Social Services*. London: HMSO.

Gutch, R. (1992) *Contracting Lessons from the United States*. London: National Council for Voluntary Organisations.

Gyford, J. (1991) 'The Enabling Council – A Third Model', *Local Government Studies 17*, 1, 1–5.

Habermas, J. (1976) *Legitimation Crisis*. London: Heinemann.

Habermas, J. (1981) 'New Social Movements', *Telos 49*, 33–37.

Habermas, J. (1987) *The Theory of Communicative Competence, Vol. 2: Lifeworld and System*. Boston: Beacon.

Haj, F. (1970) *Disability in Antiquity*. New York: Philosophical Library.

Hall, J. (1976) 'Subjective measures of quality of life in Britain 1971–1975: some developments and trends', *Social Trends 7*, 47–60.

Hansmann, H. (1980) 'The role of nonprofit enterprise', *Yale Law Journal 89*, 835–901.

Harden, I. (1992) *The Contracting State*. Buckingham: Open University Press.

Hardy, B., Wistow, G. and Rhodes, R. (1990) 'Policy Networks and the Implementation of Community Care for People with Mental Handicaps', *Journal of Social Policy 19*, 2, 141–168.

Harvey, D. (1989) *The Condition of Postmodernity*. Oxford: Basil Blackwell.

Hasler, F. (1993) 'Developments in the Disabled People's Movement'. In J. Swain, V. Finkelstein, S. French and M. Oliver (eds) (1993) *Disabling Barriers: Enabling Environments*. Milton Keynes: Open University Press/Sage.

Hayek, F. (1960) *The Constitution of Liberty*. London: Routledge.

Heiser, B. (1996) 'The nature and causes of transport disability in Britain, and how to remove it'. In G. Zarb (1996) *Removing Disabling Barrriers*. London: Policy Studies Institute.

Herbele, R. (1951) *Social Movements: an introduction to political sociology*. New York: Appleton-Century-Crofts.

Herd, D. and Stalker, K. (1996) *Involving Disabled People in Services: A document describing good practice for planners, purchasers and providers*. Edinburgh, Social Work Services Inpsectorate for Scotland.

Hevey, D. (1993) 'The Tragedy Principle: strategies for change in the representation of disabled people'. In J. Swain, V. Finkelstein, S. French and M. Oliver (eds) (1993) *Disabling Barriers: Enabling Environments*. Milton Keynes: Open University Press/Sage.

Higgins, J. (1980) 'Social control theories of social policy', *Journal of Social Policy 9*, 1, 1–23.

Hill, M. (1981) 'The Policy-Implementation Distinction; A Quest for Rational Control'. In S. Barrett and C. Fudge (eds) (1981) *Policy and Action*. London: Methuen.

Hirschman, A. (1970) *Exit, Voice and Loyalty: responses to decline in firms, organisations and states*. Harvard: Harvard University Press.

Hirst, M. (1990) 'Multidimensional Representation of Disablement: a qualitative approach'. In S. Baldwin, C. Godfrey and C. Propper (eds) (1990) *Quality of Life: perspectives and policies*. London: Routledge.

Hjern, B. (1982) 'Implementation Research – The Link Gone Missing', *Journal of Public Policy 2*, 3, 301–308.

HMSO (1990) *Community Care in the Next Decade and Beyond*. London: HMSO.

Hobsbawm, E. (1963) *Primitive Rebels: studies in archaic forms of social movement in the 19th and 20th Centuries*. Manchester: Manchester University Press.

Hogwood, B. (1987) *From Crisis to Complacency? Shaping Public Policy in Britain.* Oxford: Oxford University Press.

House of Commons Health Committee (1993) *Sixth Report: Community Care: The Way Forward.* London: HMSO, HC 482–I.

Hoyes, L. and Means, R. (1993) 'Quasi-Markets and the Reform of Community Care'. In J. LeGrand and W. Bartlett (eds) (1993) *Quasi-Markets and Social Policy.* Basingstoke: Macmillan.

Hoyes, L., Jeffers, S., Lart, R., Means, R. and Taylor, M. (1993) *User Empowerment and the Reform of Community Care.* Bristol: School for Advanced Urban Studies.

Hudson, B. (1994) *Making Sense of Markets in Health and Social Care.* Sunderland: Business Education Publishers.

Hugman, R. (1991) *Power in the Caring Professions.* Basingstoke: Macmillan.

Hunt, P. (ed.) (1966) *Stigma.* London: Chapman.

Hunt, P (1981) 'Settling Accounts with the parasite people: a critique of "A Life Apart"' by E.J. Miller and G.V. Gwynn, *Disability Challenge 1,* 37–50.

Hupe, P. (1990) 'Implementing a Meta-Policy', *Policy and Politics 18,* 3, 181–191.

Hurst, R. (1989) 'Disabled people take the initiative in Strasbourg', *Disability Now,* June 1989.

Huxley, P. and Mohamad, H. (1991) 'The development of a general satisfaction questionnaire for use in programme evaluation', *Social Work and Social Sciences Review 3,* 1, 63–74.

Illich, I. (1975) *Medical Nemesis: the expropriation of health.* London: Calder and Boyars.

Ingstad, B. and Reynolds-Whyte, S. (eds) (1995) *Disability and Culture.* Berkely: University of California Press.

James, E. and Rose-Ackerman, S. (1986) *The Nonprofit Enterprise in Market Economies.* London: Harwood Academic Publishers.

Janowitz, M. (1976) *Social Control of the Welfare State.* New York: Elsevier.

Jeewa, M. (1991) 'Conference address'. In L. Laurie (ed) (1991) *National Conference on Housing and Independent Living.* London: Shelter.

Jewson, N. (1976) 'The disappearance of the sick man from medical cosmology', *Sociology 10,* 225–244.

Johnson, N. (1987) *The Welfare State in Transition: the theory and practice of welfare pluralism.* Brighton: Wheatsheaf.

Jones, A. (1992) 'Civil rights, citizenship and the welfare agenda for the 1990s'. In National Institute for Social Work (1992) *Who Owns Welfare?* London: NISW.

Jones, R. (1996) 'Disability, discrimination and local authority social services 1: the social services context'. In G. Zarb (1996) *Removing Disabling Barrriers.* London: Policy Studies Institute.

Jones, S. (1994) '"Civil-Rights" and the normalisation of Class Rule', *Coalition,* November 1994, 31–36.

Jones-Lee, M. (1976) *The Value of Life: an economic analysis.* London: Martin Robertson and Co.

Jordan, W. (1959) *Philanthropy in England, 1480–1660: a study of the changing patterns of English social aspirations.* London: Allen and Unwin.

Jordanova, L. (1989) *Sexual Visions.* New York: Harvester Wheatsheaf.

Juckes, T. and Barresi, J. (1993) 'The subjective–objective dimension in the individual–society connection: a duality perspective'. *Journal for the Theory of Social Behaviour 23,* 197–216.

Kaplan, R. (1985) 'Quality of Life Measurement'. In P. Koroly (ed) (1985) *Measurement Strategies in Health Psychology.* New York: Wiley.

Katz, S. (1963) 'Studies of illness in the aged: the index of ADL', *Journal of the American Association 185*, 914–919.

Kay, S. (1984) *Issues for Statutory Bodies in the Transition to Integrated Living Services*, London: seminar report on 'Centres for Independent Living', Centre on Environment for the Handicapped.

Kennedy, M. (1990) 'What Quality Assurance Means to Me: expectations of consumers'. In V. Bradley and H. Bersani (eds) (1990) *Quality Assurance for Individuals with Developmental Disabilitites*. Baltimore: Paul H. Brookes.

Kestenbaum, A. (1992) *Cash for Care*. Nottingham, Independent Living Fund.

Kestenbaum, A. (1993a) *Taking care in the market: a study of agency homecare*. London: RADAR/DIG.

Kestenbaum, A. (1993b) *Making Community Care a Reality: The Independent Living Fund 1988–1993*. London: RADAR/DIG.

Kestenbaum, A. (1996) *Independent Living – a review*. York: Joseph Rowntree Foundation.

Kettner, P. and Martin, L. (1987) *Purchase of Service Contracting*. London: Sage.

Kind, P., Gudex, C. and Godfrey, C. (1990) 'Introduction: what are QALYs?'. In S. Baldwin, C. Godfrey and C. Propper (eds) (1990) *Quality of Life: perspectives and policies*. London: Routledge.

Klandermans, B. and Tarrow, S. (1988) 'Mobilization into Social Movements: synthesising European and American approaches'. In B. Klandermans, H. Kreisi and S. Tarrow (1988) *International Social Movement Research*. London: JAI Press Inc.

Klapwijk, A. (1981) 'Het Dorp, an adapted part of the City of Arnhem (The Netherlands) for severely disabled people'. In Development Trust for the Young Disabled (booklet 5/81) (1981) *An International Seminar on the Long-term Care of Disabled People*. London: Development Trust for the Young Disabled.

Klarman, H. (1965) *The Economics of Health*. New York: Columbia University Press.

Knapp, M. (1976) 'Predicting the dimensions of life satisfaction', *Journal of Gerontology 31*, 595–604.

Knapp, M. (1984) *The Economics of Social Care*. London: Macmillan.

Knoll, J. (1990) 'Defining Quality in Residential Services'. In V. Bradley and H. Bersani (eds) (1990) *Quality Assurance for Individuals with Developmental Disabilities*. Baltimore: Paul H. Brookes.

Knox, P. (1980) 'Measures of Accessibility as Social Indicators: a note', *Social Indicators Research 7*, 367–377.

Kramer, R. and Grossman, B. (1987) 'Contracting for social services: process management and resource dependencies', *Social Service Review*, March 1987, 32–55.

Kriegal, L. (1987) 'The crippled in literature'. In A. Gartner and T. Joe (eds) (1987) *Images of the Disabled: Disabling Images*. New York: Praeger.

Kriesi, H. (1988) 'The Interdependence of Structure and Action: some perspectives on the state of the art'. In B. Klandermans, H. Kriesi and S. Tarrow (eds) (1988) *From Structure to Action: comparing social movement research across cultures*. London: JAI Press.

Kristeva, J. (1982) *Power of Horror: an esay in abjection*. New York: Columbia University Press.

Laclau, E. and Mouffe, C. (1985) *Hegemony and Socialist Strategy: towards a radical democratic politics*. London: Verso Press.

Laing, R. (1960) *The Divided Self: An Existential Study in Sanity and Madness*. London: Tavistock.

Lakey, J. (1994) *Caring about Independence: Disabled People and the Independent Living Fund*. London: Policy Studies Institute.

Lamb, B. and Layzell, S. (1994) *Disabled in Britain: Behind Closed Doors*. London: Scope.

Lamb, B. and Layzell, S. (1995) *Disabled in Britain: Counting on Community Care*. London: Scope.

Lawrence, E. (1982) 'In the abundance of water the fool is thirsty'. In Centre for Contemporary Cultural Studies (1982) *The Empire Strikes Back*. London: Hutchinson.

Le Grand, J. (1991) 'Quasi-markets and social policy', *The Economic Journal 101*, 1256–1267.

Le Grand, J. and Bartlett, W. (eds) (1993) *Quasi-Markets and Social Policy*. Basingstoke: Macmillan.

Leat, D. (1988) 'Residential Care for Younger Physically Disabled Adults'. In I. Sinclair (ed) (1988) *Residential Care: The Research Reviewed*. London: HMSO.

Lenny, J. (1993) 'Do disabled people need counselling?'. In J. Swain, V. Finkelstein, S. French and M. Oliver (eds) (1993) *Disabling Barriers: Enabling Environments*. Milton Keynes: Open University/Sage.

Leonard, P. (1997) *Postmodern Welfare: Reconstructing an Emancipatory Project*. London: Sage.

Lipsky, M. (1978) 'Standing the Study of Implementation on Its Head'. In W. Burnham and M. Weinberg (eds) (1978) *American Politics and Public Policy*. Cambridge, MA.: MIT Press.

Lipsky, M. and Smith, S. (1989) 'Nonprofit organisations, government and the welfare state', *Poitical Science Quarterly 104*, 626–648.

Lis, C. and Soly, H. (1979) *Poverty and Capitalism in Pre-Industrial Europe*. Brighton: The Harvester Press.

Liu, B. (1976) *Quality of Life Indicators in U.S. Metropolitan Areas: a statistical analysis*. New York: Praeger Publishers.

Lloyd, M. (1992) 'Does She Boil Eggs?', *Disability, Handicap and Society 7*, 3, 207–223.

Local Government Management Board (1991) *Quality and Equality: services to the whole community*. Birmingham: University of Birmingham/LGMB.

Longmore, P. (1987) 'Screening stereotypes, images of disabled people in television and motion pictures'. In A. Gartner and T. Joe (eds) (1987) *Images of the Disabled: Disabling Images*. New York: Praeger.

Lonsdale, S. (1990) *Women and Disability: The Experience of Physical Handicap Amongst Women*. Basinstoke: Macmillan.

Loomes, G. and McKenzie, L. (1990) 'The Scope and Limitations of QALY Measures'. In S. Baldwin, C. Godfrey and C. Propper (eds) (1990) *Quality of Life: perspectives and policies*. London: Routledge.

Lorde, A. (1988) 'Age, Race, Class and Sex: women redefining difference'. In C. McEwan and S. O'Sullivan (eds) (1988) *Out the Other Side: Contemporary Lesbian Writing*. London: Virago.

Lugones, M. and Spelman, E. (1983) 'Have We Got a Theory for You! Feminist theory, cultural imperialism and the demand for "the woman's voice"', *Women's Studies International Forum 6*, 573–581.

Macaulay, S. (1963) 'Non-contractual relations in business', *American Sociological Review 28*, 55–67.

MacNeil, I. (1978) 'Contracts: adjustments of long-term economic relations under classical, neo-classical, and relational contract law', *Northwestern University Law Review 72*, 854–905.

Manser, G. (1972) 'Implications of purchase of service for voluntary agencies', *Social Casework 53*, 335–340.

Manser, G. (1974) 'Further thoughts on purchase of service', *Social Casework 55*, 421–427.

Marans, R. and Rogers, W. (1975) 'Towards an Understanding of Community Satisfaction'. In A. Hawley and V. Rock (eds) (1975) *Metropolitan America in Contemporary Perspective*. New York: Halstead Press.

Marshall, T. (1952) *Citizenship and Social Class.* Cambridge: Cambridge University Press.

Martin, J. and White, A. (1988) *The Financial Circumstances of Disabled Adults Living in Private Households.* London: HMSO.

Mastekaasa, A. and Kaasa, S. (1989) 'Measurement Error and Research Design: a note on the utility of panel data in quality of life research', *Social Indicators Research 21*, 315–335.

Mauss, A. (1975) *Social Problems as Social Movements.* Philadelphia: J. P. Lippincott Co.

McKnight, J. (1981) 'Professionalised service and disabling help'. In A. Brechin, P. Liddiard and J. Swain (eds) (1981) *Handicap in a Social World.* London: Hodder and Stoughton.

McNay, L. (1992) *Foucoult and Feminism.* Cambridge: Polity Press.

Means, R. and Smith, R. (1994) *Community Care: policy and practice.* Basingstoke: Macmillan.

Megone, C. (1990) 'The Quality of Life: starting from Aristotle'. In S. Baldwin, C. Godfrey and C. Propper (eds) (1990) *Quality of Life: perspectives and policies.* London: Routledge.

Melucci, A. (1985) 'The Symbollic Challenge of Contemporary Movements', *Social Research 52*, 789–816.

Melucci, A. (1989) *Nomads of the Present.* London: Hutchinson Radius.

Mishra, R. (1977) *Society and Social Policy.* London: Macmillan.

Moe, R. (1988) 'Law versus performance as objective standard', *Public Administration Review 48*, 674–675.

Morgan, D. and England, R. (1988) 'The two faces of privatisation', *Public Administration Review 48*, 989–997.

Morris, J. (1991a) *Pride Against Prejudice: transforming attitudes to disability.* London: Women's Press.

Morris, J. (1991b) *Able Lives: Women's Experience of Paralysis.* London: Women's Press.

Morris, J. (1992) *Interim Evaluation of the post of Independent Living Advocate at the National Spinal Injuries Association.* London: unpublished report for SIA.

Morris, J. (1993a) *Community care or independent living?* York: Joseph Rowntree Foundation.

Morris, J. (1993b) *Independent Lives? Community care and disabled people.* Basingstoke: Macmillan.

Morris, J. (1993c) 'Feminism and Disability', *Feminist Review 43*, 57–70.

Morris, J. (ed.) (1995) *Encounters with Strangers: feminism and disability.* London: Women's Press.

Morris, J. and Lindow, V. (1993) *User Participation in Community Care Services: key recommendations.* Leeds, Department of Health, Community Care Support Force.

Morrison, E. and Finkelstein, V. (1993) 'Broken Arts and Cultural Repair: the role of culture in the empowerment of disabled people'. In J. Swain, V. Finkelstein, S. French and M. Oliver (eds) (1993) *Disabling Barriers: Enabling Environments.* Milton Keynes: Open University Press/Sage.

Moum, T. (1988) 'Yea-Saying and Mood-of-the-Day Effects in Self-Reported Quality of Life', *Social Indicators Research 20*, 117–139.

Munday, B. (1985) *Report of the European Expert Meeting on Established Social Services versus new social initiatives.* Vienna, European Centre for Social Welfare Training and Research.

Murray, R. (1991) 'The State after Henry', *Marxism Today*, May 1991, 22–27.

National Council for Voluntary Organisations (1993) *Local Authority Funding for Voluntary Organisations.* London: NCVO.

National League of the Blind and Disabled (1988) 'A brief history of the national league of the blind and disabled'. In NLBD, *Year Book 1988*, Manchester: NLBD.

Nelson, P. (1970) 'Information and Consumer Behaviour', *Journal of Political Economy 78*, 311–329.

Neugarten, B., Havighurst, R. and Tobin, S. (1961) 'The measurement of life satisfaction', *Journal of Gerontology 16*, 134–143.

Nocon, A. and Qureshi, H. (1996) *Outcomes of Community Care for Users and Carers.* Buckingham: Open University Press.

Nordon, M. (1995) *The Cinema of Isolation: Physical Handicap in the Movies.* New Jersey: Rutgers University Press.

Northern Officer Group (1996) *The Disability Discrimination Act: a policy and practice guide for local government by disabled people.* Wakefield, Northern Officer Group.

Norwich, B. (1994) *Segregation and Inclusion: English LEA Statistics 1988–92.* Bristol: Centre for Studies on Inclusive Education.

O'Brien, J. (1990) 'Developing High Quality Services for People with Developmental Disabilities'. In V. Bradley and H. Bersani (eds) (1990) *Quality Assurance for Individuals with Developmental Disabilities.* Baltimore: Paul H. Brookes.

O'Connor, J. (1973) *The Fiscal Crisis of the State.* New York: St Martin's Press.

O'Toole, L. (1986) 'Policy Recommendations for Multi-Actor Implementation: An assessment of the field', *Journal of Public Policy 6*, 2, 181–210.

Offe, C. (1980) 'The Separation of Form and Content in Liberal Democratic Politics', *Studies in Political Economy 3*, 5–16.

Offe, C. (1984) *Contradictions of the Welfare State.* London: Hutchinson.

Offe, C. (1985) 'New Social Movements: challenging the boundaries of industrial politics', *Social Research 52*, 817–868.

Oliver, M. (1990) *The Politics of Disablement.* Basingstoke: Macmillan.

Oliver, M. (1991) 'Speaking Out: disabled people and the welfare state'. In G. Dalley (ed) (1991) *Disability and Social Policy.* London: Policy Studies Institute.

Oliver, M. (1992a) 'Changing the Social Relations of Research Production?', *Disability, Handicap and Society 7*, 2, 101–114.

Oliver, M. (1992b) 'A case of disabling welfare'. In National Institute for Social Work (1992) *Who Owns Welfare?: Questions on the social services agenda.* London: NISW.

Oliver, M. (1996a) *Understanding Disability: from theory to practice.* Basingstoke: Macmillan.

Oliver, M. (1996b) 'A Sociology of Disability or a Disablist Sociology?'. In L. Barton (ed) (1996) *Disability and Society: emerging issues and insights.* Harlow: Longman.

Oliver, M. and Barnes, C. (1991) 'Discrimination, Disability and Welfare: from needs to rights'. In I. Bynoe, M. Oliver and C. Barnes (eds) (1991) *Equal Rights and Disabled People: the case for a new law.* London: Institute for Public Policy Research.

Oliver, M. and Barnes, C. (1993) 'Discrimination, disability and welfare: from needs to rights'. In J. Swain, V. Finkelstein, S. French and M. Oliver (eds) (1993) *Disabling Barriers: Enabling Environments.* Milton Keynes: Open University Press/Sage.

Oliver, M. and Hasler, F. (1987) 'Disability and Self Help: a case study of the Spinal Injuries Association', *Disability, Handicap and Society 2*, 2, 113–125.

Oliver, M. and Zarb, G. (1992) *Greenwich Personal Assistance Schemes: An Evaluation.* London: Greenwich Association of Disabled People Ltd.

Osborne, S. (1992) 'The Quality Dimension: evaluating quality of service and quality of life in human services', *British Journal of Social Work 22*, 437–453.

Pagel, M. (1988) *On Our Own Behalf: an introduction to the self-organisation of disabled people.* Manchester: Greater Manchester Council of Disabled People.

Parmar, P. (1988) 'Rage and desire: confronting pornography'. In C. McEwan and S. O'Sullivan (eds) (1988) *Out the Other Side: Contemporary Lesbian Writing.* London: Virago.

Parmenter, T. (1988) 'An analysis of the dimensions of quality of life for people with physical disabilities'. In R. Brown (ed) (1988) *Quality of Life for Handicapped People.* London: Routledge.

Perry, J. and Felce, D. (1995) 'Objective indicators of the quality of life: how much do they agree with each other?', *Journal of Community, Applied and Social Psychology 5*, 1–19.

Phelan, P. and Cole, S. (1991) 'Social Work in a Traditional Setting'. In M. Oliver (ed) (1991) *Social Work: disabled people and disabling environments.* London: Jessica Kingsley Publishers.

Pirie, M. and Butler, E. (1989) *Extending Care.* London: Adam Smith Institute.

Piven, F. and Cloward, R. (1977) *Poor People's Movements: why they succeed. How they fail.* New York: Pantheon Books.

Plant, R. (1992) 'Citizenship, Rights and Welfare'. In A. Coote (ed) (1992) *The Welfare of Citizens: developing new social rights.* London: IPPR/Rivers Oram Press.

Priestley, M. (1994a) 'Blind Prejudice', *Community Care,* 3 February 1994, 28–29.

Priestley, M. (1994b) *Organising for Change: ABA (Leeds) Research Paper.* Leeds, Association of Blind Asians/Leeds City Council Health Unit.

Priestley, M. (1995a) 'Commonality and Difference in the Movement: an "Association of Blind Asians" in Leeds', *Disability and Society 10,* 157–169.

Priestley, M. (1995b) 'The Disabled Peoples' Movement: class or post-class?'. In W. Bottero (ed) (1996) (1995b) *Post Class Society?* Cambridge: Cambridge University Sociological Research Group.

Priestley, M. (1995c) 'Dropping 'E's: the missing link in quality assurance for disabled people', *Critical Social Policy 44,* 7–21.

Priestley, M. (1996a) *From Strength to Strength: a report on the recent development of ABA (Leeds) 1995–1996.* Leeds: Association of Blind Asians/Leeds City Council Health Unit.

Priestley, M. (1996a) 'Evaluating quality in services for disabled and older people', by Doria Pilling and Graham Watson (eds) *Disability and Society 11,* 4, 596–598.

Priestley, M. (1996b) 'Making Effective Use of User Inputs'. In Derbyshire Centre for Integrated Living (1996) *Giving Greater Voice and Influence to Disabled People in Commissioning and Providing Services.* Ripley: NHS Management Executive/DCIL.

Priestley, M. (1996c) *Perceptions of Quality: user views on DCIL's Personal Support Service.* Ripley: Disability Research Unit, University of Leeds/Derbyshire Centre for Integrated Living.

Priestley, M. (1997a) 'The origins of a legislative disability category in England: a speculative history', *Disability Studies Quarterly,* Spring 1997.

Priestley, M. (1997b) 'Who's Research?: a personal audit'. In C. Barnes and G. Mercer (eds) (1997) *Doing Disability Research.* Leeds: Disability Press.

Priestley, M. (1998a) 'Constructions and Creations: idealism, materialism and disability theory', *Disability and Society 13,* 1, 75–94.

Priestley, M. (1998b) 'Discourse and Resistance in Care Assessment: integrated living and community care', *British Journal of Social Work 28,* 5, (forthcoming).

Propper, C. (1993) 'Quasi-Markets, Contracts and Quality in Health and Social Care: the US experience'. In J. LeGrand and W. Bartlett (eds) (1993) *Quasi-Markets and Social Policy.* Basingstoke: Macmillan.

Rae, A. (1993) 'Equal Opportunities, Independent Living and Personal Assistance'. In C. Barnes (ed) (1993) *Making Our Own Choices: independent living, personal assistance and disabled people.* Clay Cross: British Council of Organisations of Disabled People.

Ramon, S. (ed.) (1991) *Beyond Community Care: normalisation and integration work.* London: Macmillan.

Rescher, N. (1972) *Welfare: social issues in philosophical perspective.* Pittsburg: Pittsburg University Press.

Rhodes, R. (1987) 'Developing the Public Service Orientation', *Local Government Studies 13,* 63–73.

Ridout, M. (1995) 'Independent Living, Legislation and Direct/Indirect Payments'. In C. Barnes, M. McCarthy and S. Comerford (eds) (1995) *Assessment, Accountability and Independent Living: confirmation and clarification of a disability led perspective.* Coventry, report of a conference organised by Coventry Independent Living Group (CLIG) and Coventry Social Services Department, Coombe Abbey, Coventry, 23–24 May 1995.

Rieser, R. and Mason, M. (1992) *Disability Equality in the Classroom: A Human Rights Issue.* London: Disability Equality in the Classroom.

Rioux, M. and Bach, M. (1994) *Disability Is Not Measles: New Research Paradigms in Disability.* Ontario: L'Institut Roeher.

Ritchie, P. (1994a) 'Community Care – a quick look at some of the big issues'. In R. Davidson and S. Hunter (eds) (1994) *Community Care in Practice.* London: Batsford.

Ritchie, P. (1994b) 'The process of quality assurance'. In R. Davidson and S. Hunter (eds) (1994) *Community Care in Practice.* London: Batsford.

Ritchie, P. and Ash, A. (1990) 'Quality in Action: improving services through quality action groups'. In T. Booth (ed) (1990) *Better Lives: changing services for people with learning difficulties.* Sheffield: Joint Unit for Social Services Research, Sheffield University.

Roberts, R. and Kloss, R. (1974) *Social Movements: between the balcony and the barricade.* St Louis: C. V. Mosby Co.

Robertson, A. (1985) 'Social Services Planning and the Quality of Life'. In A. Robertson and A. Osborn (eds) (1985) *Planning to Care.* Aldershot: Gower.

Rose, N. (1989) *Governing the Soul.* London: Routledge.

Ryan, J. and Thomas, F. (1980) *The Politics of Mental Handicap.* Harmondsworth: Penguin.

Salamon, L. (1987) 'Partners in Public Service: the scope and theory of governmental-nonprofit relations'. In W. Powell (ed) (1987) *The Nonprofit Sector: a research handbook.* New Haven: Yale University Press.

Saxton, M. and Howe, F. (eds) (1987) *With Wings: an anthology of literature by and about women with disabilities.* New York: The Feminist Press, City University of New York.

Schalock, R., Kieth, K., Hoffman, K. and Karan, O. (1989) 'Quality of Life: its measurement and use', *Mental Retardation 27,* 25–31.

Scheff, T. (1966) *Being Mentally Ill – a sociological theory.* London: Weidenfeld and Nicolson.

Schmalz, A. (1972) *Social Indicators.* New York: New World Systems/INL.

Schneider, M. (1976) 'The "quality of life" and social indicators research', *Public Administration Review 36,* 297–305.

Scotch, R. (1985) 'Disability as a basis for a social movement; advocacy and the politics of definition', *Journal of Social Issues 44,* 1, 159–172.

Scott-Parker, S. (1989) *They Aren't in the Brief: advertising people with disabilities.* London: Kings Fund Centre.

Sedgewick, P. (1982) *Psycho Politics.* London: Pluto.

Shakespeare, T. (1994) 'Cultural Representation of Disabled People: dustbins for disavowal?' *Disability and Society 9,* 283–299.

Shakespeare, T. (1995) 'Back to the Future? New genetics and disabled people', *Critical Social Policy 44,* 22–35.

Shakespeare, T. (1996) 'Disability, Identity, Difference'. In C. Barnes and G. Mercer (eds) (1996) *Accounting for Illness and Disability: bridging the divide*. Leeds: Disability Press.

Shaw, J. (1734) *Parish law: or, A guide to justices of the peace, ministers, church-wardens, overseers of the poor, constables, surveyors of the highways, vestry clerks, and all other concerned in parish business...[etc.]*. [London] In the Savoy, Printed by E. and R. Nutt, and R. Gosling (assigns of E. Sayer) for F. Cogan, [etc.].

Shiell, A., Pettipher, C., Raynes, N. and Wright, R. (1990) 'Economic approaches to measuring quality of life: conceptual convenience or methodological straightjacket?'. In S. Baldwin, C. Godfrey and C. Propper (eds) (1990) *Quality of Life: perspectives and policies*. London: Routledge.

Shilling, C. (1993) *The Body and Social Theory*. London: Sage.

Simpkins, R. (1993) *Planning and Evaluating Disability Information Services*. London: Policy Studies Institute.

Simpson, F. (1995) 'Personal Assistance Support Schemes'. In C. Barnes, M. McCarthy and S. Comerford (eds) (1995) *Assessment, Accountability and Independent Living: confirmation and clarification of a disability led perspective*. Coventry, report of a conference organised by Coventry Independent Living Group (CLIG) and Coventry Social Services Department, Coombe Abbey, Coventry, 23–24 May 1995.

Simpson, F. and Campbell, J. (1996) *Facilitating and supporting independent living: A guide to setting up a Personal Assistance Support Scheme*. London: Disablement Income Group.

Slaughter, T. (1982) 'Epidermalizing the World: a basic mode of being Black'. In L. Harris (ed) (1982) *Philosophy Born of Struggle*. Dubuque, Io, Hunt.

Smelser, N. (1963) *Theory of Collective Behaviour*. New York: Free Press.

Smith, D. (1988) *The Everyday Worlds a Problematic: a feminist sociology*. Milton Keynes: Open University Press.

Smith, G. (1981) 'Discretionary Decision-Making in Social Work'. In M. Adler and R. Asquith (eds) (1981) *Discretion and Welfare*. London: Heinemann.

Smith, S. and Jordan, A. (1991) *What the Papers Say and Don't Say About Disability*. London: Spastics Society.

Social Services Inspectorate (1991) *Assessment Systems and Community Care*. London: HMSO.

Solomos, J. (1985) 'Problems, but Whose Problems? The social construction of Black youth unemployment', *Journal of Social Policy 14*, 527–554.

Sombart, W. (1909) *Socialism and the Social Movement*. London: Dent.

Spelman, E. (1990) *Inessential Women: problems of exclusion in feminist thought*. London: Women's Press.

Stanley, L. (1990) *Feminist Praxis: Research, Theory and Epistemology in Feminist Sociology*. London: Routledge.

Stewart, J. (1993) 'The limitations of government by contract', *Public Money and Management 13*, 7–12.

Stewart, J. and Ranson, S. (1988) 'Management in the public domain', *Public Money and Management 8*, 13–20.

Stone, D. (1984) *The Disabled State*. Philadelphia, PA: Temple University Press.

Stone, E. and Priestley, M. (1996) 'Parasites, Pawns and Partners: disability research and the role of non-disabled researchers', *British Journal of Sociology 47*, 4, 699–716.

Stuart, O. (1992) 'Race and disability: just a double oppression?', *Disability, Handicap and Society 7*, 177–88.

Stuart, O. (1993) 'Double Oppression: an appropriate starting point?'. In J. Swain, V. Finkelstein, S. French and M. Oliver (eds) (1993) *Disabling Barriers: Enabling Environments*. Milton Keynes: Open University Press/Sage.

Sullivan, H. (1987) 'Privatisation of public services: a growing threat to constitutional rights', *Public Administration Review 47*, 461–467.

Sutherland, A. (1981) *Disabled We Stand*. London: Souvenir.

Szasz, T. (1973) *Ideology and Insanity: essays on the psychiatric dehumanisation of man*. London: Calder and Boyers.

Thomas, C. (1993) 'Deconstructing concepts of care', *Sociology 27*, 649–669.

Thompson, P. (1993) *Cause for Concern: What Directors of Social Services Think about the Impact of Changes to the Independent Living Fund*. London: Disablement Income Group.

Thompson, P., Lavery, M. and Curtice, J. (1990) *Short Changed by Disability*. London: Disability Income Group.

Thomson, W. (1992) 'Realizing Rights Through Local Service Contracts'. In A. Coote (ed) (1992) *The Welfare of Citizens*. London: IPPR/Rivers Oram Press.

Tilly, C., Tilly, L. and Tilly, R. (1975) *The Rebellious Century, 1830–1930*. Cambridge, MA: Harvard University Press.

Touraine, A. (1981) *The Voice and the Eye: An Analysis of Social Movements*. Cambridge: Cambridge University Press.

Touraine, A. (1985) 'An Introduction to the study of social movements', *Social Research 52*, 749–87.

Townsend, P. (1981) 'The structural dependency of the elderly: the creation of social policy in the twentieth century', *Ageing and Society 1*, 5–28.

Tuckett, D. (ed.) (1985) *Meetings Between Experts: an approach to sharing ideas in medical consultations*. London: Tavistock.

Turner, B. (1984) *The Body and Society*. Oxford: Blackwell.

Turner, B. (1990) *Theories of Modernity and Postmodernity*. London: Sage.

Turner, B. (1992) *Regulating Bodies*. London: Routledge.

Turner, R. (1969) 'The theme of contemporary social movements', *British Journal of Sociology 20*, 390–405.

Ungerson, C. (1994) *The Commodification of Care: current policies and future politics*. Southampton, paper presented at the International Sociological Association's 13th World Congress of Sociology, July 1994.

Union of Physically Impaired Against Segregation (UPIAS) and The Disability Alliance (1976) *Fundamental Principles of Disability*. London: UPIAS/Disability Alliance.

United Nations (1993) *Standard Rules on the Equalization of Opportunities for People with Disabilities*. General Assembly, Resolution 48/96, 20 December 1993.

Useem, B. (1980) 'Solidarity Model, Breakdown Model, and the Boston Anti-Busing Movement', *American Sociological Review 45*, 357–69.

Von Stein, L. (1850) *Geschichte der Socialen Bewegung Frankreichs von 1789 bis auf unsere Tage*. Munchen: Drei Masken Verlag.

Waitzkin, H. (1979) 'Medicine, superstructure and micropolitics', *Social Science and Medicine 13*, 601–609.

Waitzkin, H. (1989) 'A critical theory of medical discourse', *Journal of Health and Social Behaviour 30*, 220–239.

Walby, S. (1990) *Theorizing Patriarchy*. Oxford: Basil Blackwell.

Walker, A. (1989) 'Community Care'. In M. McCarthy (ed) (1989) *The New Politics of Welfare: an agenda for the 1990s?* Basingstoke: Macmillan.

Walker, A. (1996) 'Universal access and the built environment'. In G. Zarb (1996) *Removing Disabling Barrriers.* London: Policy Studies Institute.

Walzer, M. (1982) 'Politics in the Welfare State: concerning the role of American radicals'. In I. Howe (ed) (1982) *Beyond the Welfare State.* New York: Shocken.

Warburton, W. (1993) 'Performance indicators: what was all the fuss about?' *Community Care Management and Planning 1,* 4, 99–105.

Warner, K. and Hutton, R. (1980) 'Cost-benefit and cost-effectiveness analysis in health care', *Medical Care 18,* 1069–1084.

Weber, M. (1952) *The Protestant Ethic and the Spirit of Capitalism.* New York: Scribner.

Weinstein, M. and Stason, W. (1977) *Hypertension: a policy perspective.* Cambridge, MA: Harvard University Press.

Weisbrod, B. (1961) *Economics of Public Health.* Philadelphia, University of Philadelphia.

Weisbrod, B. (ed) (1977) *The Voluntary Nonprofit Sector.* Lexington, MA: D. C. Heath.

Wendell, S. (1996) *The Rejected Body: Feminist Philosophical Reflections on Disability.* London: Routledge.

Widdicombe Committee (1986) *Report of the Committee of Enquiry into the Conduct of Local Authority Business.* London: HMSO (Cmnd 9797).

Wilding, P. (1982) *Professional Power and Social Welfare.* London: Routledge.

Williams, A. (1987) 'Measuring Quality of Life'. In G. Teeling Smith (ed) (1987) *Health Economics: prospects for the future.* Beckenham: Croom Helm.

Williams, F. (1989) *Social Policy: a critical introduction.* Cambridge: Polity Press.

Williams, F. (1991) *Somewhere over the rainbow: Universality and selectivity in social policy.* Nottingham, paper presented at the 25th Annual Conference of the Social Policy Association, University of Nottingham, UK, 9–11 July 1991.

Williams, G. (1983) 'The Movement for Independent Living: an evaluation and critique', *Social Science and Medicine 17,* 1003–1010.

Williamson, O. (1978) *The Economic Institutions of Capitalism.* New York: The Free Press.

Williamson, O. (1975) *Markets and Heirachies: analysis and anti-trust implications.* New York: The Free Press.

Winkler, J. (1981) 'The Political Economy of Administrative Discretion'. In M. Adler and R. Asquith (eds) (1981) *Discretion and Welfare.* London: Heinemann.

Wistow, G., Knapp, M., Hardy, B. and Allen, C. (1994) *Social Care in a Mixed Economy.* Buckingham: Open University Press.

Wolfensberger, W. (1989) 'Human Services Policies: The Rhetoric versus the Reality'. In L. Barton (ed) (1989) *Disability and Dependency.* Lewes: Falmer Press.

Wood, R. (1991) 'Care of Disabled People'. In G. Dalley (ed) (1991) *Disability and Social Policy.* London: Policy Studies Institute.

Young, I. (1990) *Justice and the Politics of Difference.* Princeton, NJ: Princeton University Press.

Young, K. (1981) 'Discretion as an implementation problem: a framework for interpretation. In M. Adler and R. Asquith (eds) *Discretion and Welfare.* London: Heinemann.

Zarb, G. (1992) 'On the Road to Damascus: first steps towards changing the relations of disability research production', *Disability, Handicap and Society 7,* 2, 125–138.

Zarb, G. (1995b) 'Direct Payments Legislation: Prospects and Pitfalls'. In C. Barnes, M. McCarthy and S. Comerford (eds) (1995) *Assessment, Accountability and Independent Living:*

confirmation and clarification of a disability led perspective. Coventry, report of a conference organised by Coventry Independent Living Group (CLIG) and Coventry Social Services Department, Coombe Abbey, Coventry, 23–24 May 1995.

Zarb, G. and Oliver, M. (1993) *Ageing with a Disability: what do they expect after all these years?* London: University of Greenwich.

Zarb, G. and Nadash, P. (1994) *Cashing in on Independence.* Clay Cross: British Council of Organisations of Disabled People.

Zarb, G., Nadash, P. and Berthoud, R. (1996) *Direct Payments for Personal Assistance: comparing the costs and benefits of cash services for meeting disabled people's support needs.* London: Policy Studies Institute for British Council for Organisations of Disabled People.

Zautra, A. and Goodhart, D. (1979) 'Quality of life indicators: a review of the literature', *Community Mental Health Review 4,* 3–10.

Zola, I. (1977) 'Healthism and Disabling Medicalisation'. In I. Illich (ed) (1977) *Disabling Professions.* London: Marion Boyars.

Zola, I. (1982) *Missing Pieces: A Chronicle of Living with a Disability.* Philadelphia: Temple University Press.

Zola, I. (1987) 'The Politicization of the Self-Help Movement', *Social Policy 18,* 32–33.

Subject Index

rights, civil 11, 210
  and anti-discriminatory laws
    205–9, 225
  collective approach 65–6,
    188–9
  vs consumerism 158–9,
    211–12
  vs needs 53, 188, 200, 211

St Thomas Hospital direct
  payment scheme 201
SASM 79, 94–108, 204 see also
  personal assistance
satisfaction
  life 176, 182–3
  ratings in QA 151–3
segregation/desegregation
  49–51, 189–90, 200
self-assessment 94–8
self-management 98–108 see also
  personal assistance
service contracting
  and providers pressures 119,
    120, 133, 134, 134–5
  purchasing 114–16, 129
  vs integrated living 129–30,
    132–4, 134, 167, 175,
    175
  see also quality of services
sexism 29, 216
  see also feminism
Sherwood Peak 61
Shropshire Disability
  Consortium 95
single issue groups 60, 61
social constructionist approaches
  29, 53
social creationism 29–30
social indicators 181–2
social model of disability 7, 8, 9
  and disabled people's
    movement 65–6, 219
  and ecological theory 183–4
  and functionalism 184
  and tragedy 53–4
  vs individual model see under
    individual model
social movements 55–9, 65, 66
  see also disabled people's
    movement
Social Security (Incapacity for
  Work) Act (1995) 48
solidarity model of social
  movements 58, 59, 65

Spinal Injuries Association 61,
  196
staffing of PA schemes 99–102,
  146–7
support for PA schemes (PAS)
  96–7, 203–4 see also peer
  support
support schemes, self-managed
  see personal assistance
  in Derbyshire see under DCIL

tragedy, disability as 30, 31–4,
  47, 53–4
training, staff 97–8, 153–5

UPIAS 61, 65, 66–7
user involvement 75, 166–7,
  196–7
  checklist 163–5
  and quality 157–9, 187–8
  LOP project 19–20,
    159–65
user satisfaction 151–3

values
  disabling and ideology 29,
    30–1, 48–9, 215–17
  organisational and QA 156
'voice' 113, 158, 159
voluntary sector 115–16, 117
  and contracting 128, 130–1

welfare capitalism and disability
  11–12, 30, 38, 50, 53,
  216–17
welfare pluralism and integrated
  living 117–21, 118
well-being and life quality
  174–6, 182–3
West of England CIL 83, 95
Wiltshire 195
  Independent Living Fund
    (WILF) 82, 95
women as carers 45, 87

Author Index